AF291749

TearSheet PDX

First Annual Retrospective

Introduction

We at TearSheet PDX wanted to thank our readers and contributors for supporting us. We figured that there was no better way to thank you than to present to you a coffee table book.

You have sent us some of your best work and we have given you our best as well.

Please know that if an image doesn't say who the Photographer is, it is New Illusions Photo. If it doesn't say who the Muah or Stylist is, it is Illusions by Melanie.

Our friends and editors have chosen the best images to present in this publication. It wasn't an easy task, as these are our babies!

We hope that you will enjoy this as much as we enjoyed putting it together.

Warmest Regards,

Melanie
Editor in Chief

Front and back cover
Mikyla Bordner
Paper Dress and Lampshade Hat by Jackson Couture of Portland
with assistance from Get Sushi Designs & Rei Rei Nguyen

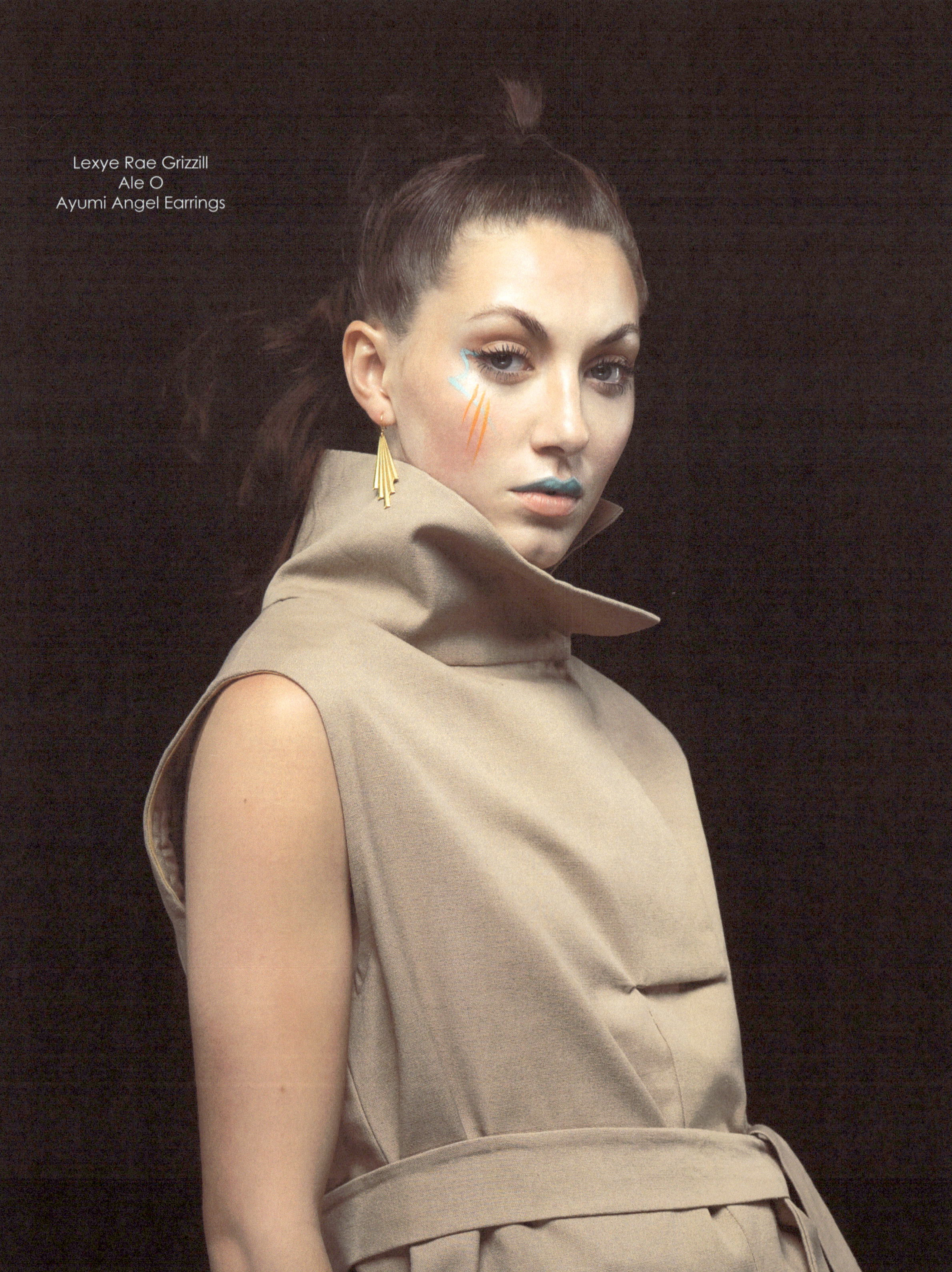

Lexye Rae Grizzill
Ale O
Ayumi Angel Earrings

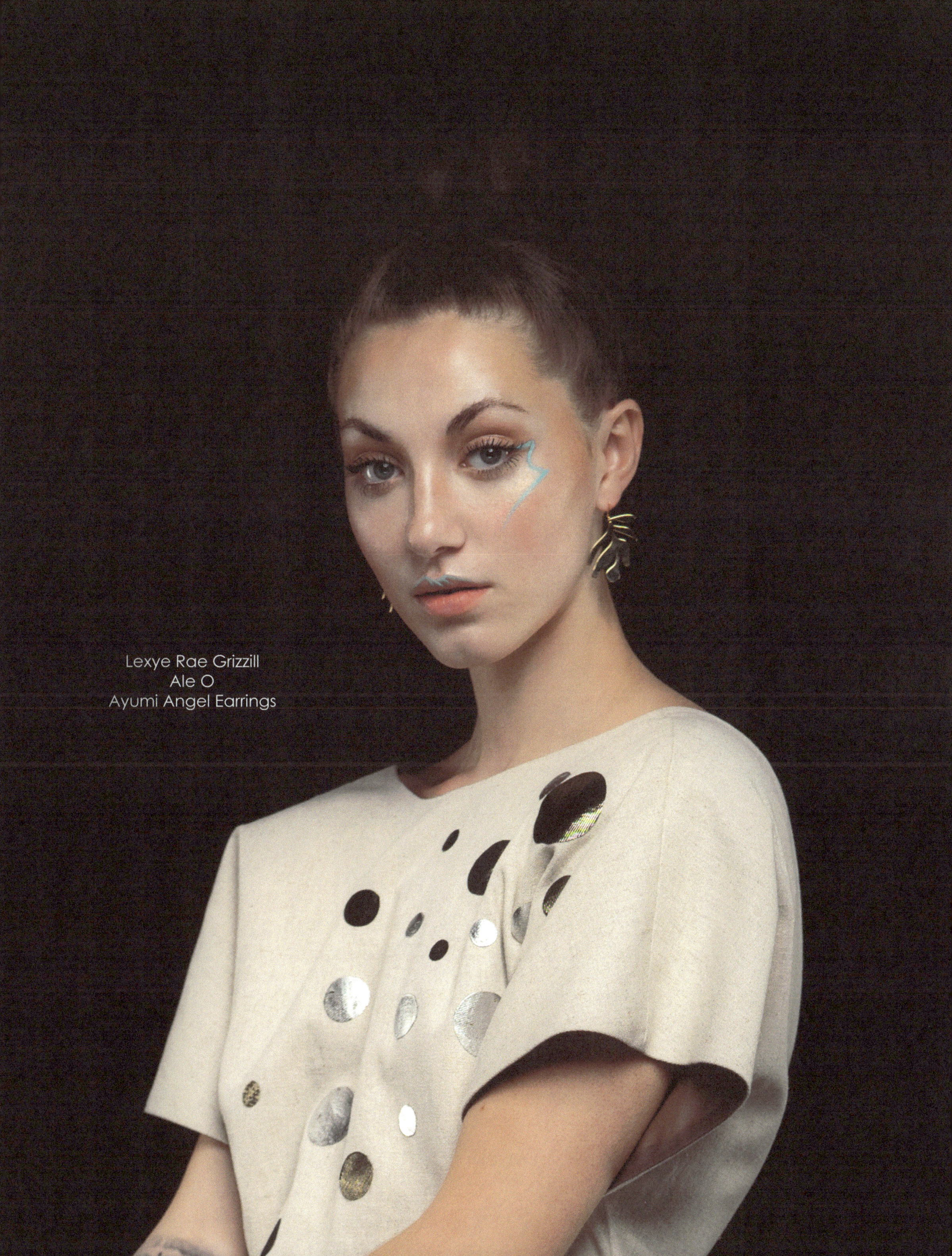
Lexye Rae Grizzill
Ale O
Ayumi Angel Earrings

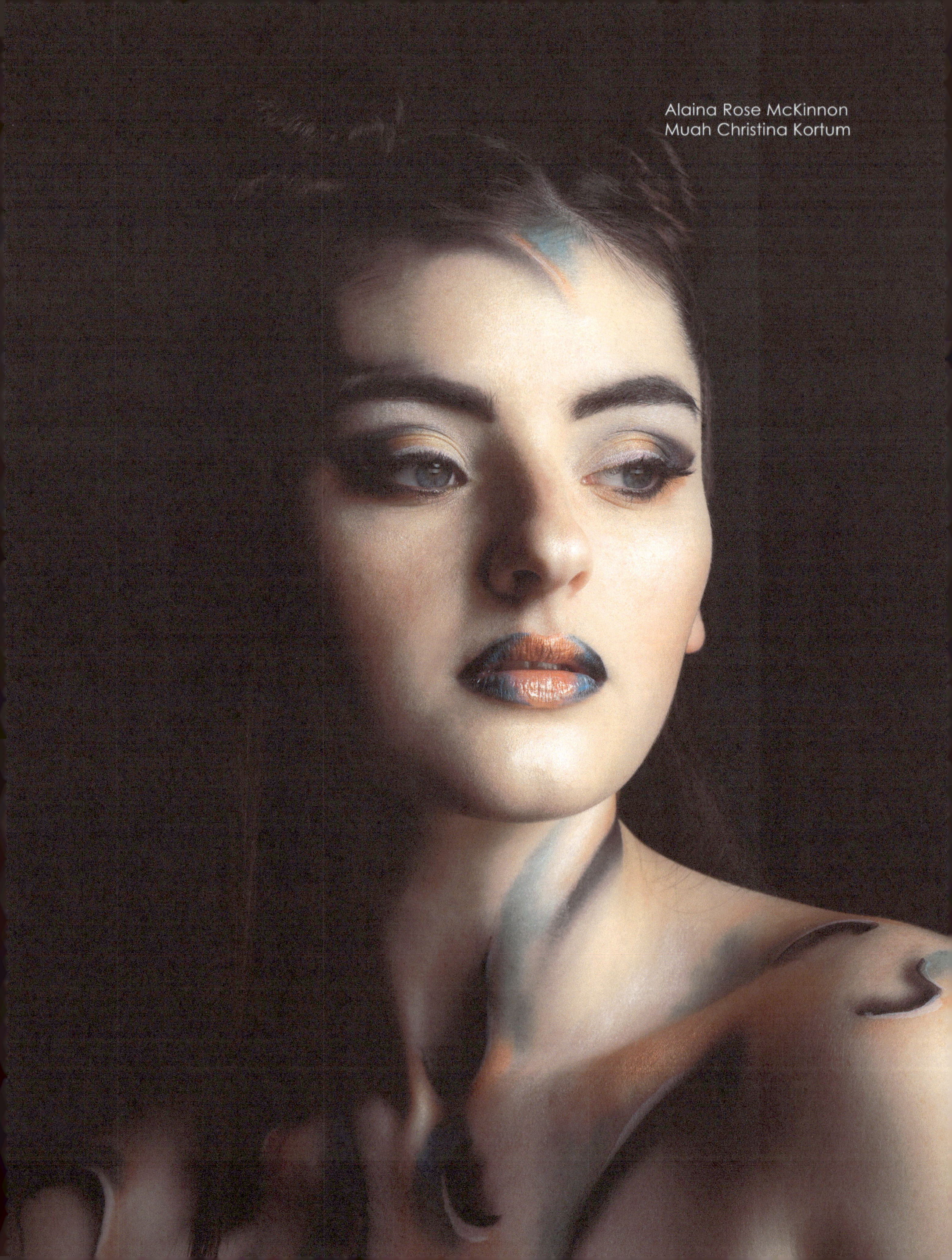
Alaina Rose McKinnon
Muah Christina Kortum

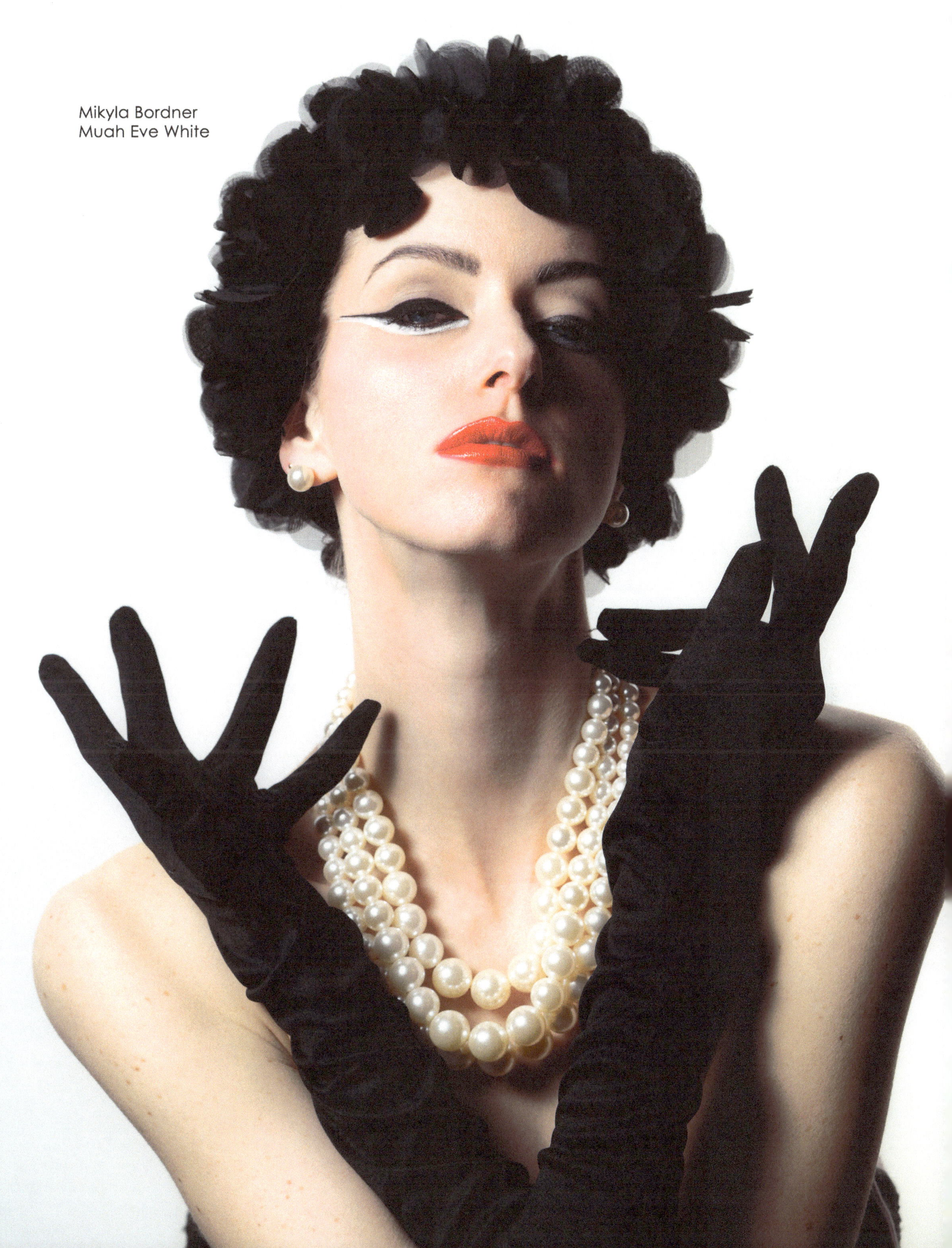
Mikyla Bordner
Muah Eve White

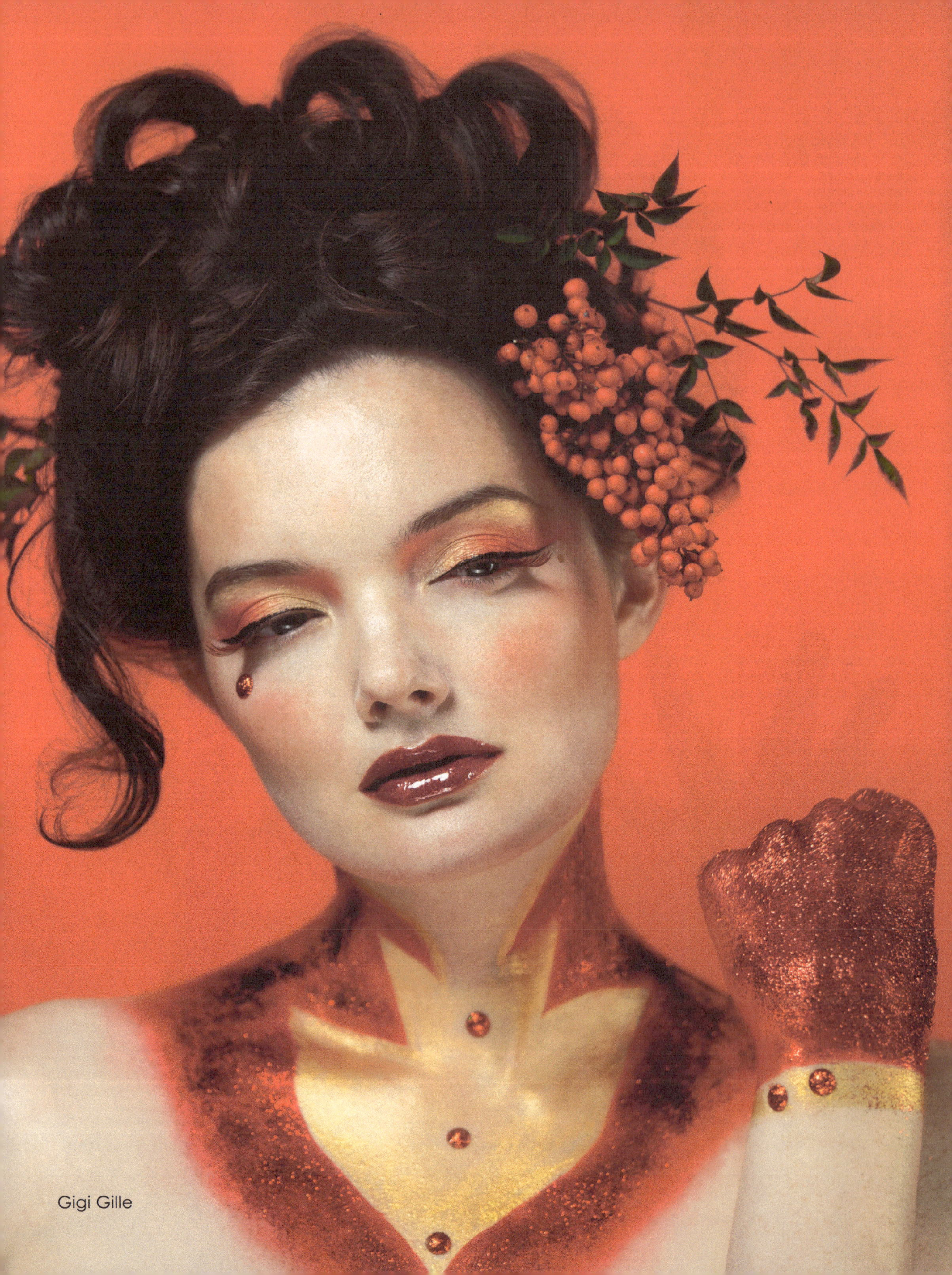

Gigi Gille

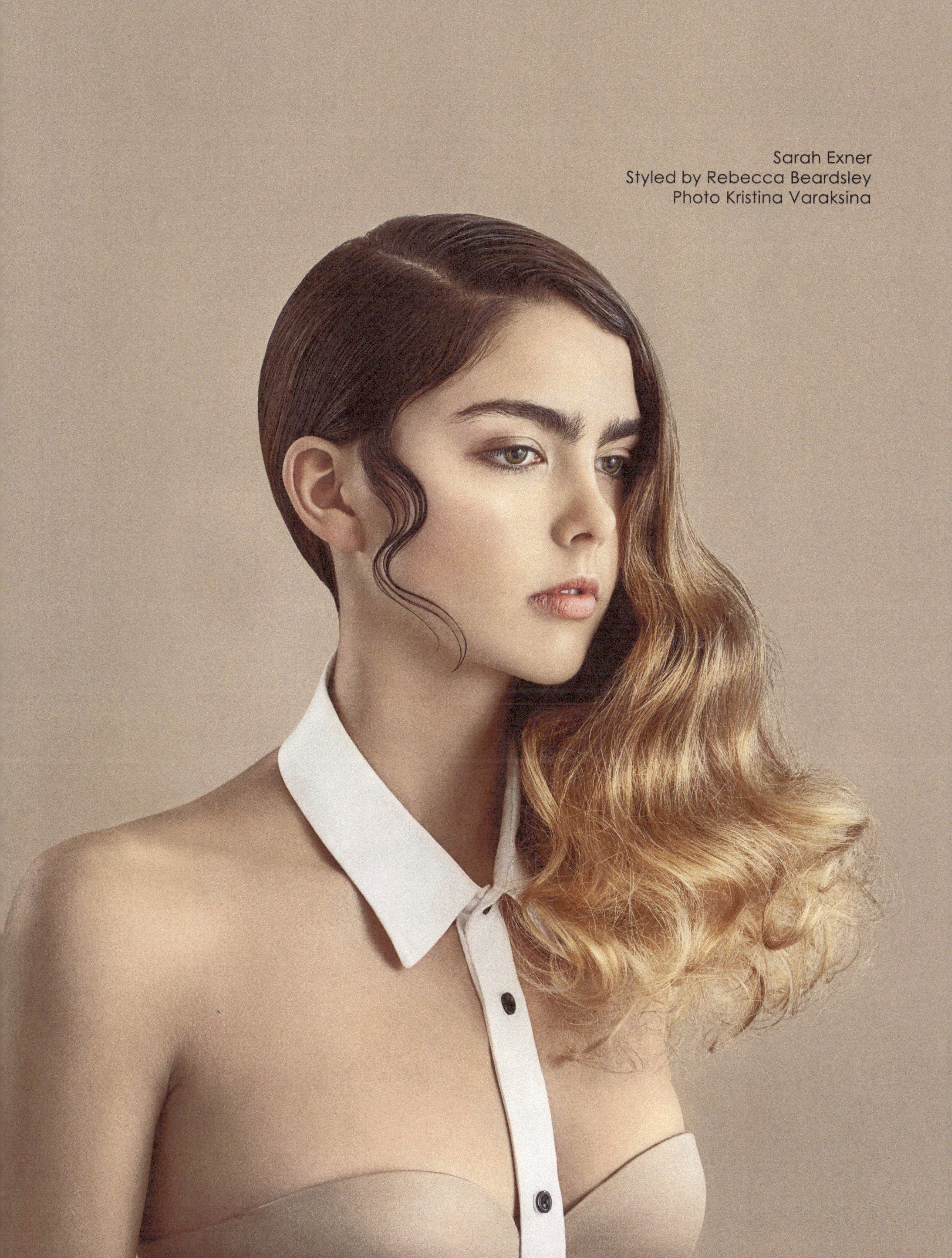

Sarah Exner
Styled by Rebecca Beardsley
Photo Kristina Varaksina

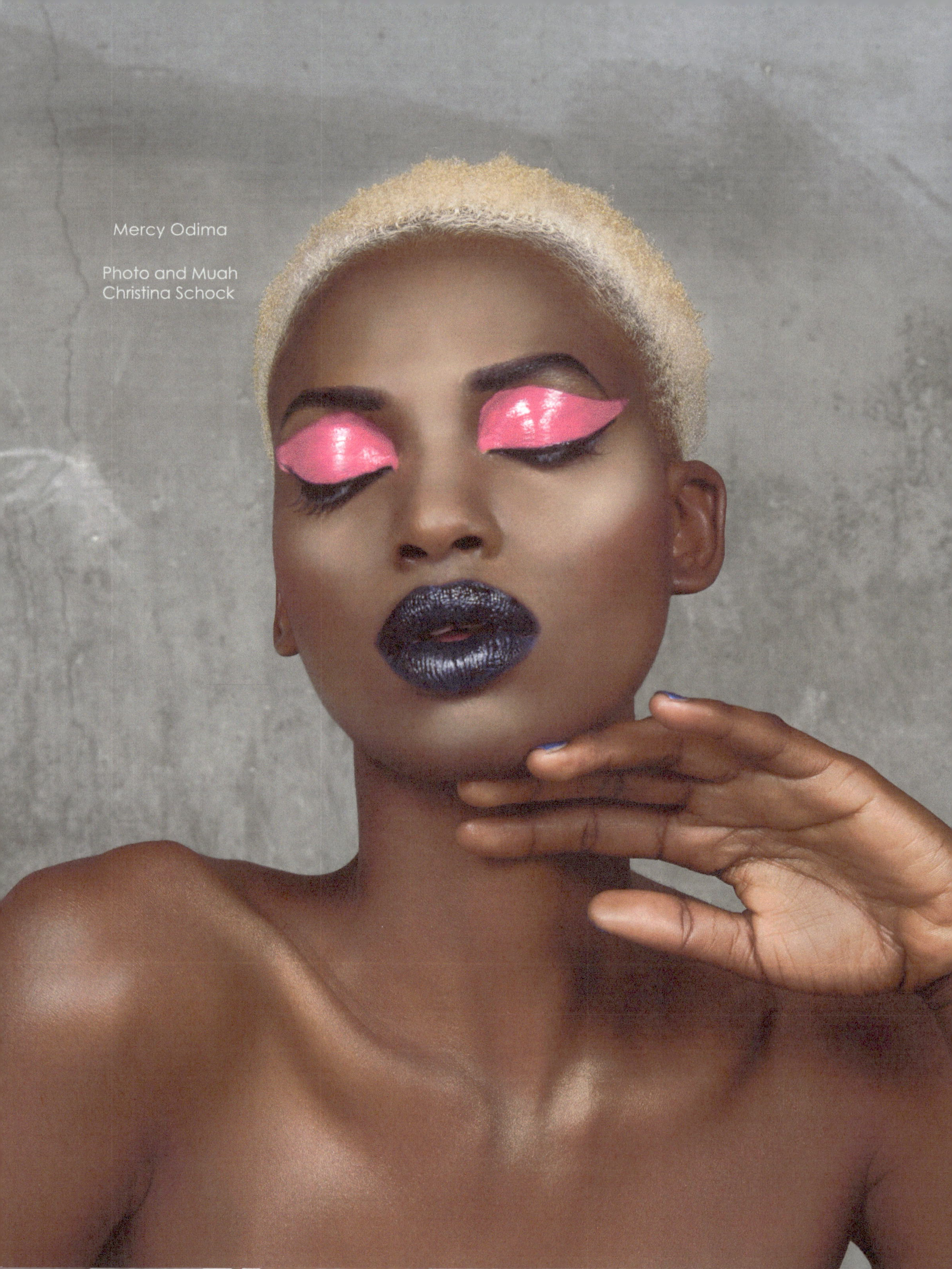

Mercy Odima

Photo and Muah
Christina Schock

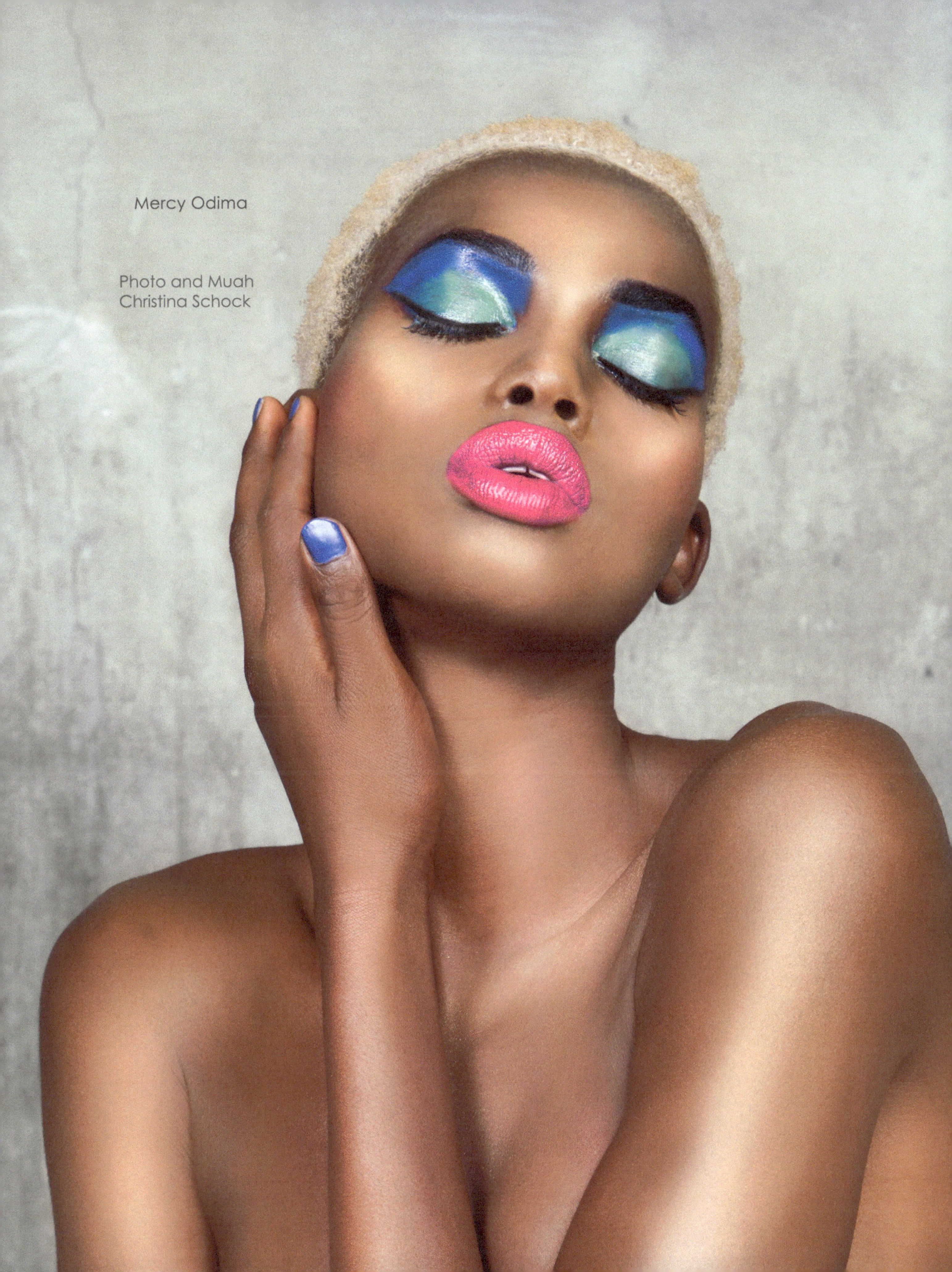
Mercy Odima

Photo and Muah
Christina Schock

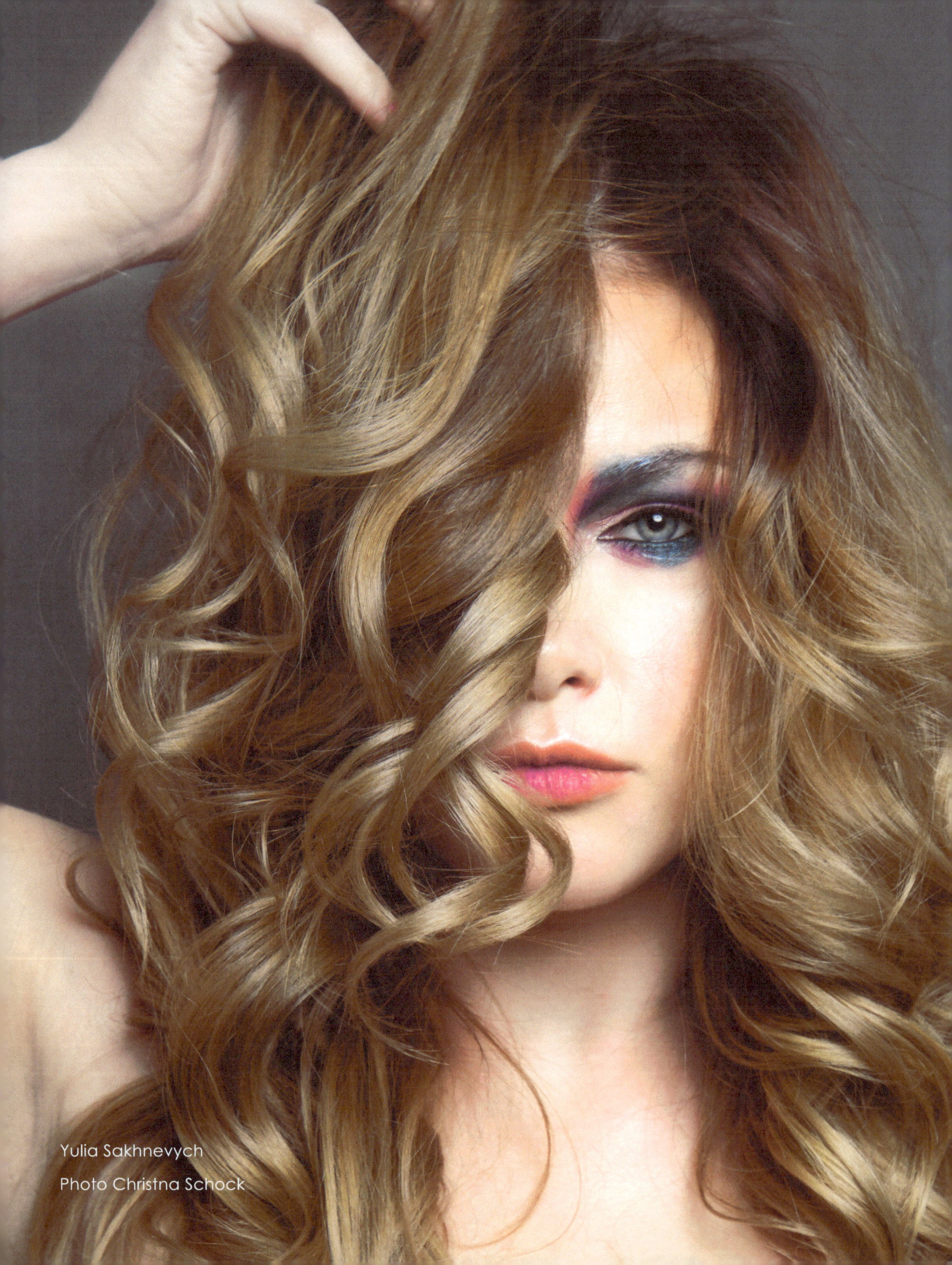

Yulia Sakhnevych
Photo Christna Schock

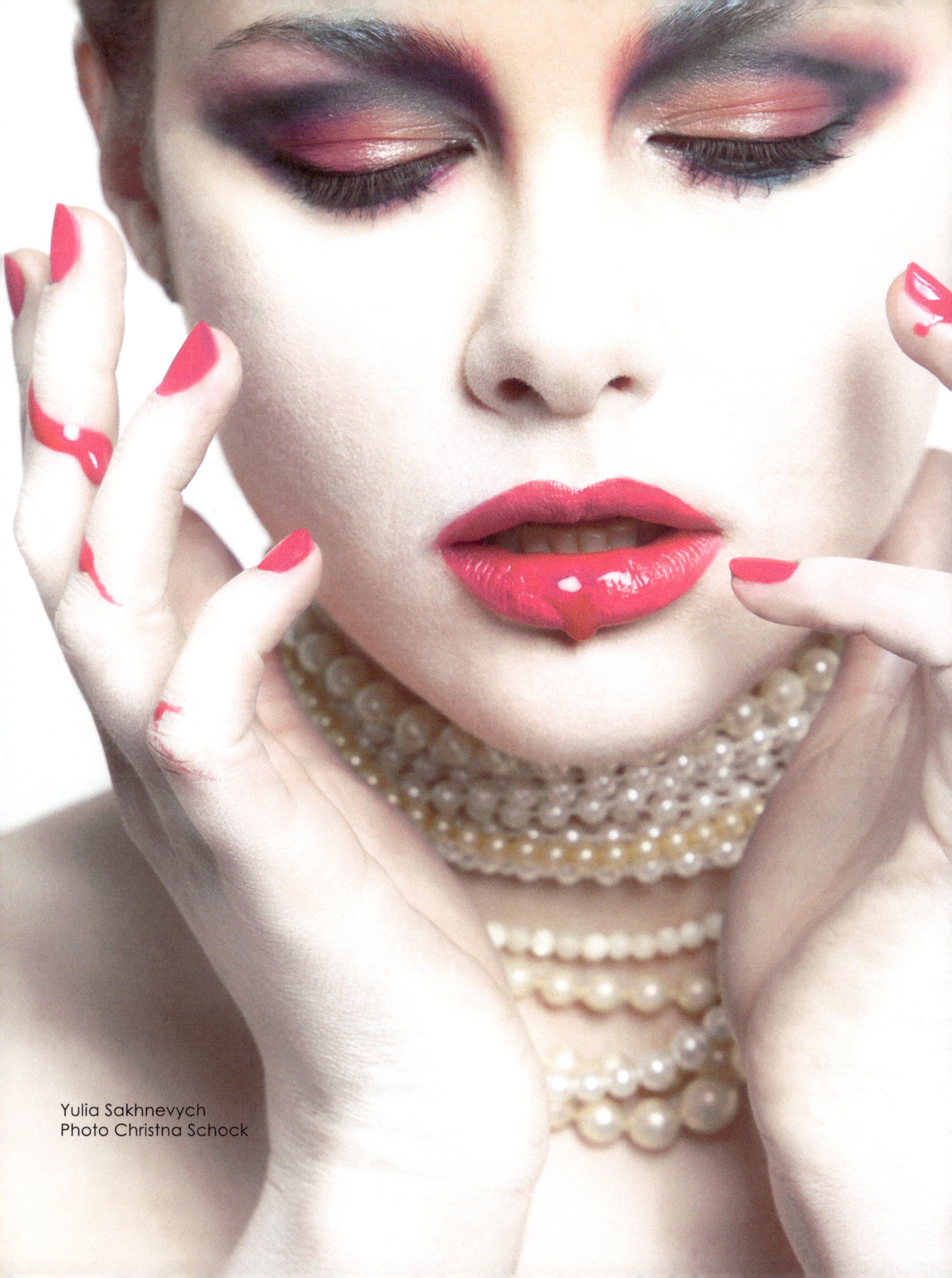

Yulia Sakhnevych
Photo Christna Schock

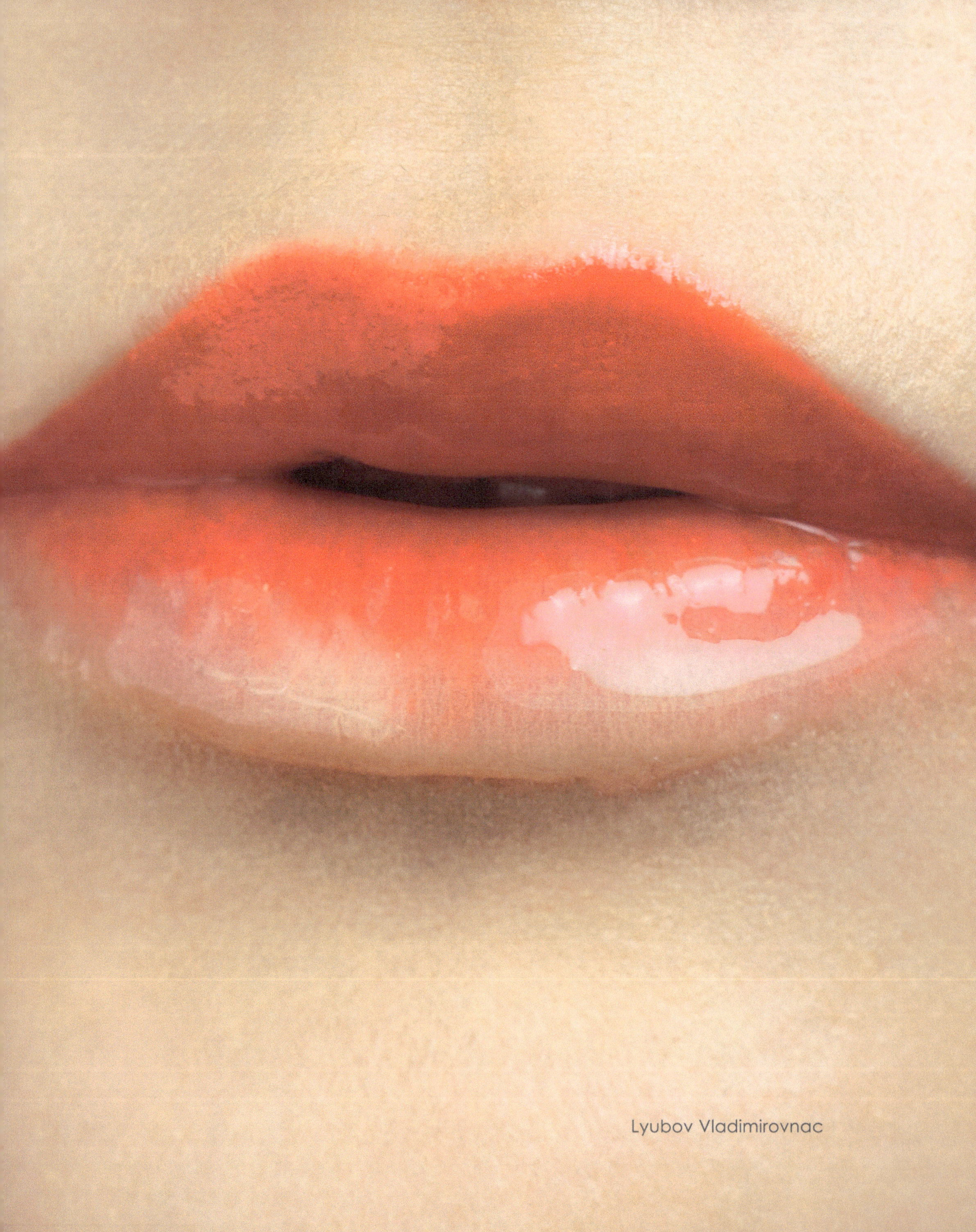

Lyubov Vladimirovnac

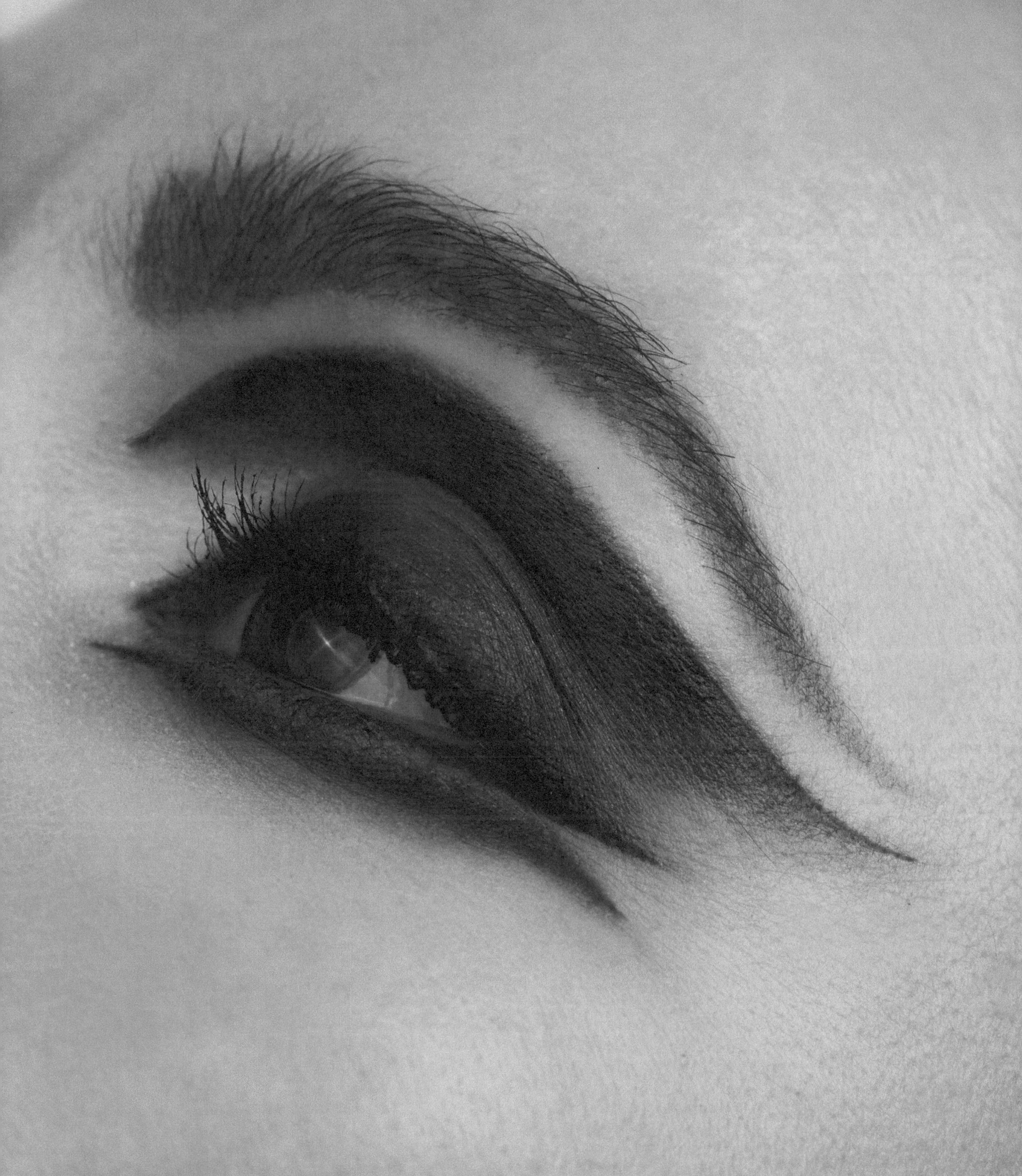
Lyubov Vladimirovnac

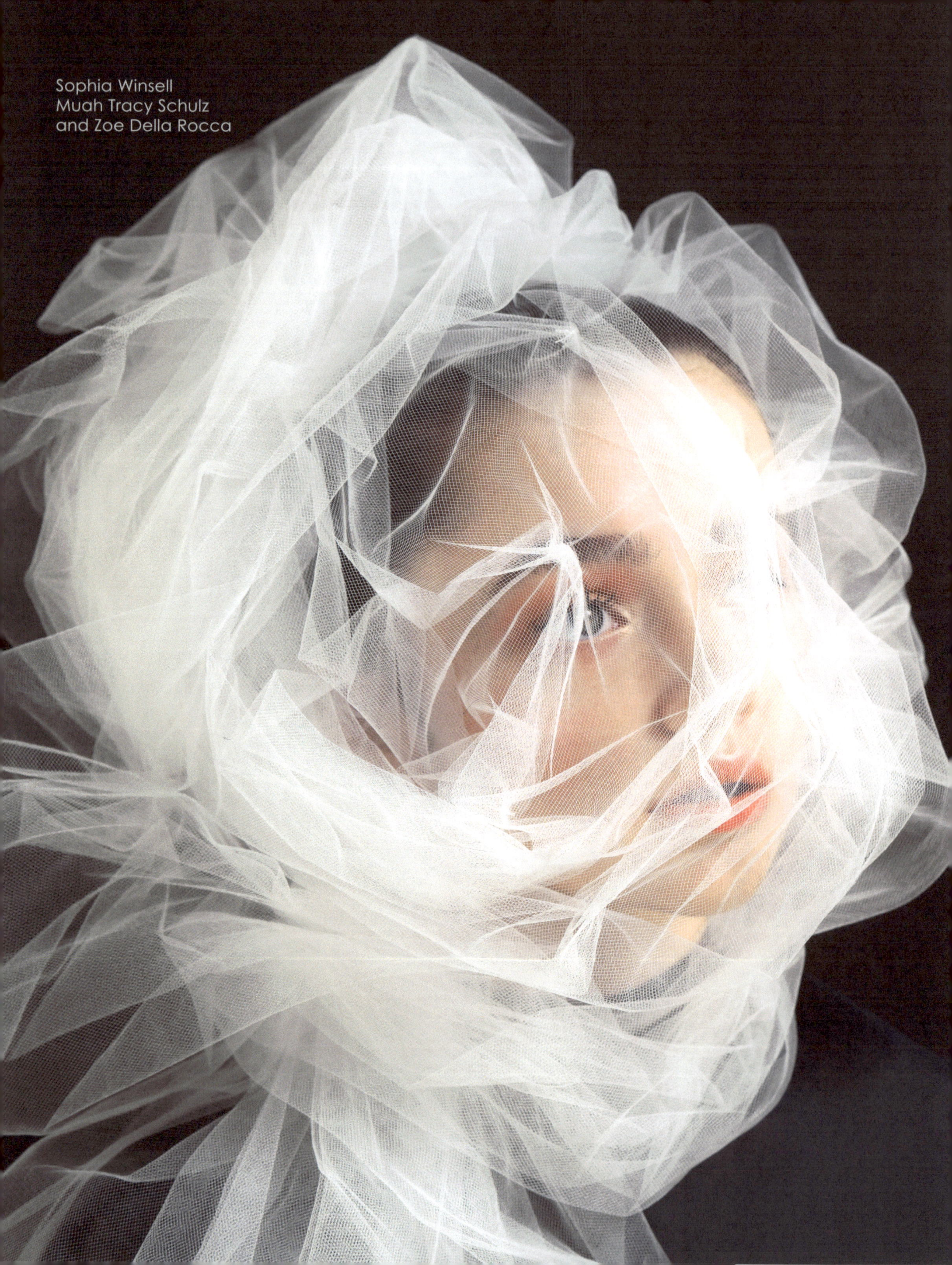
Sophia Winsell
Muah Tracy Schulz
and Zoe Della Rocca

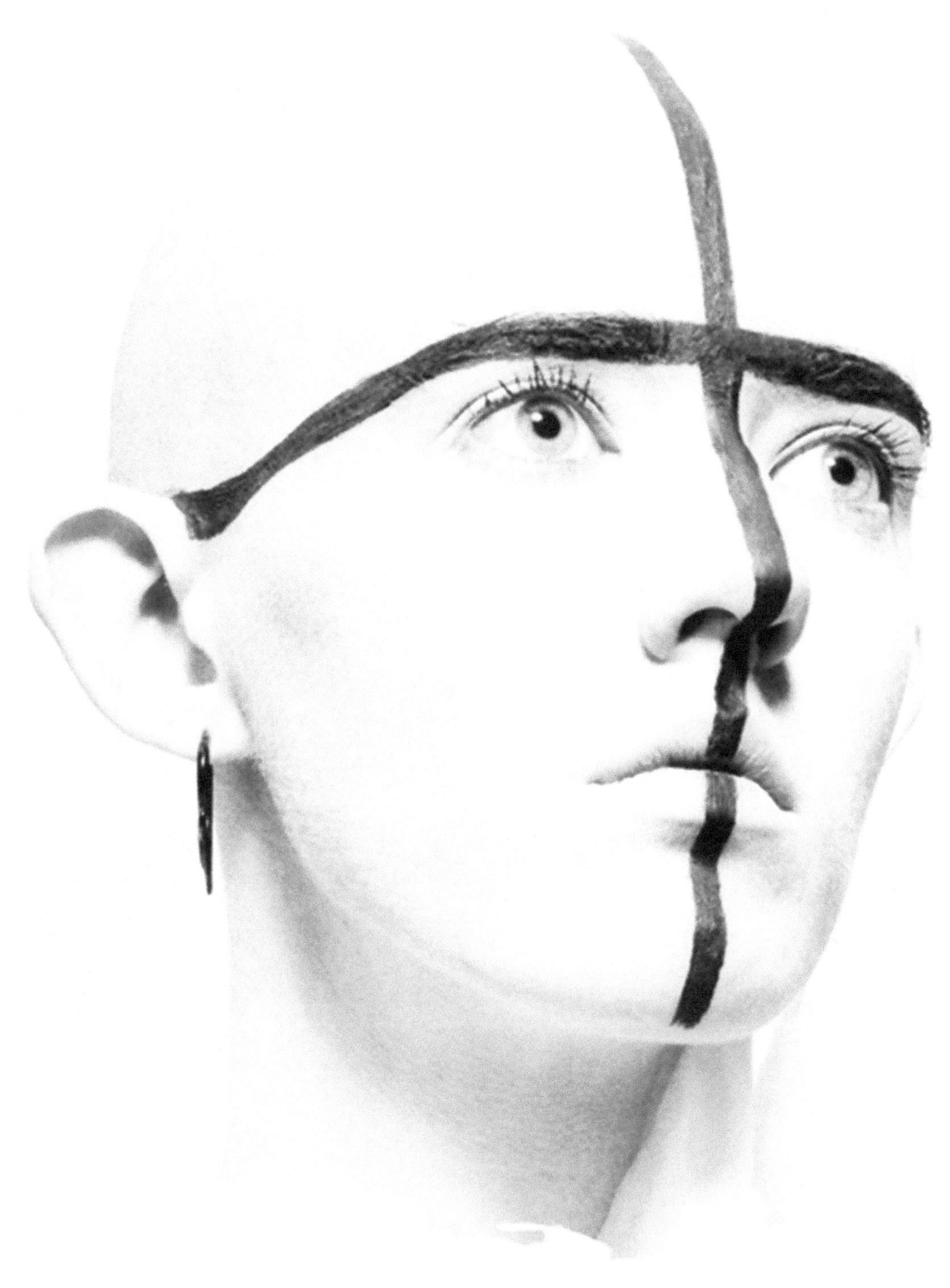

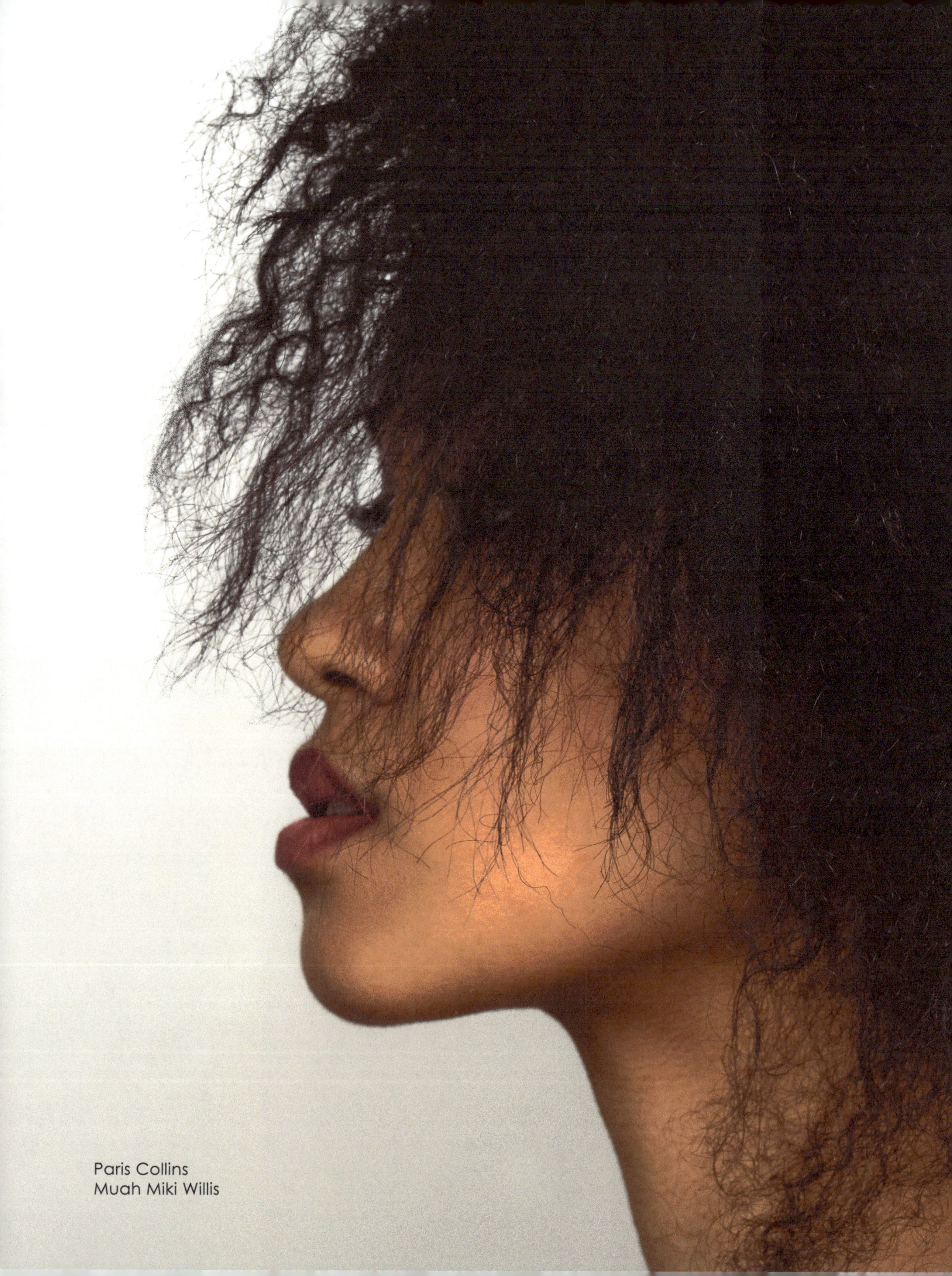

Paris Collins
Muah Miki Willis

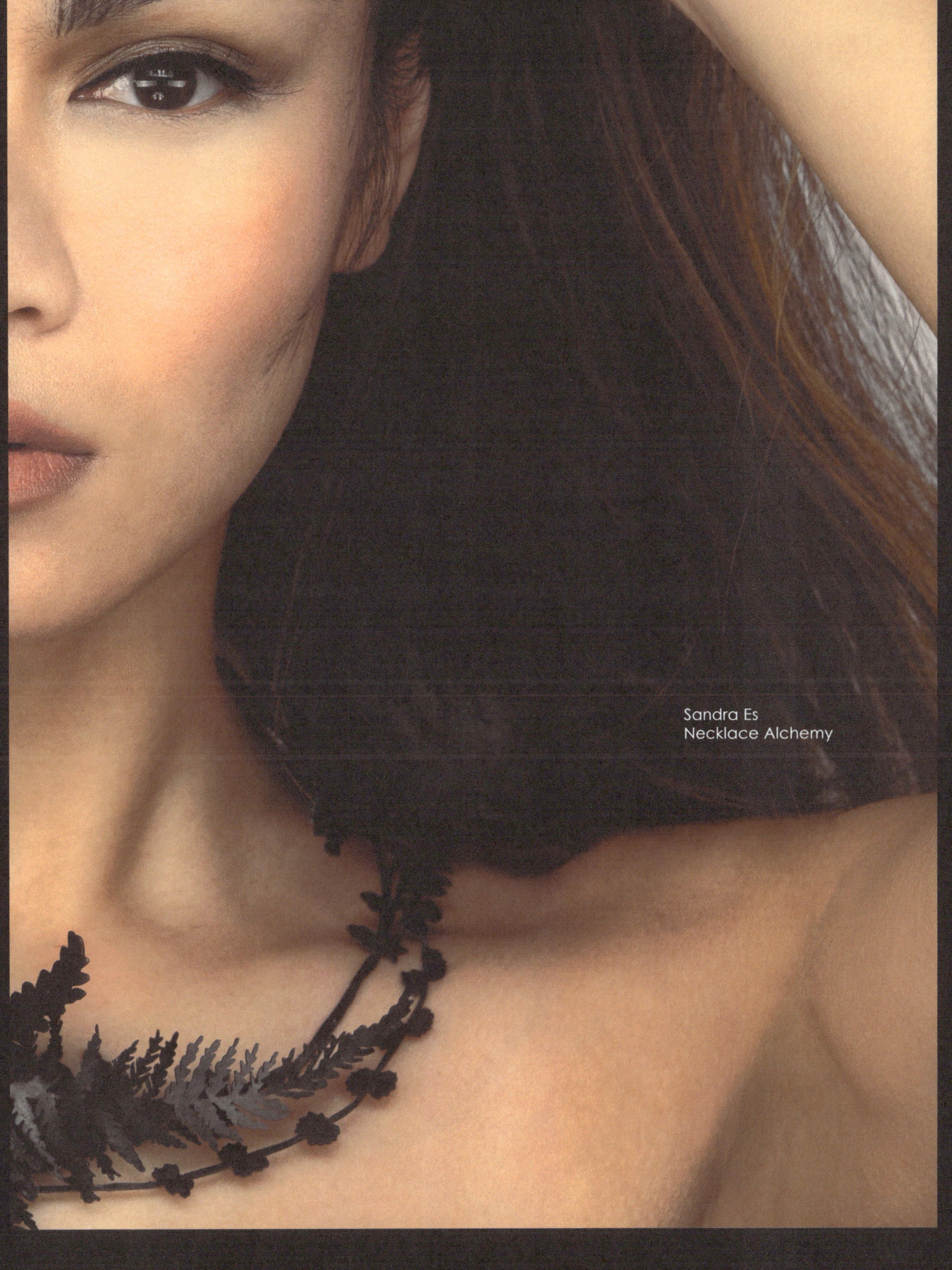

Sandra Es
Necklace Alchemy

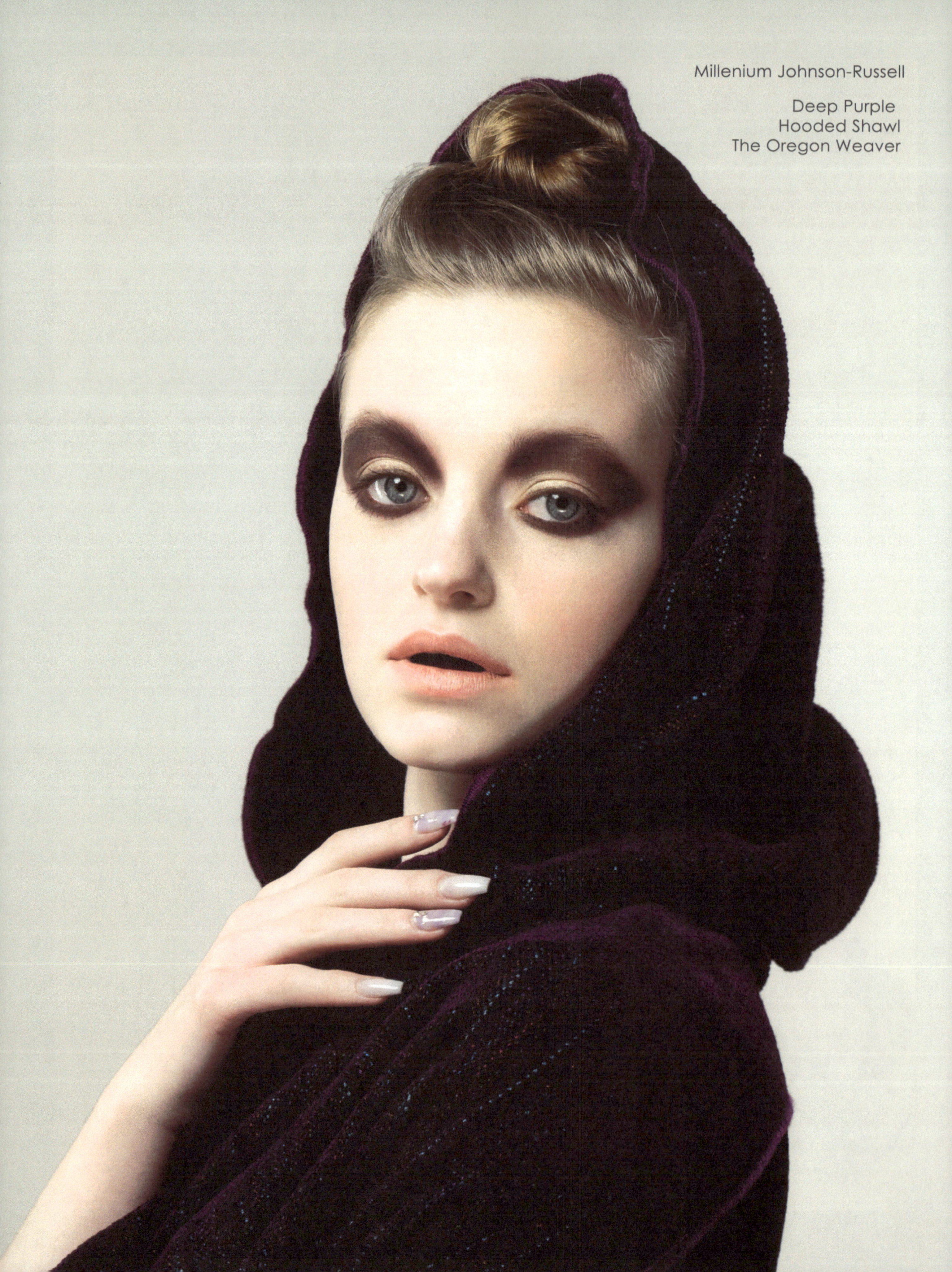

Millenium Johnson-Russell

Deep Purple
Hooded Shawl
The Oregon Weaver

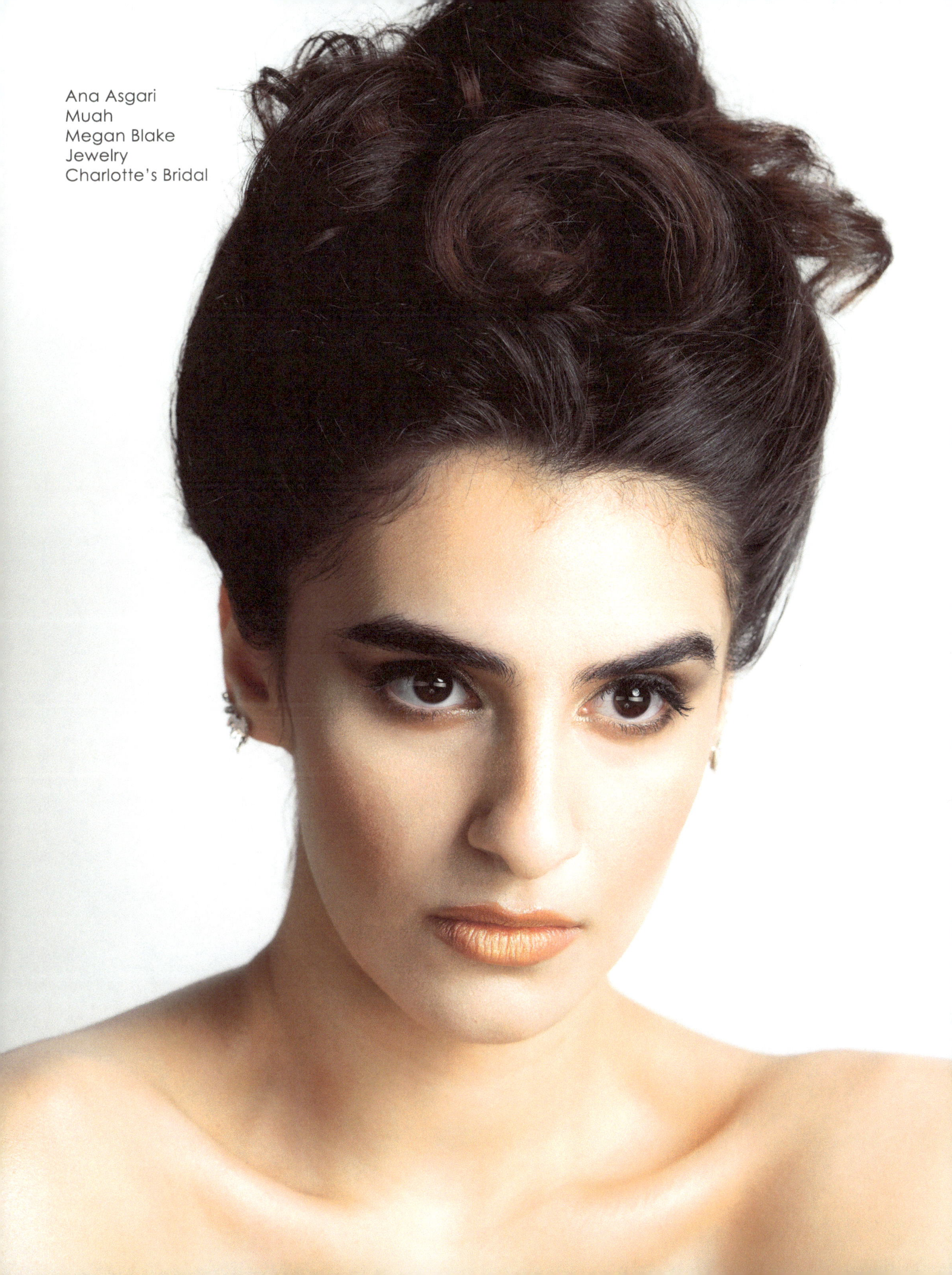
Ana Asgari
Muah
Megan Blake
Jewelry
Charlotte's Bridal

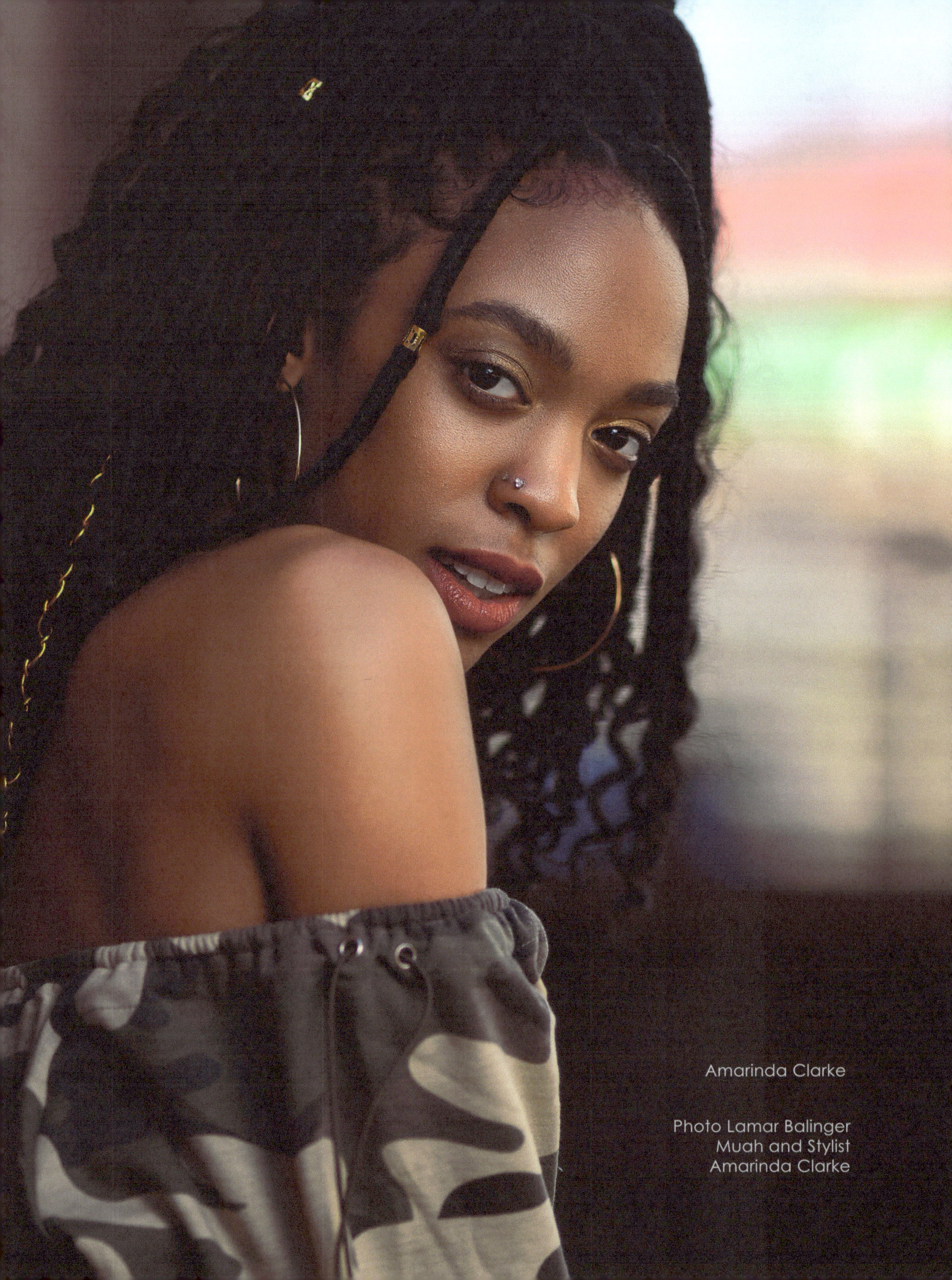
Amarinda Clarke

Photo Lamar Balinger
Muah and Stylist
Amarinda Clarke

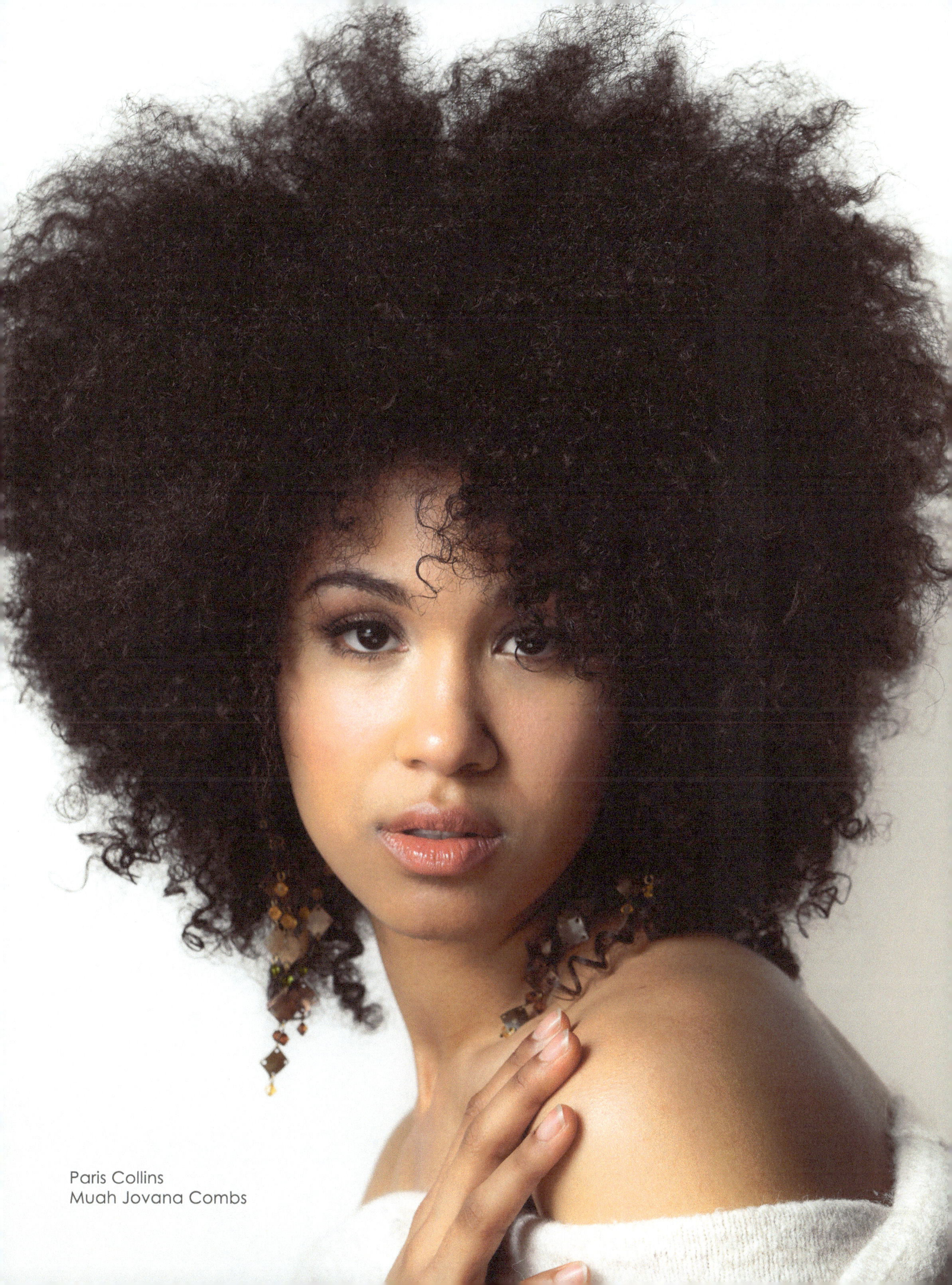

Paris Collins
Muah Jovana Combs

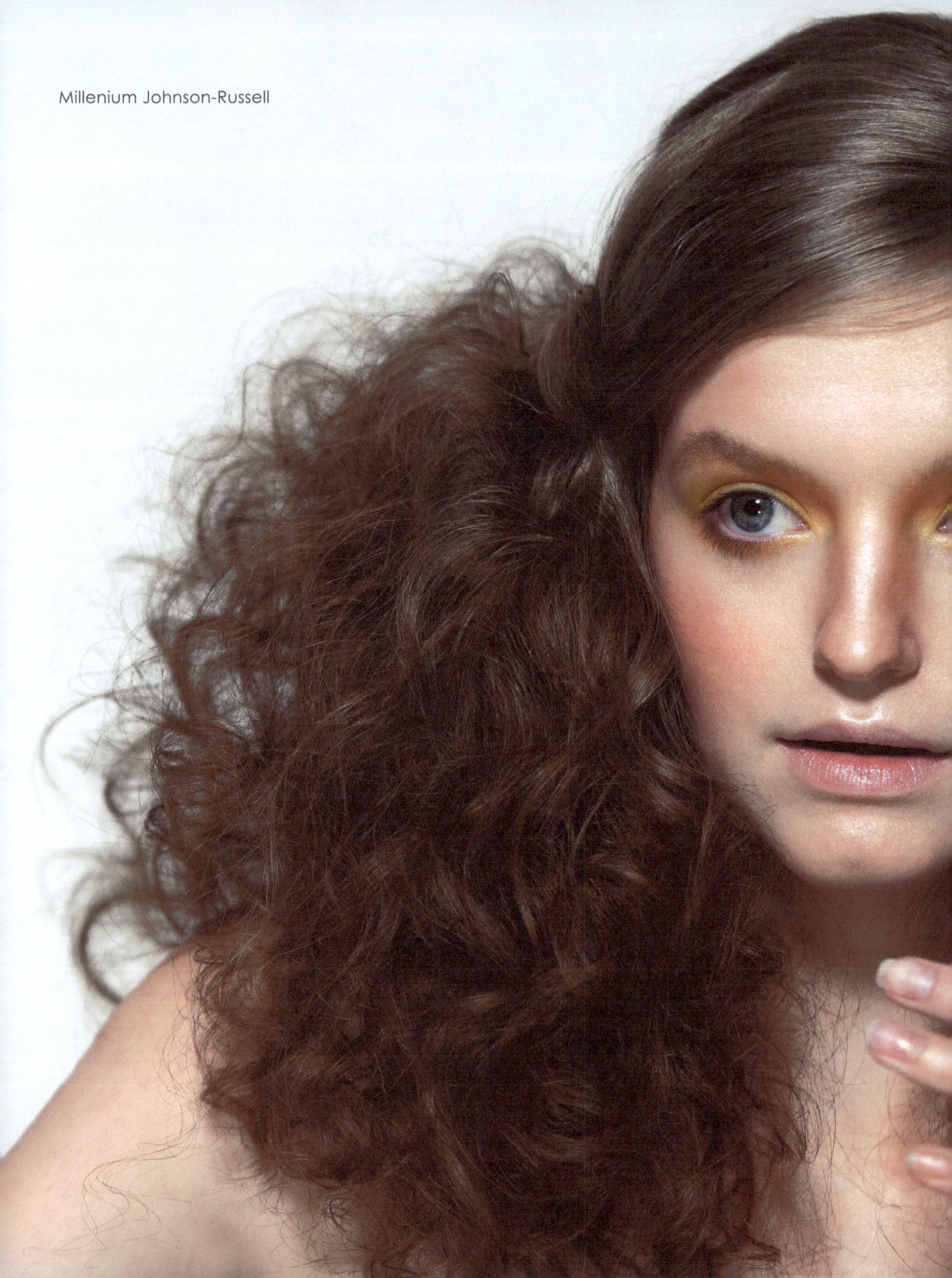
Millenium Johnson-Russell

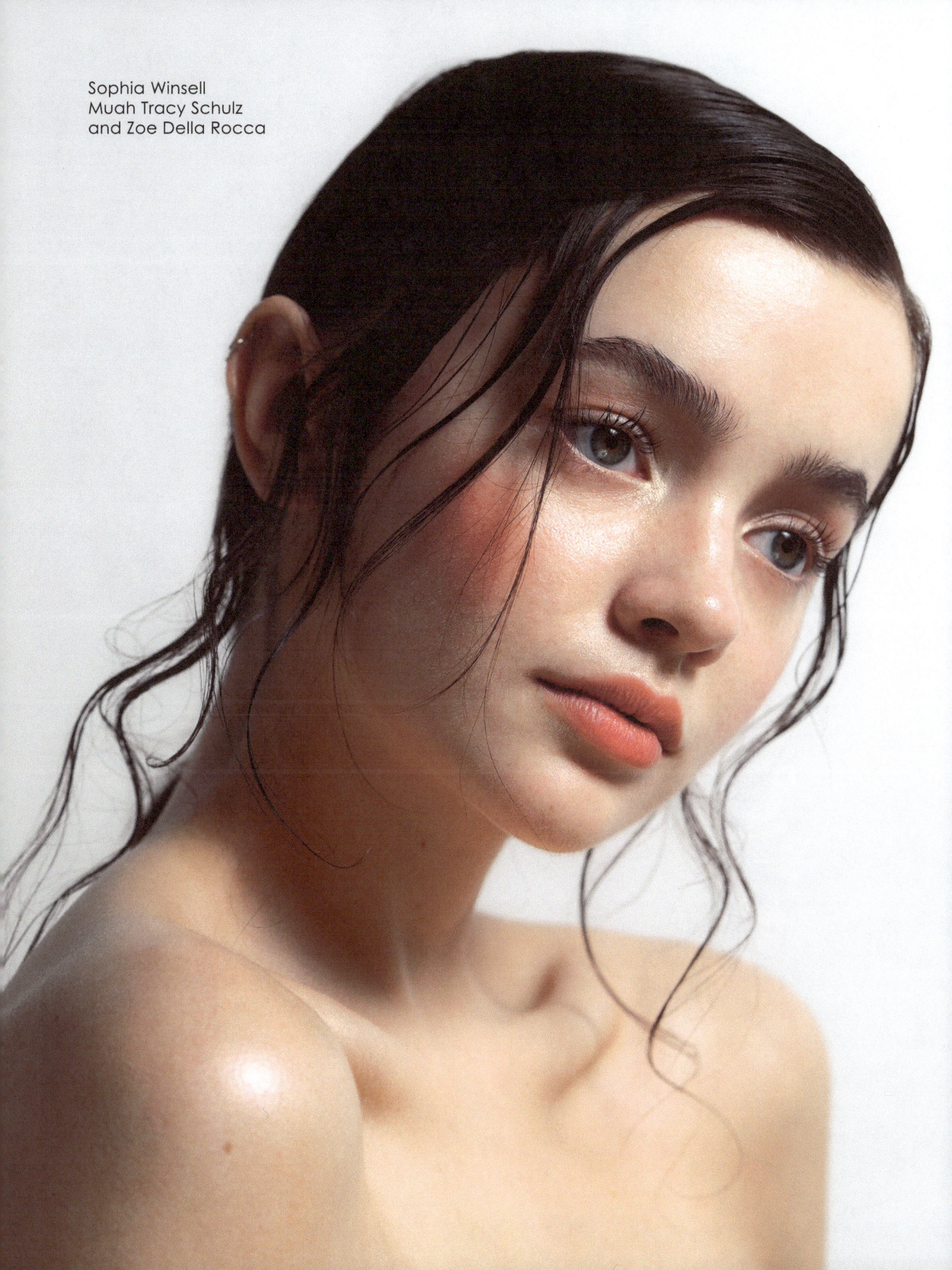
Sophia Winsell
Muah Tracy Schulz
and Zoe Della Rocca

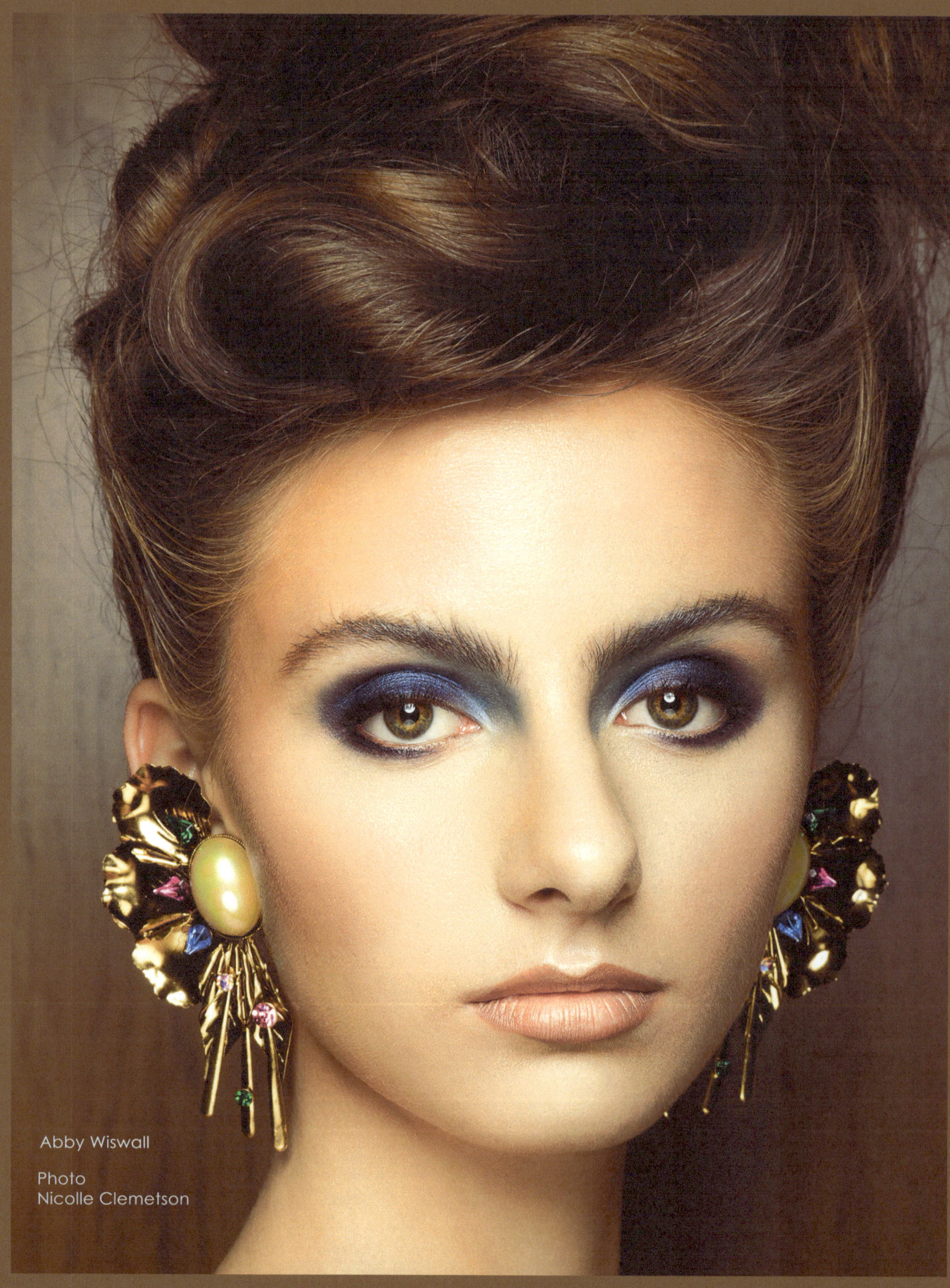

Abby Wiswall

Photo
Nicolle Clemetson

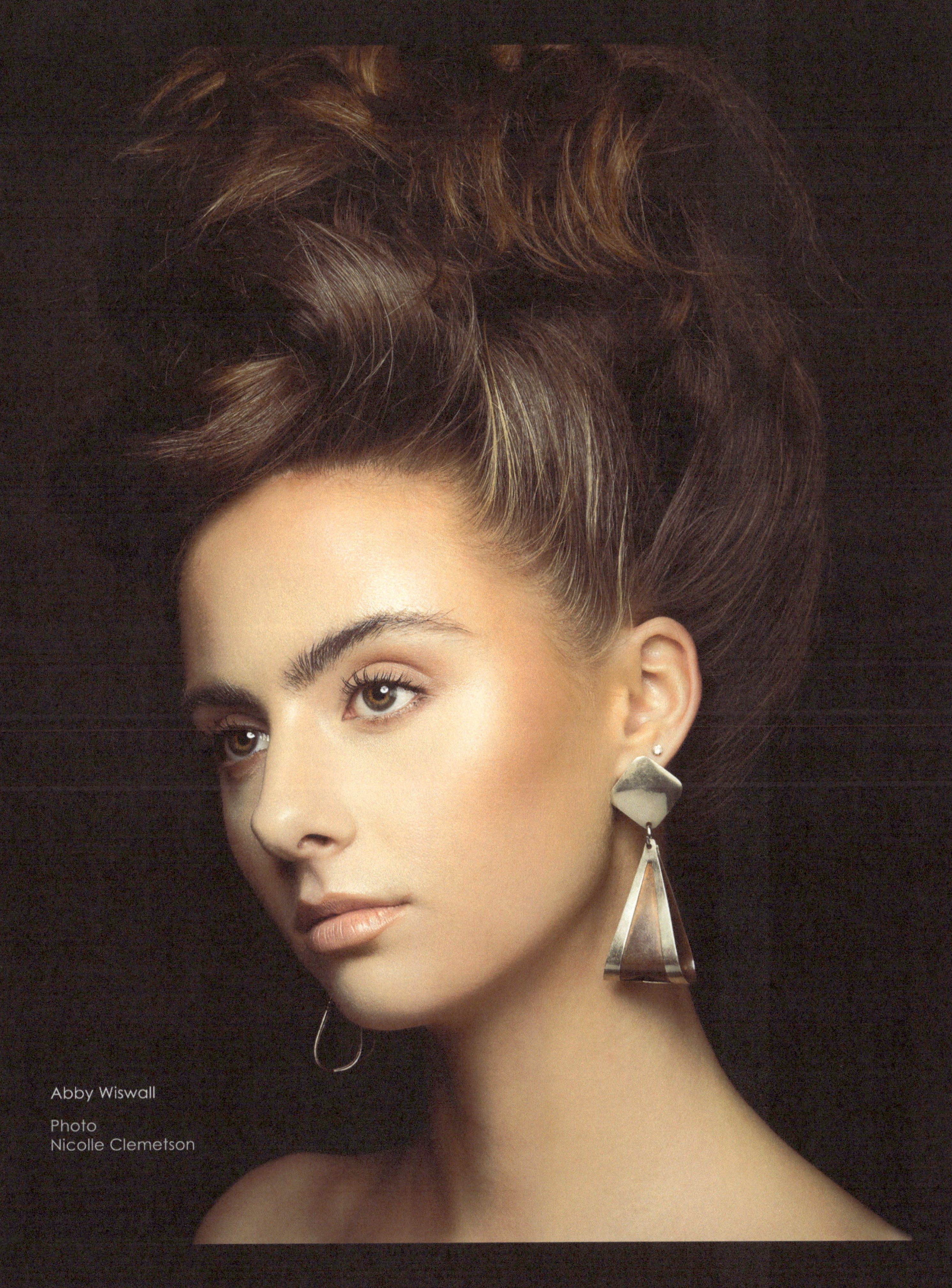

Abby Wiswall

Photo
Nicolle Clemetson

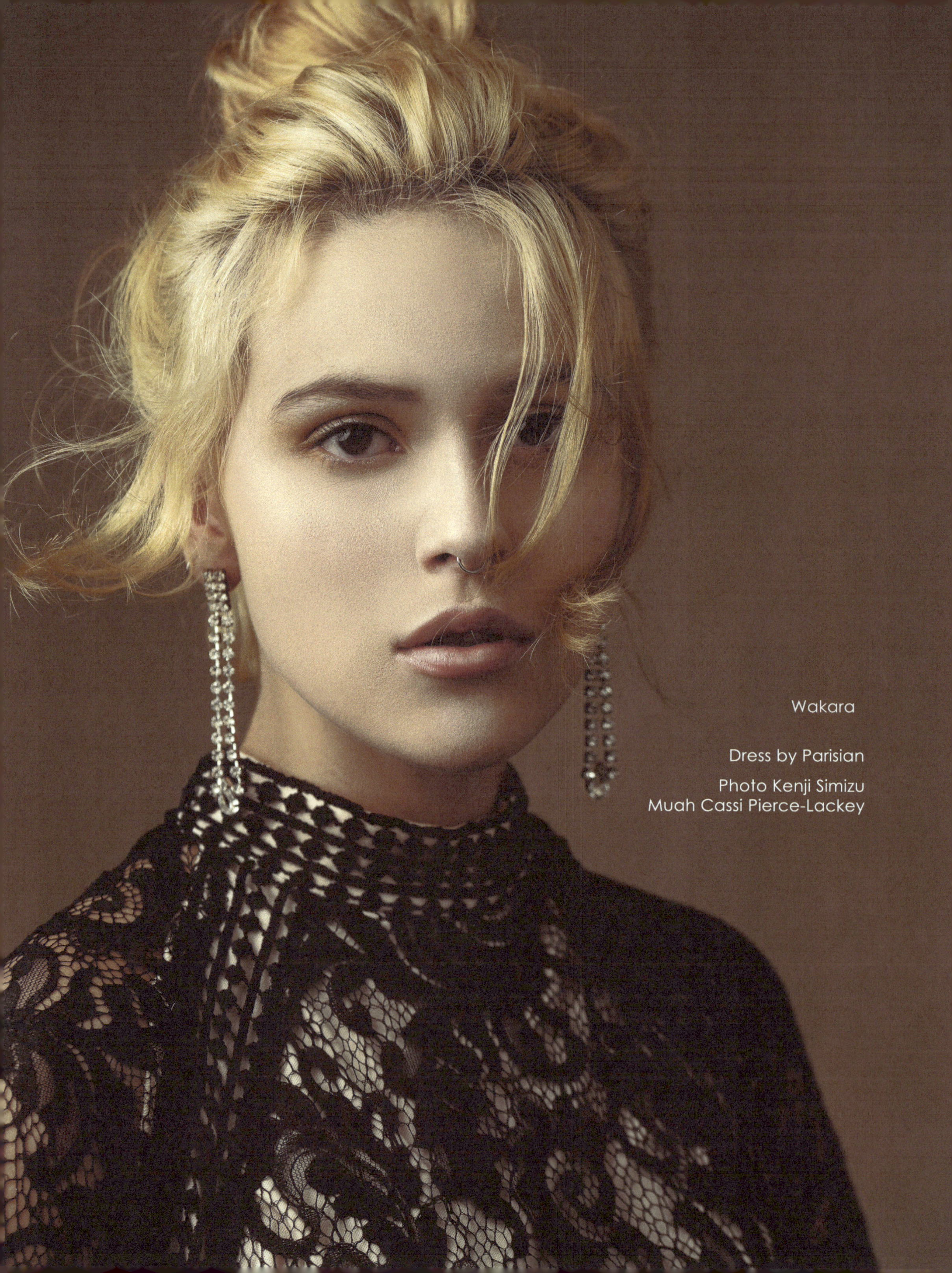
Wakara

Dress by Parisian
Photo Kenji Simizu
Muah Cassi Pierce-Lackey

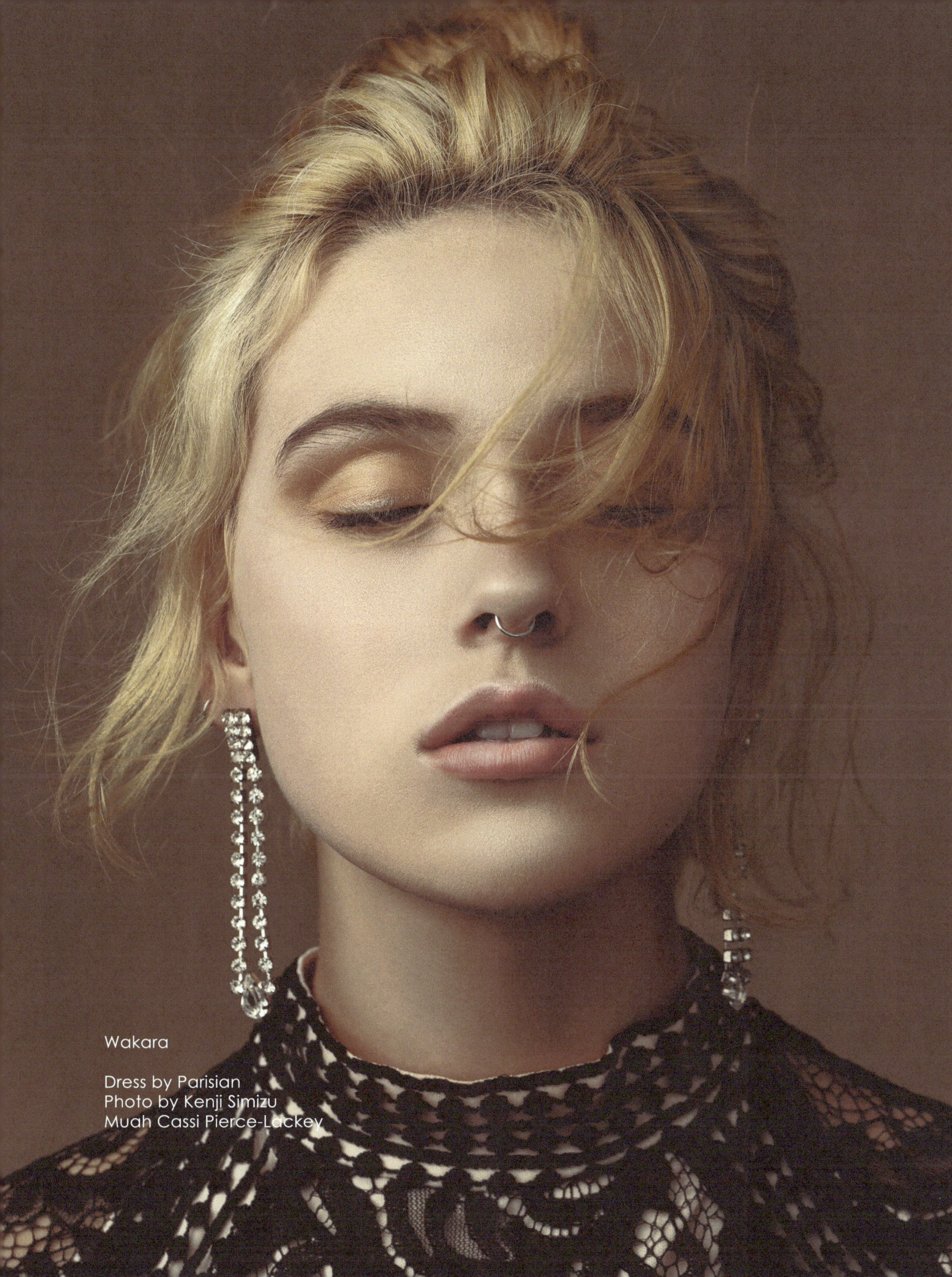

Wakara

Dress by Parisian
Photo by Kenji Simizu
Muah Cassi Pierce-Lackey

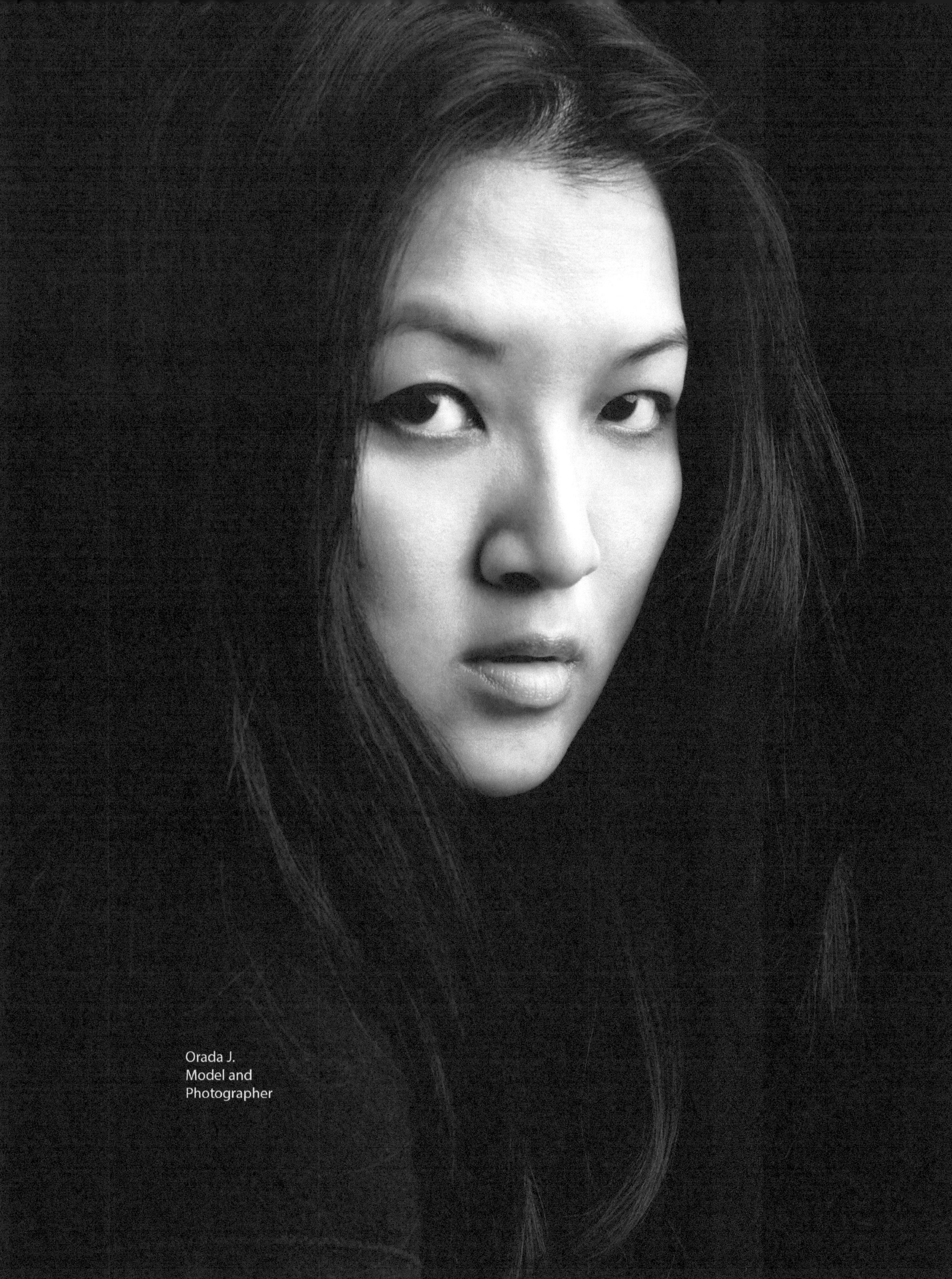

Orada J.
Model and
Photographer

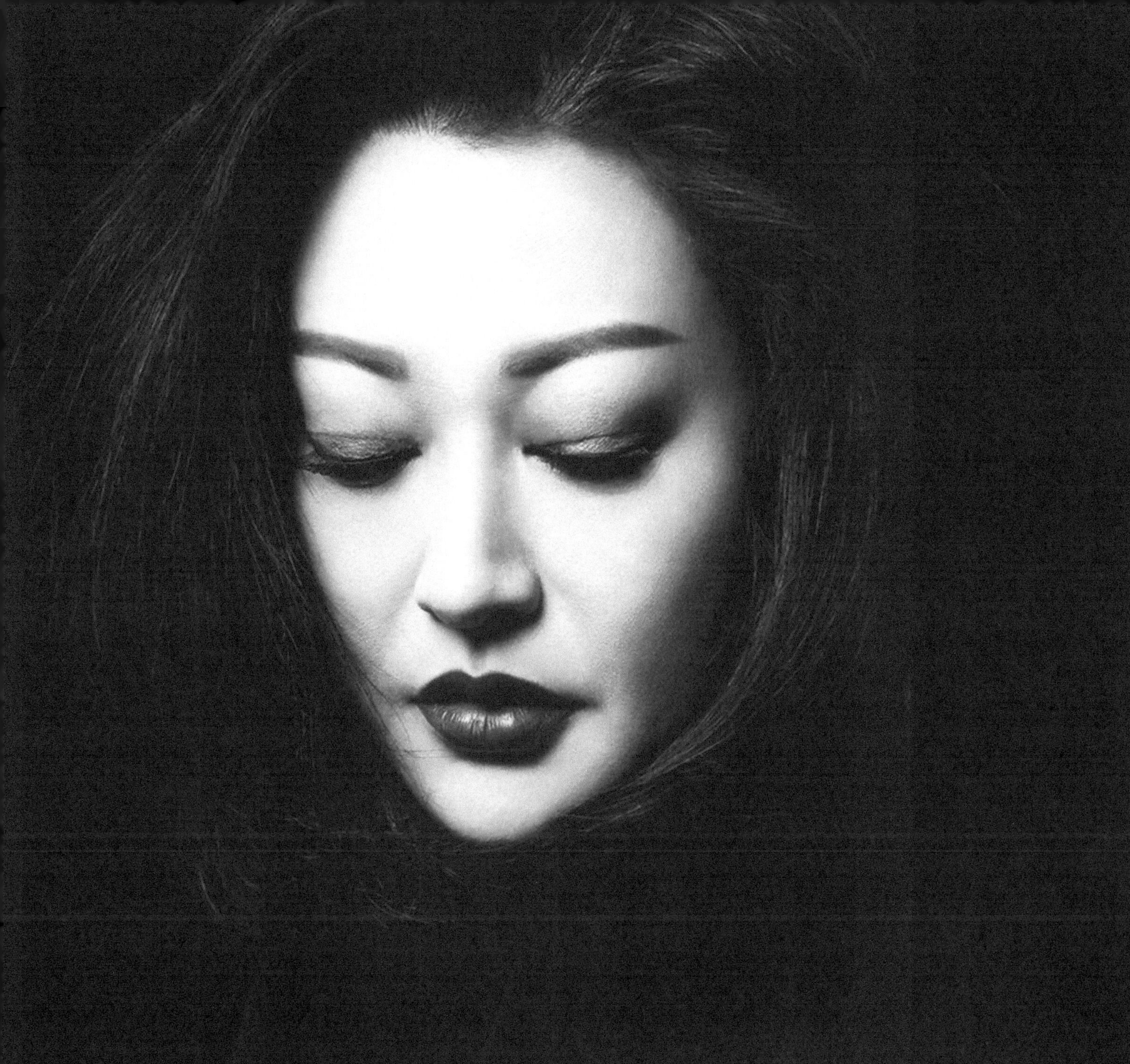

Song Hong
Designer Cashmere Song Collection
Photo Kevin Mock

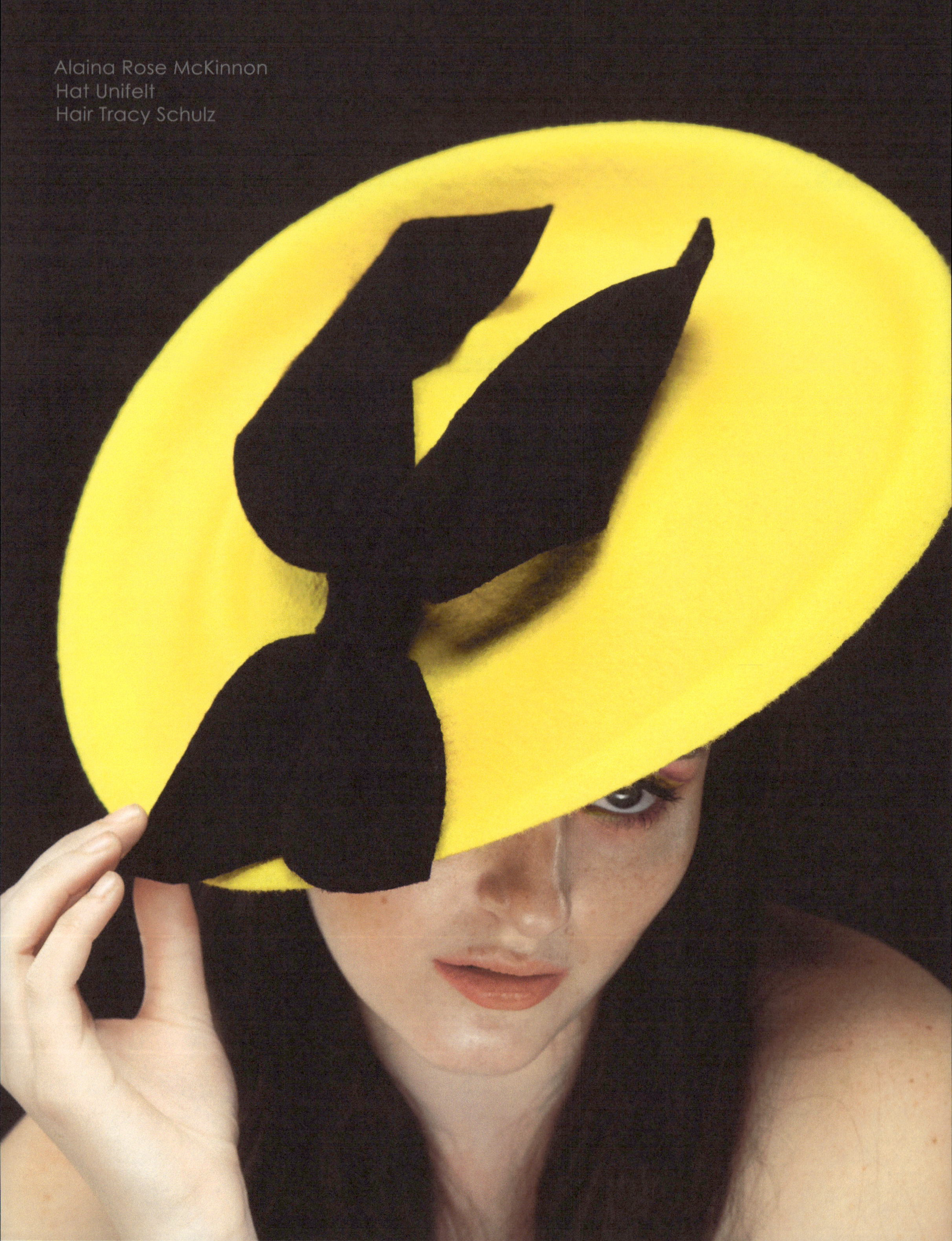

Alaina Rose McKinnon
Hat Unifelt
Hair Tracy Schulz

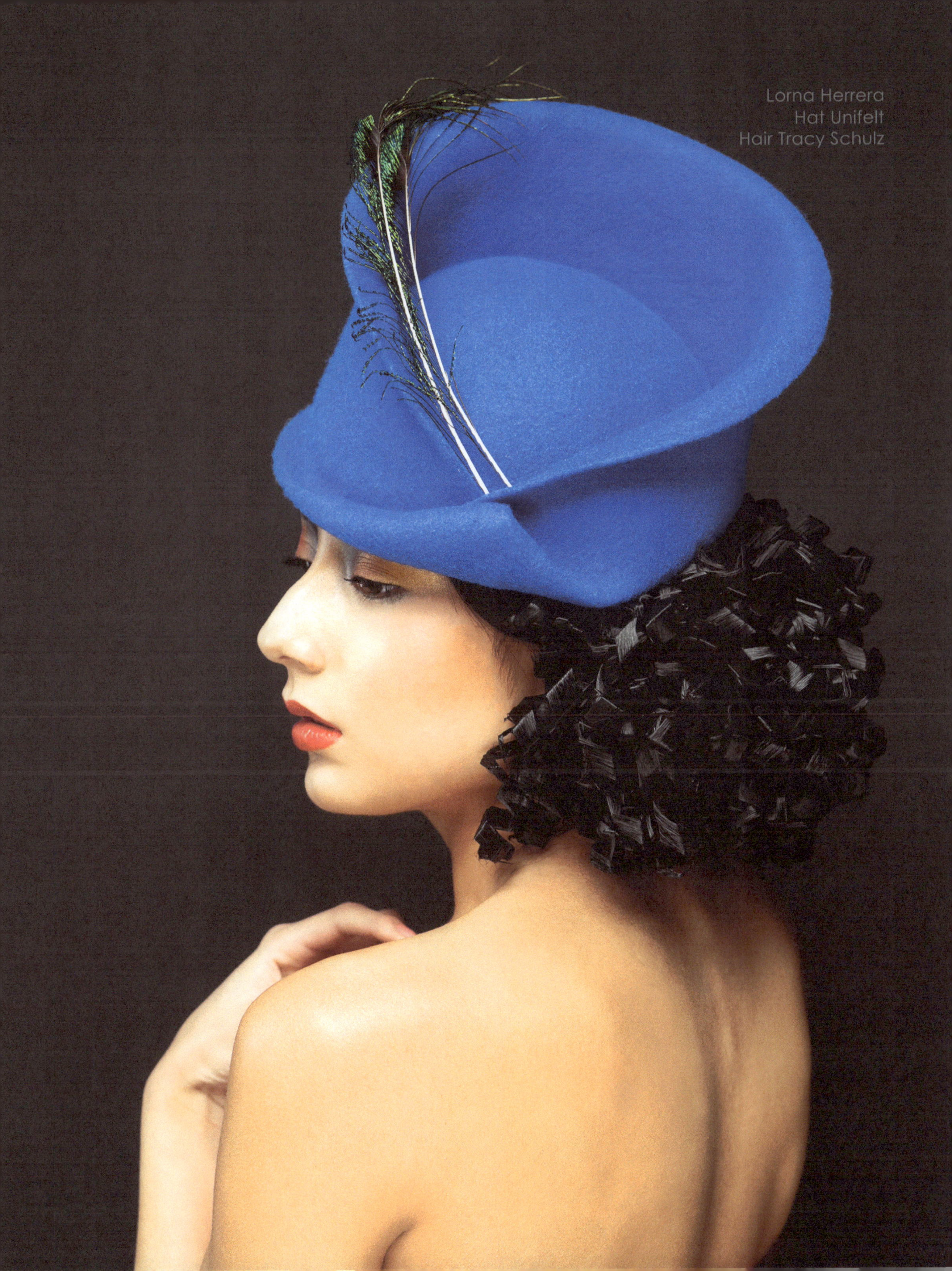
Lorna Herrera
Hat Unifelt
Hair Tracy Schulz

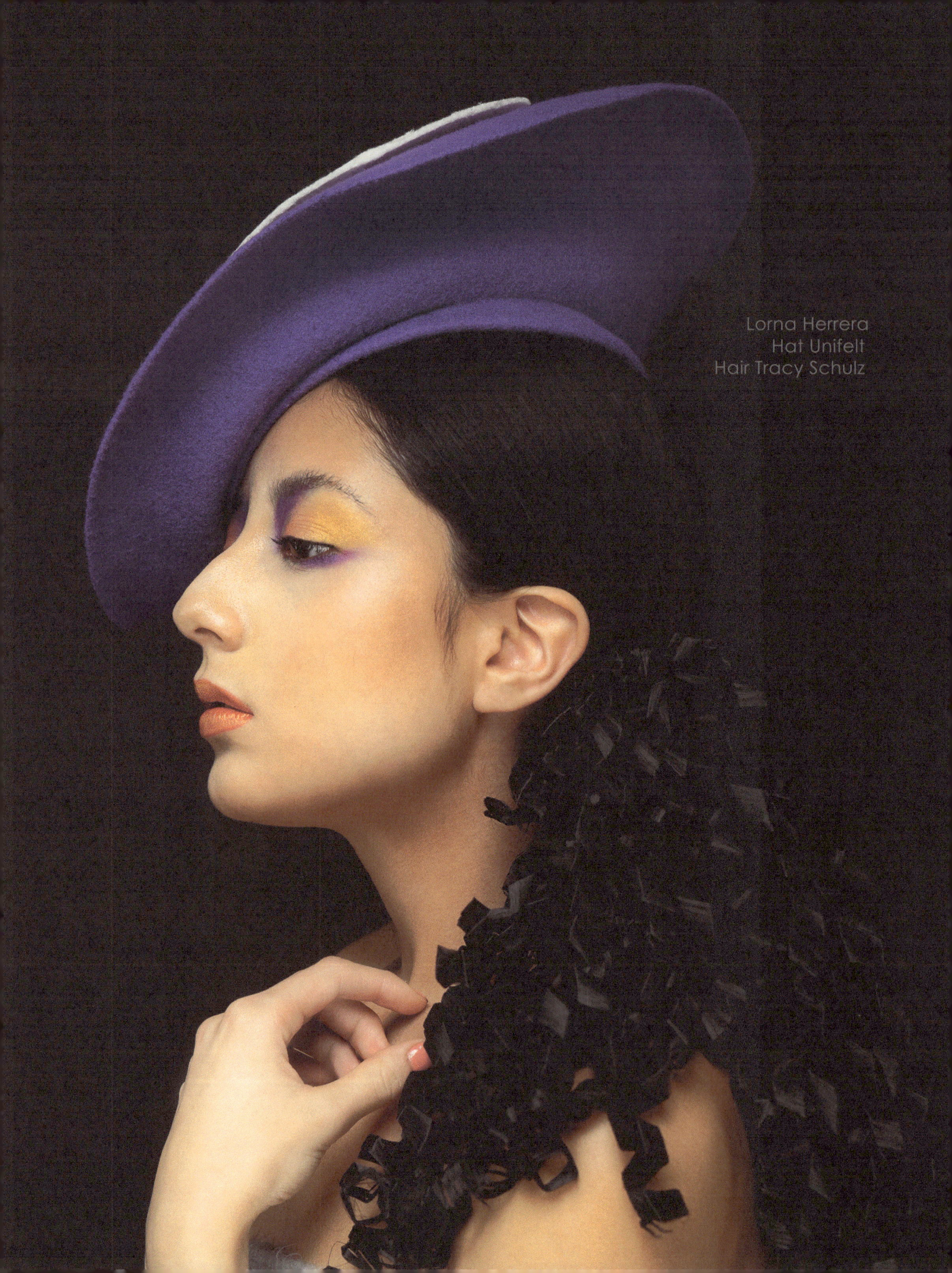
Lorna Herrera
Hat Unifelt
Hair Tracy Schulz

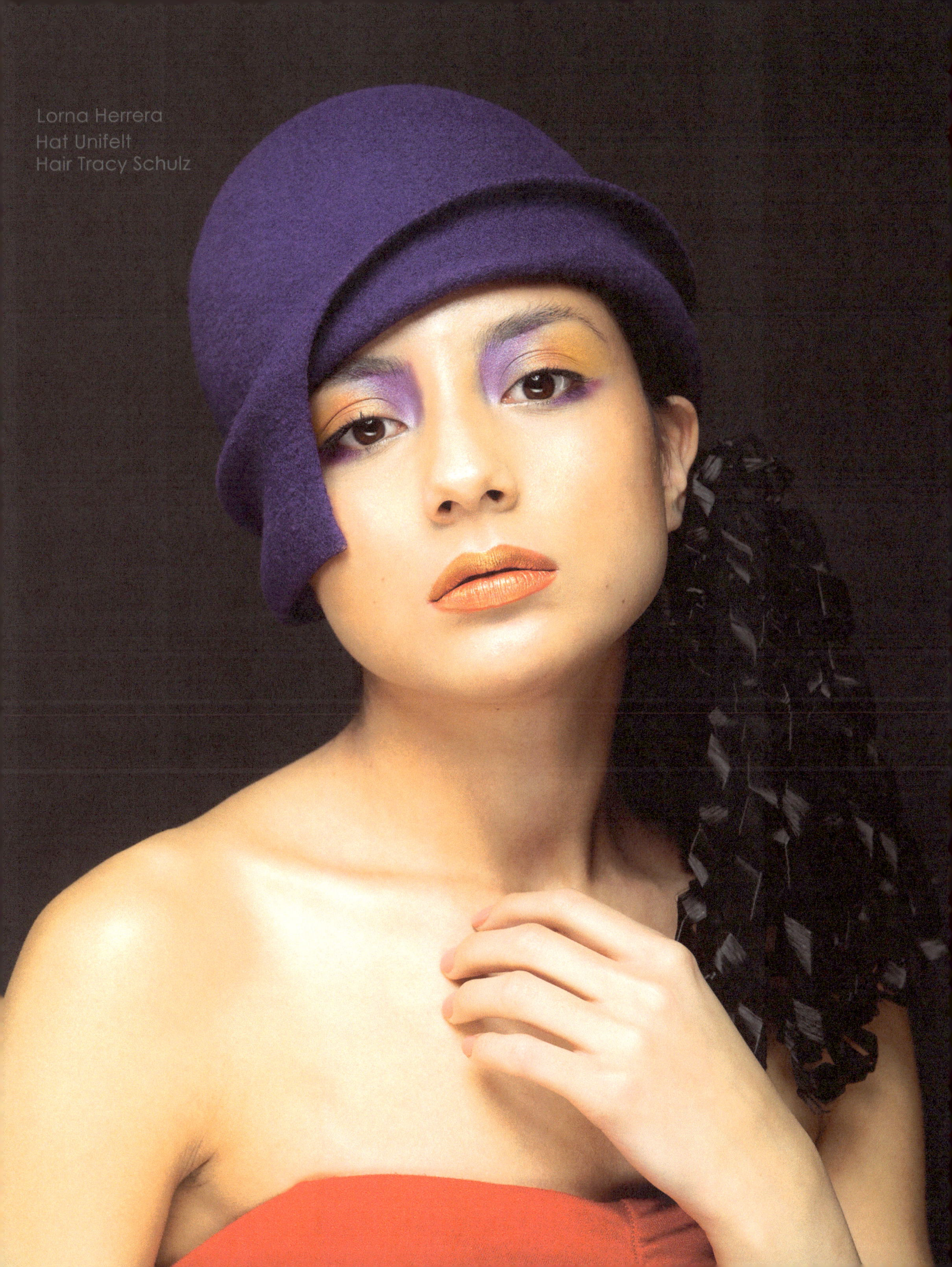

Lorna Herrera
Hat Unifelt
Hair Tracy Schulz

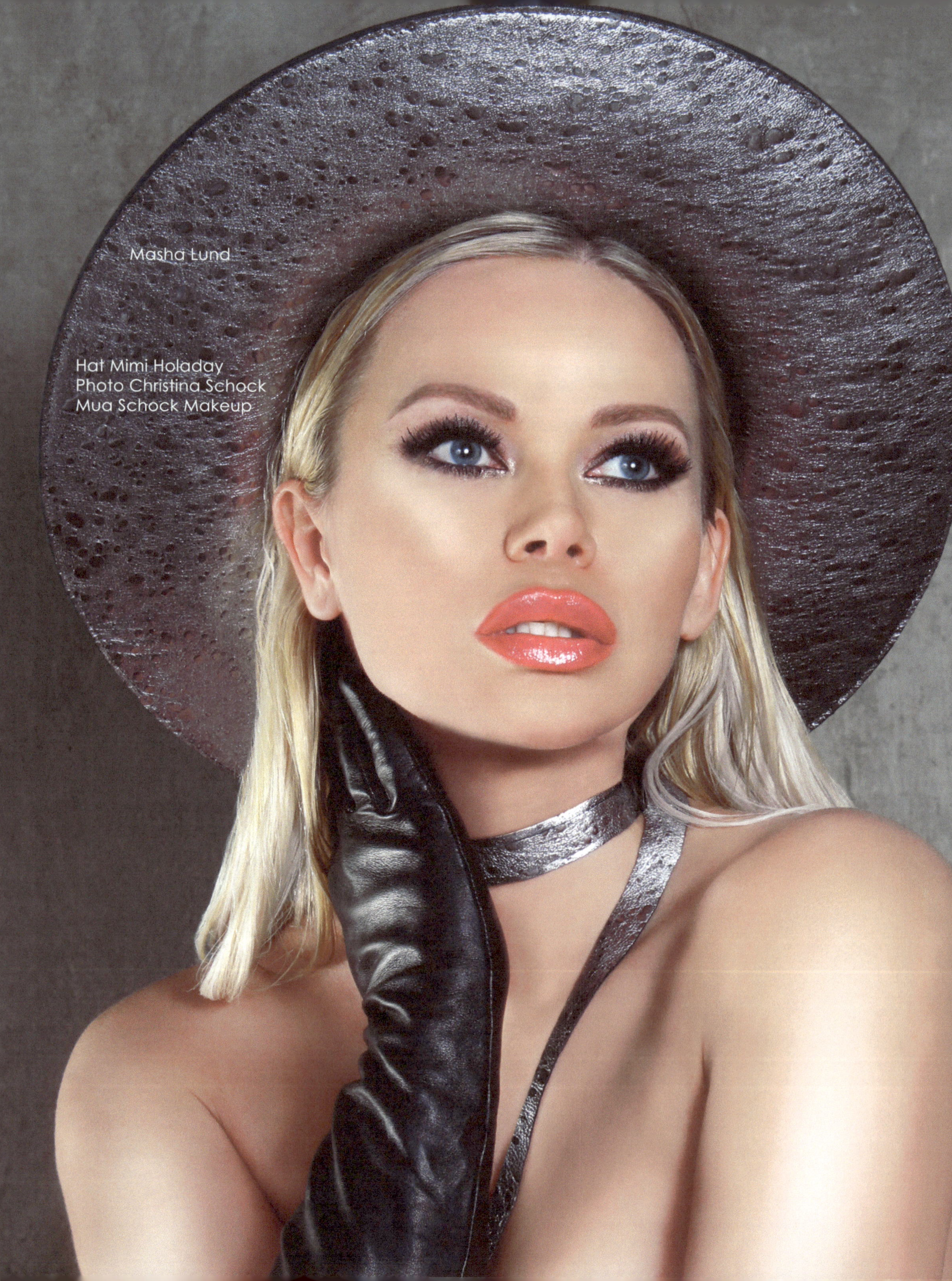

Masha Lund

Hat Mimi Holaday
Photo Christina Schock
Mua Schock Makeup

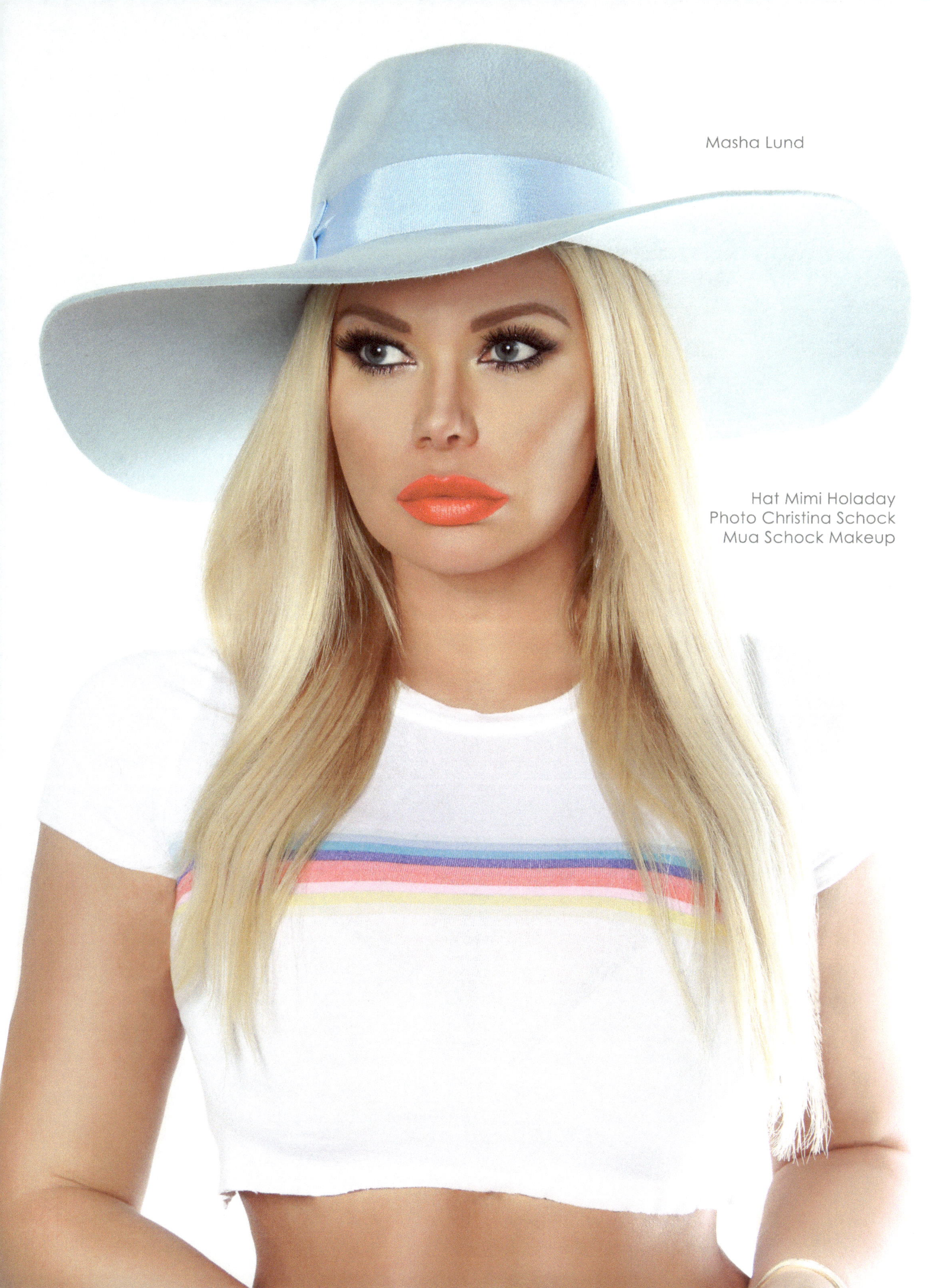

Masha Lund

Hat Mimi Holaday
Photo Christina Schock
Mua Schock Makeup

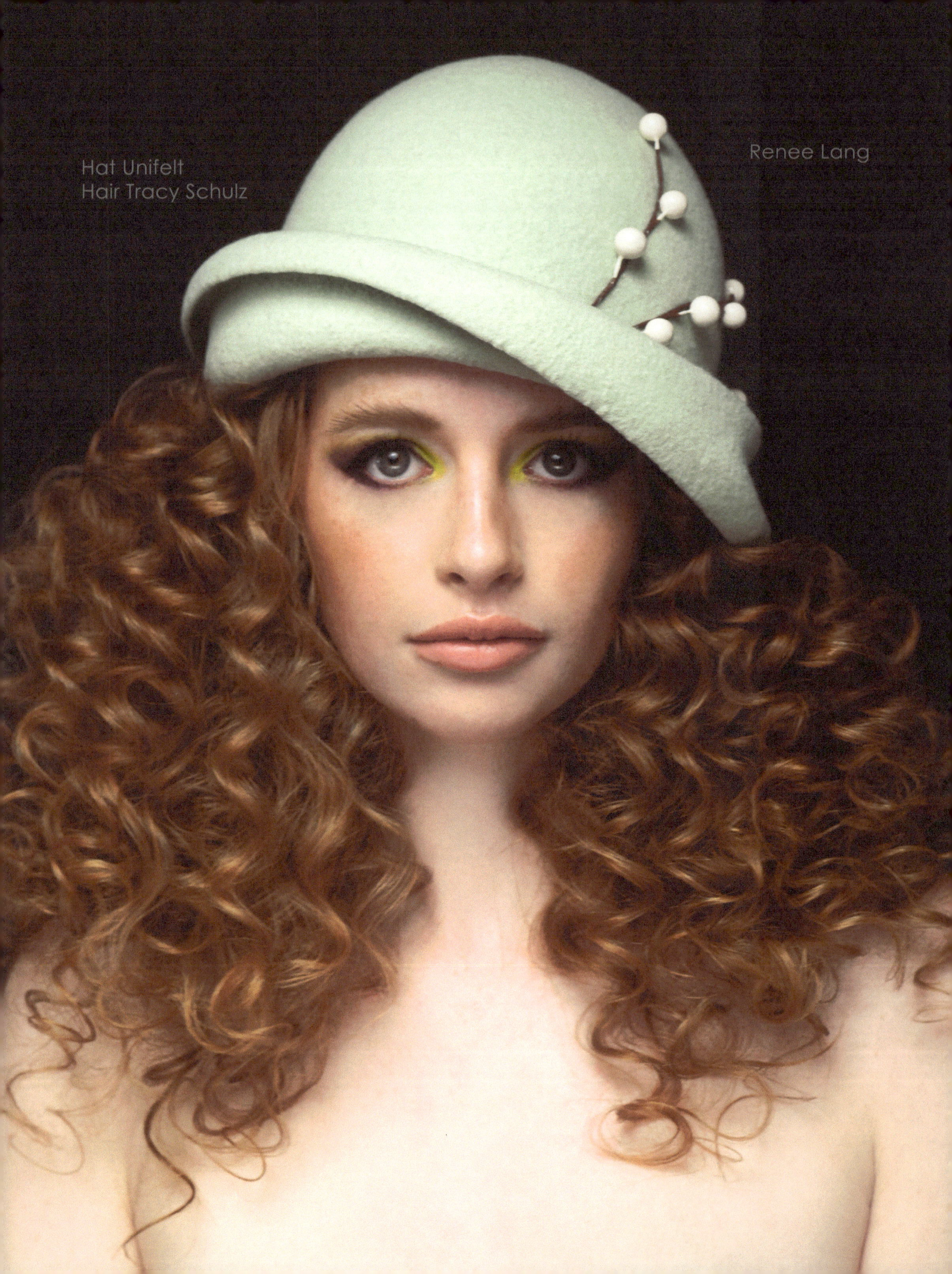

Hat Unifelt
Hair Tracy Schulz
Renee Lang

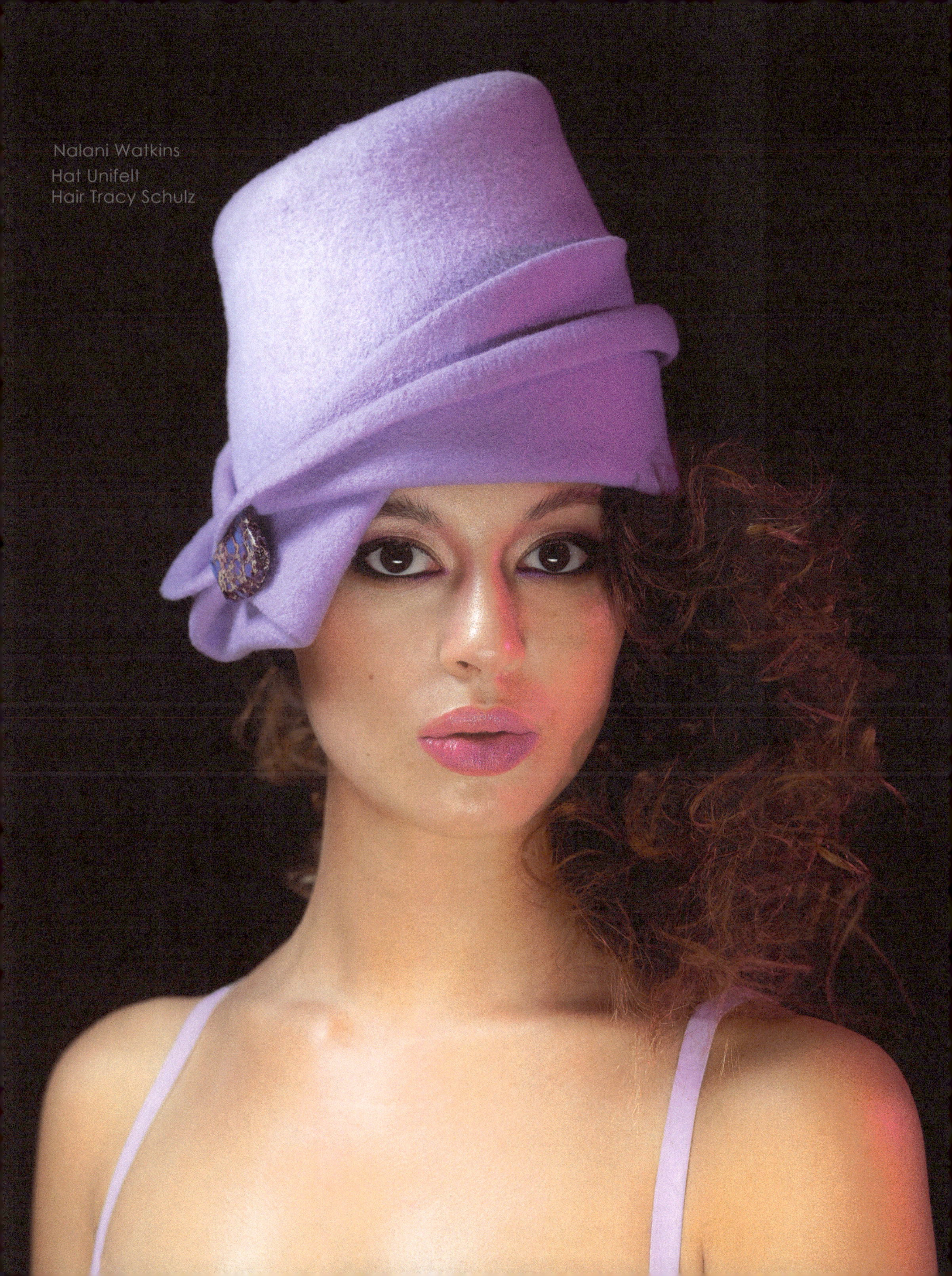

Nalani Watkins
Hat Unifelt
Hair Tracy Schulz

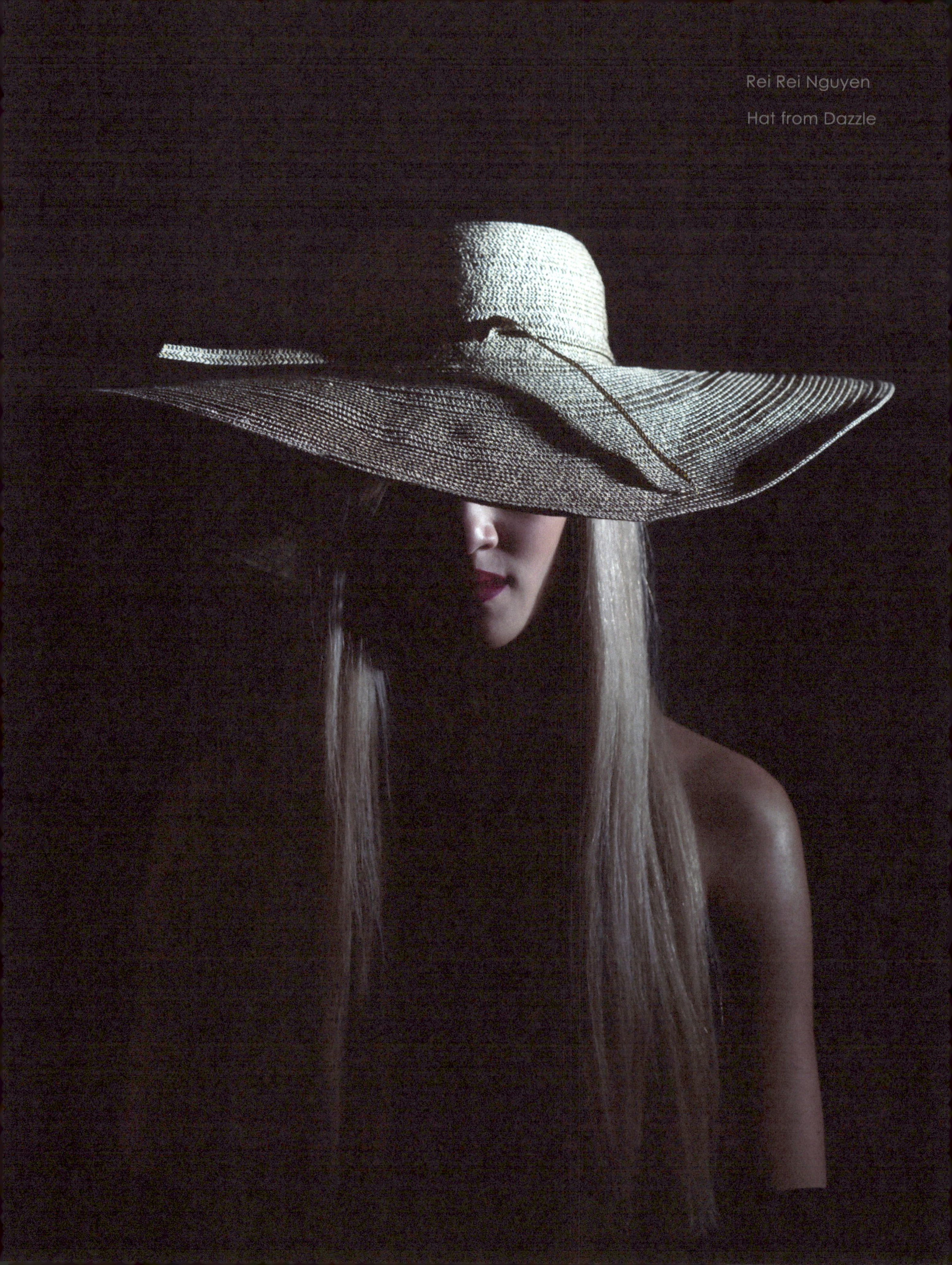

Rei Rei Nguyen
Hat from Dazzle

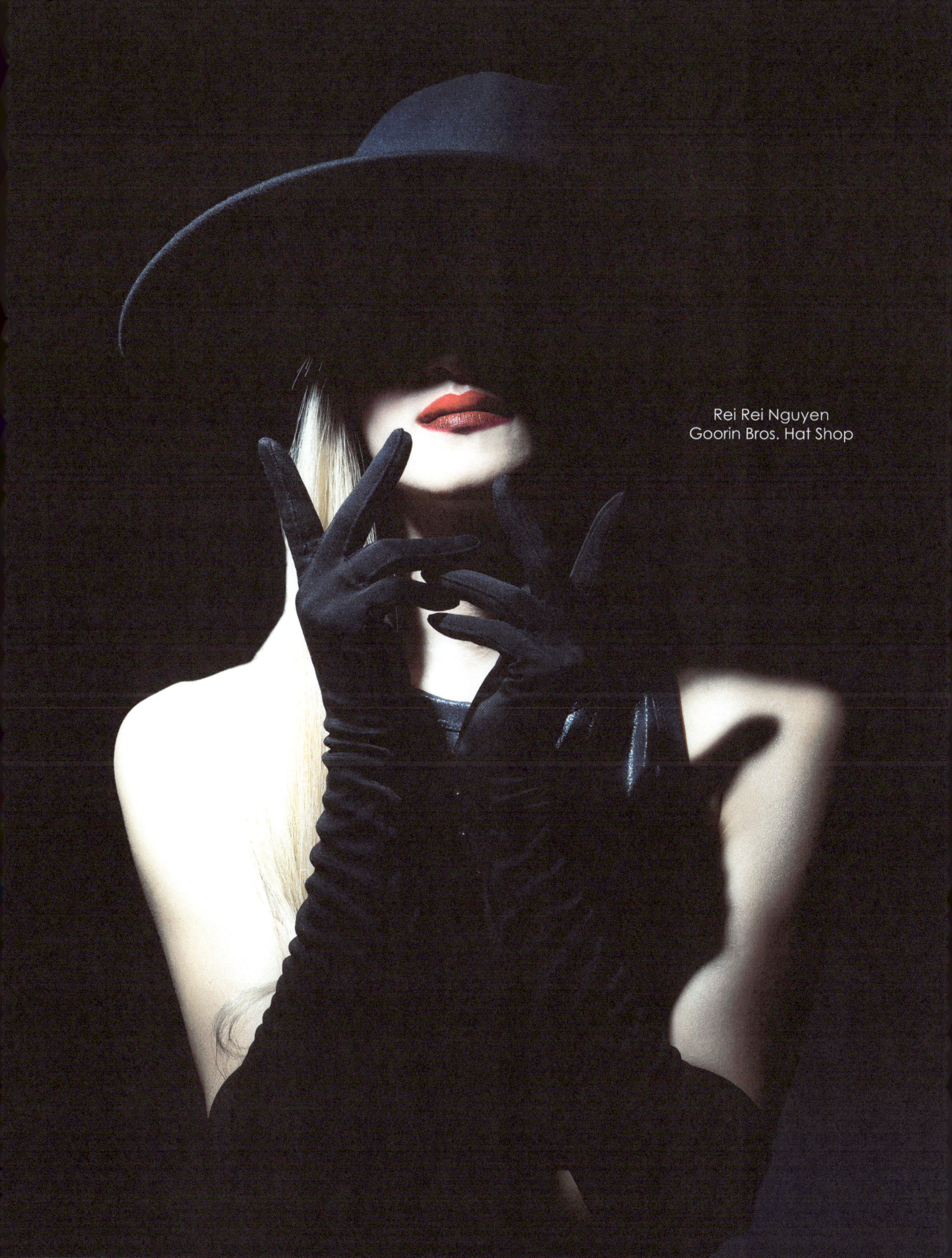
Rei Rei Nguyen
Goorin Bros. Hat Shop

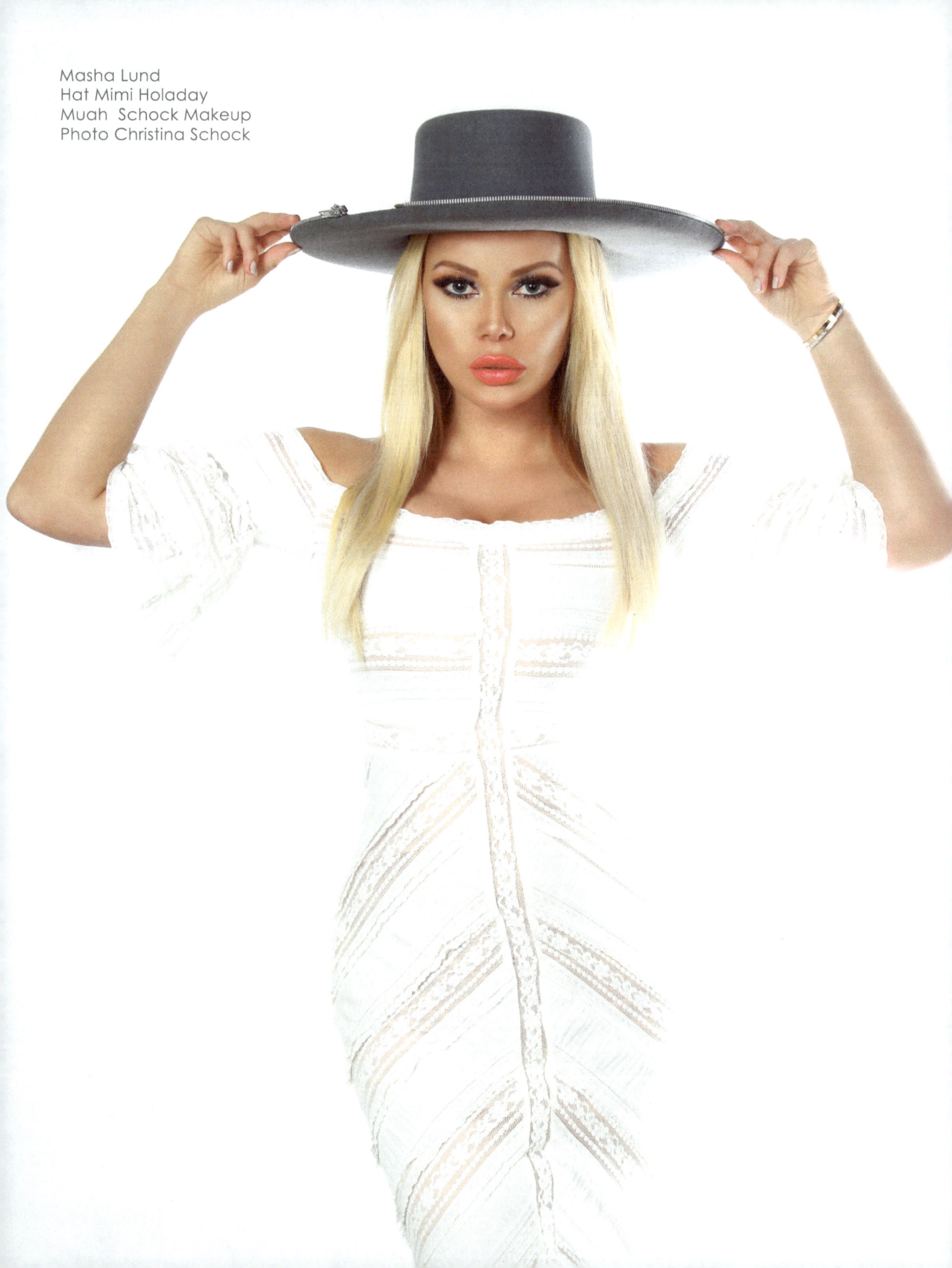

Masha Lund
Hat Mimi Holaday
Muah Schock Makeup
Photo Christina Schock

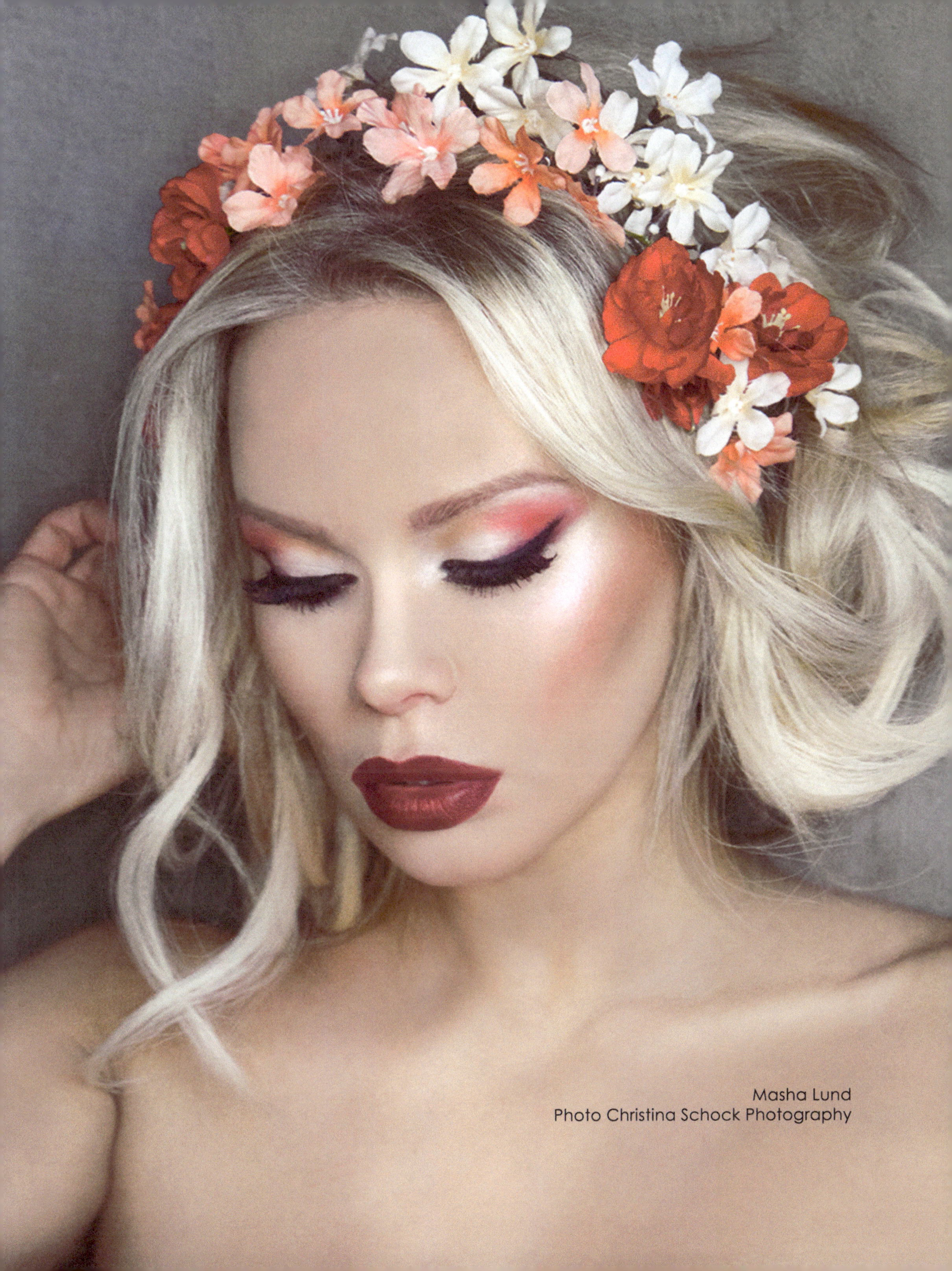

Masha Lund
Photo Christina Schock Photography

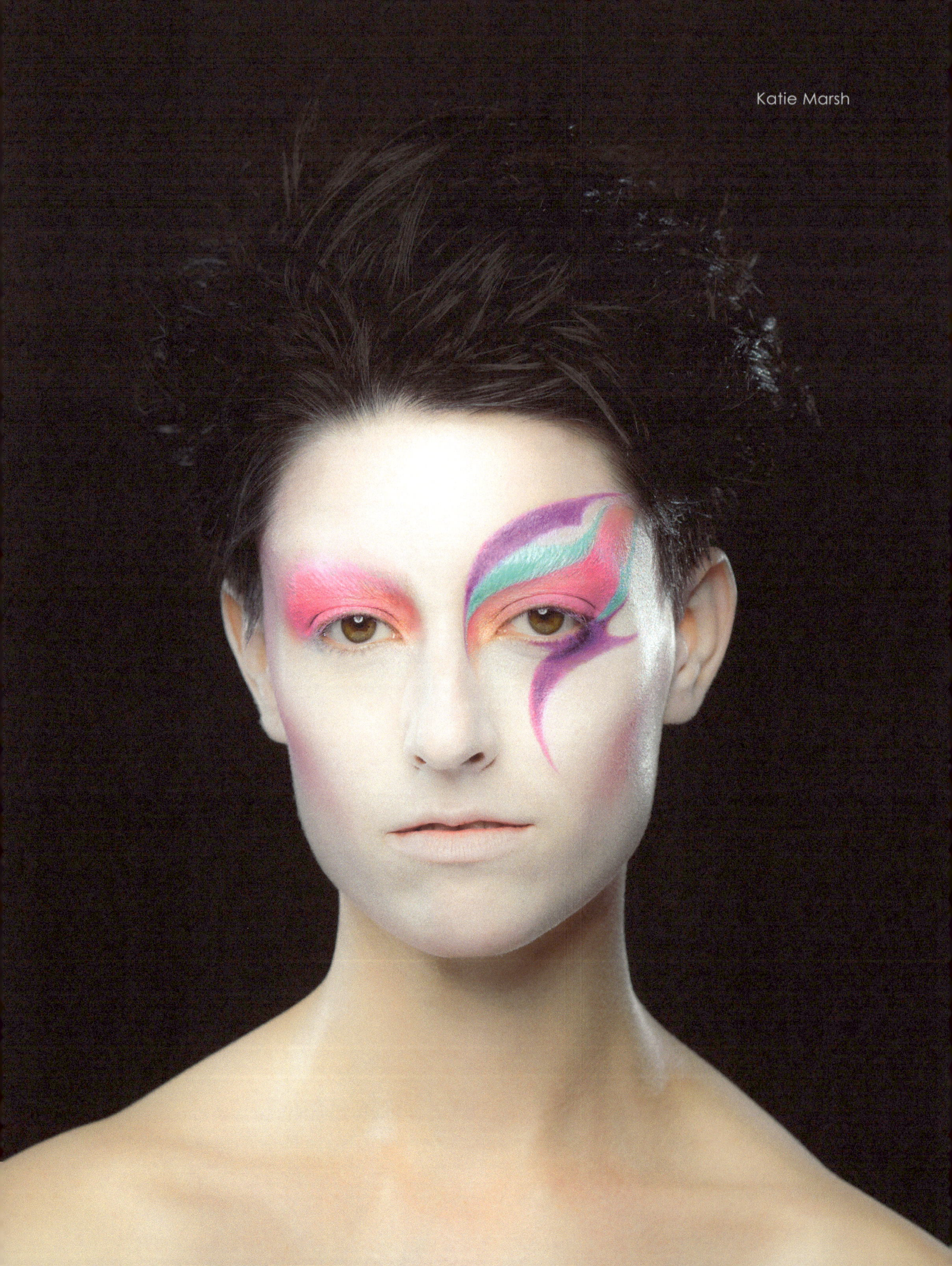
Katie Marsh

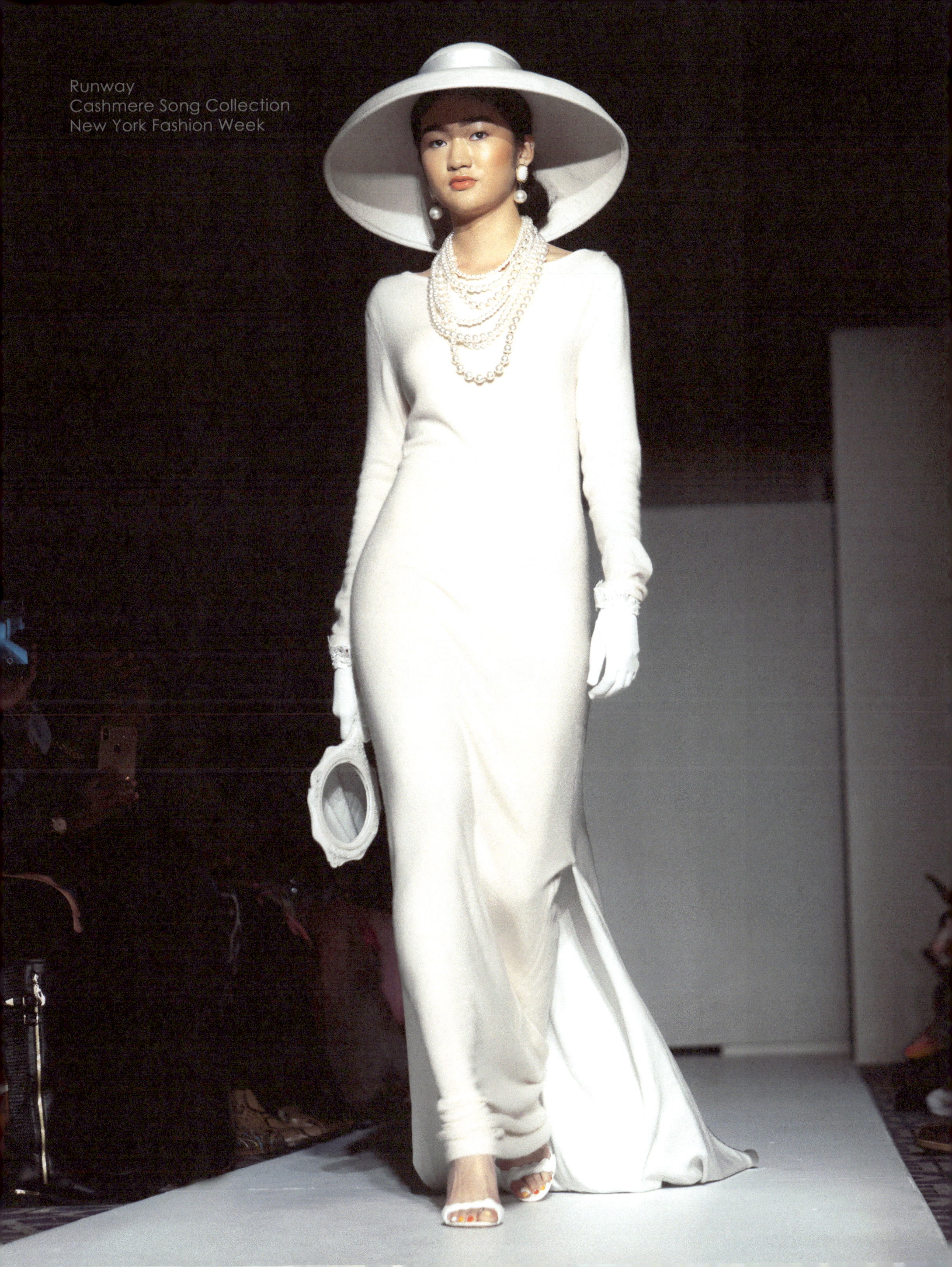
Runway
Cashmere Song Collection
New York Fashion Week

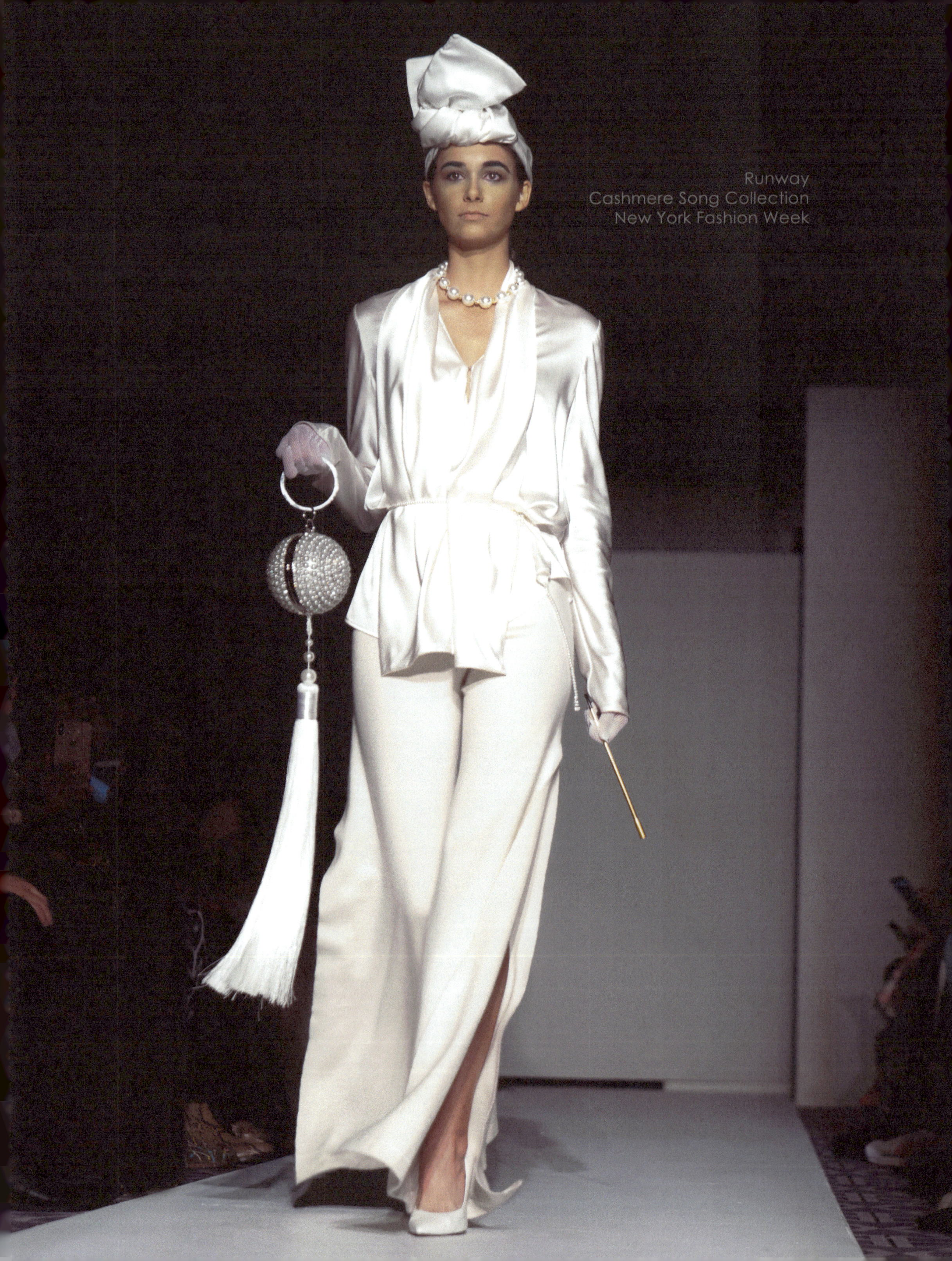
Runway
Cashmere Song Collection
New York Fashion Week

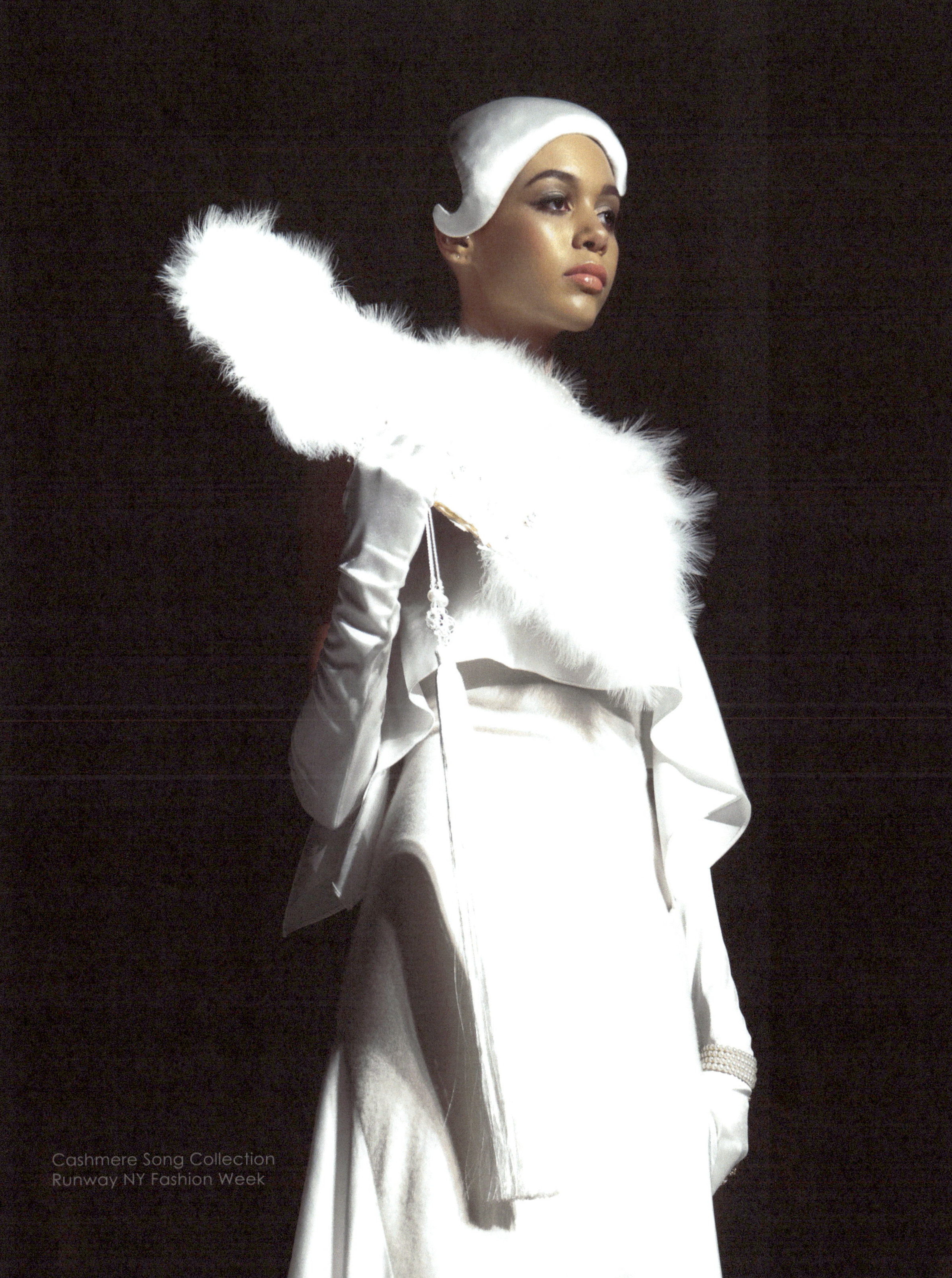

Cashmere Song Collection
Runway NY Fashion Week

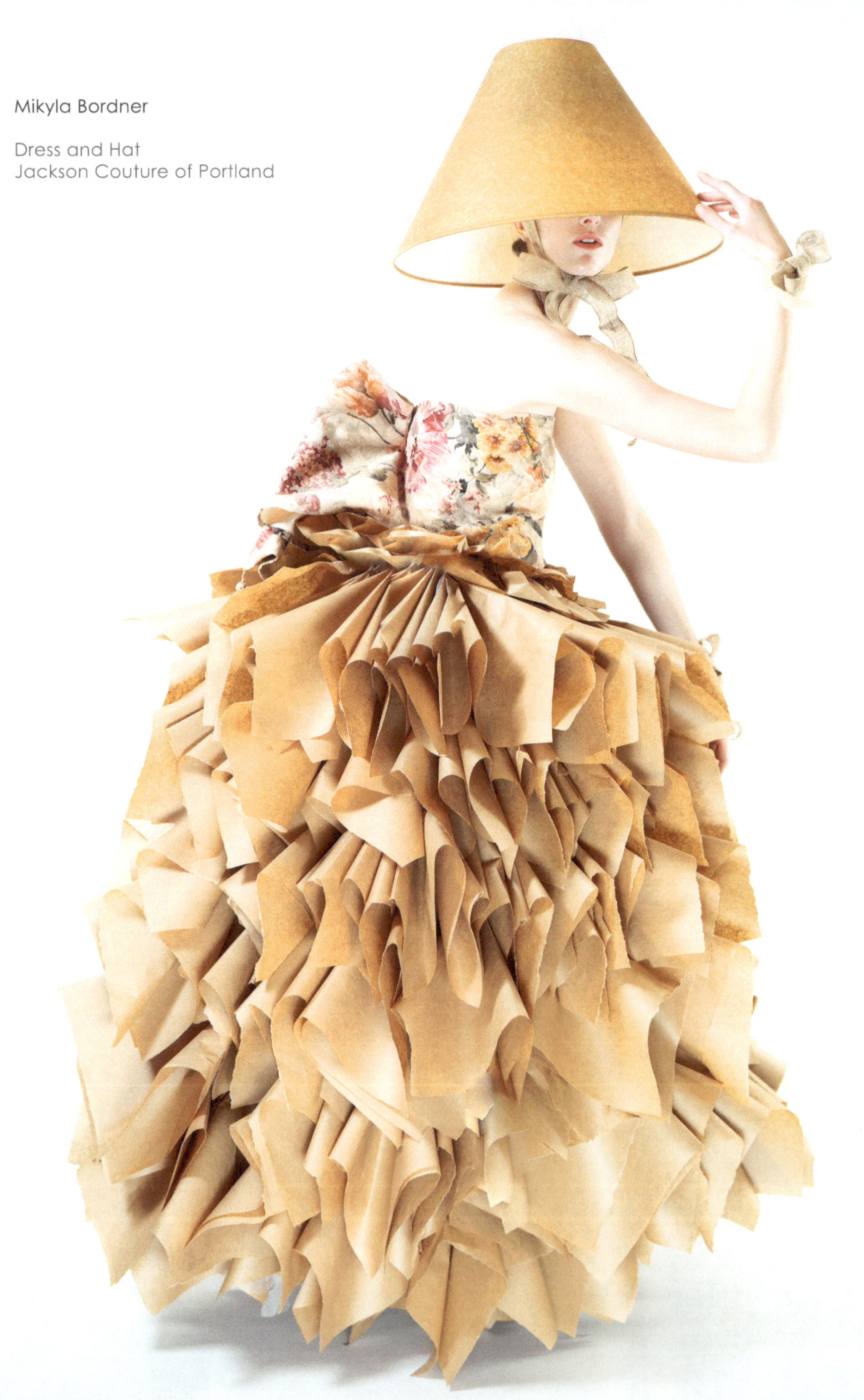

Mikyla Bordner

Dress and Hat
Jackson Couture of Portland

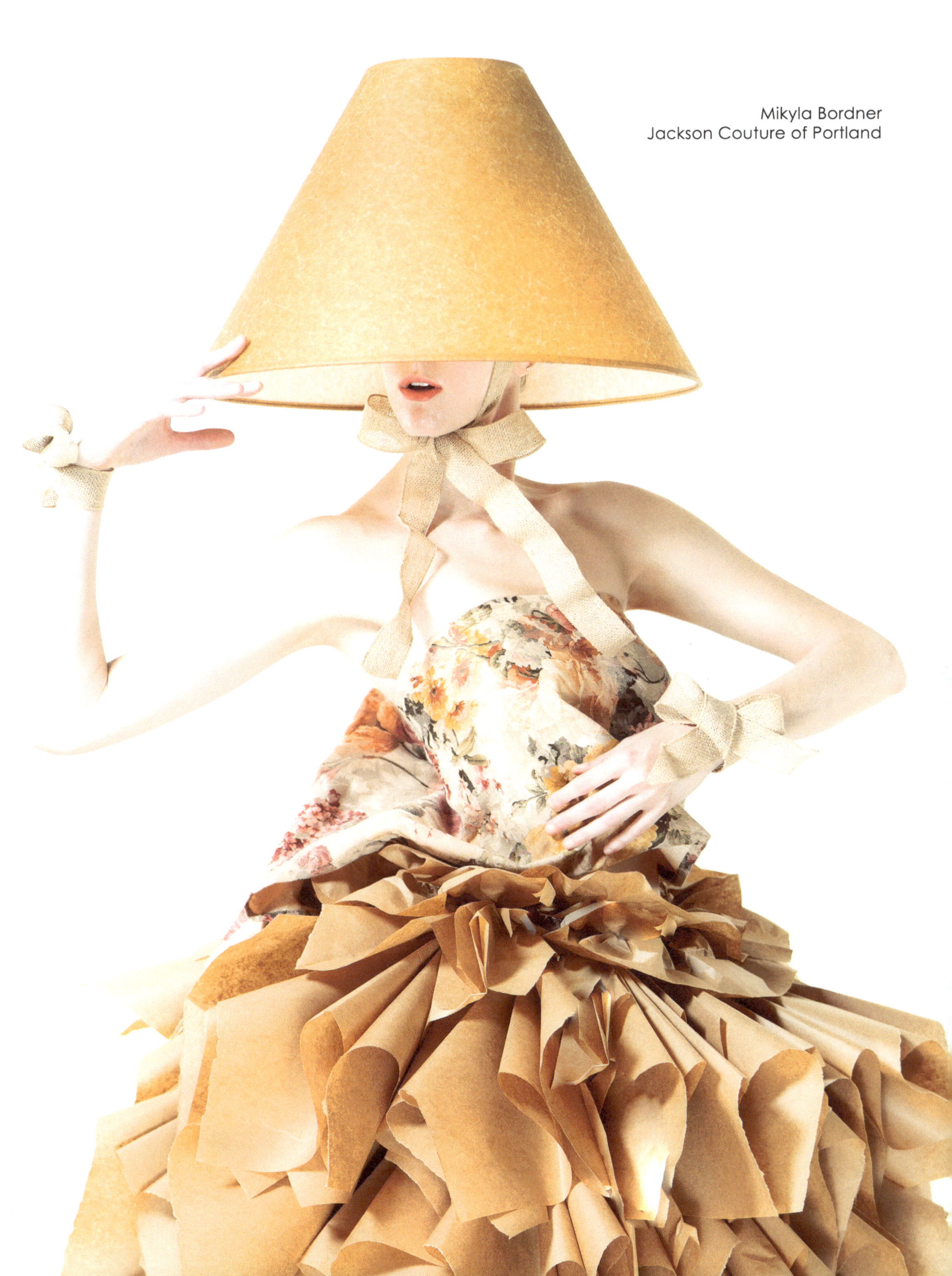

Mikyla Bordner
Jackson Couture of Portland

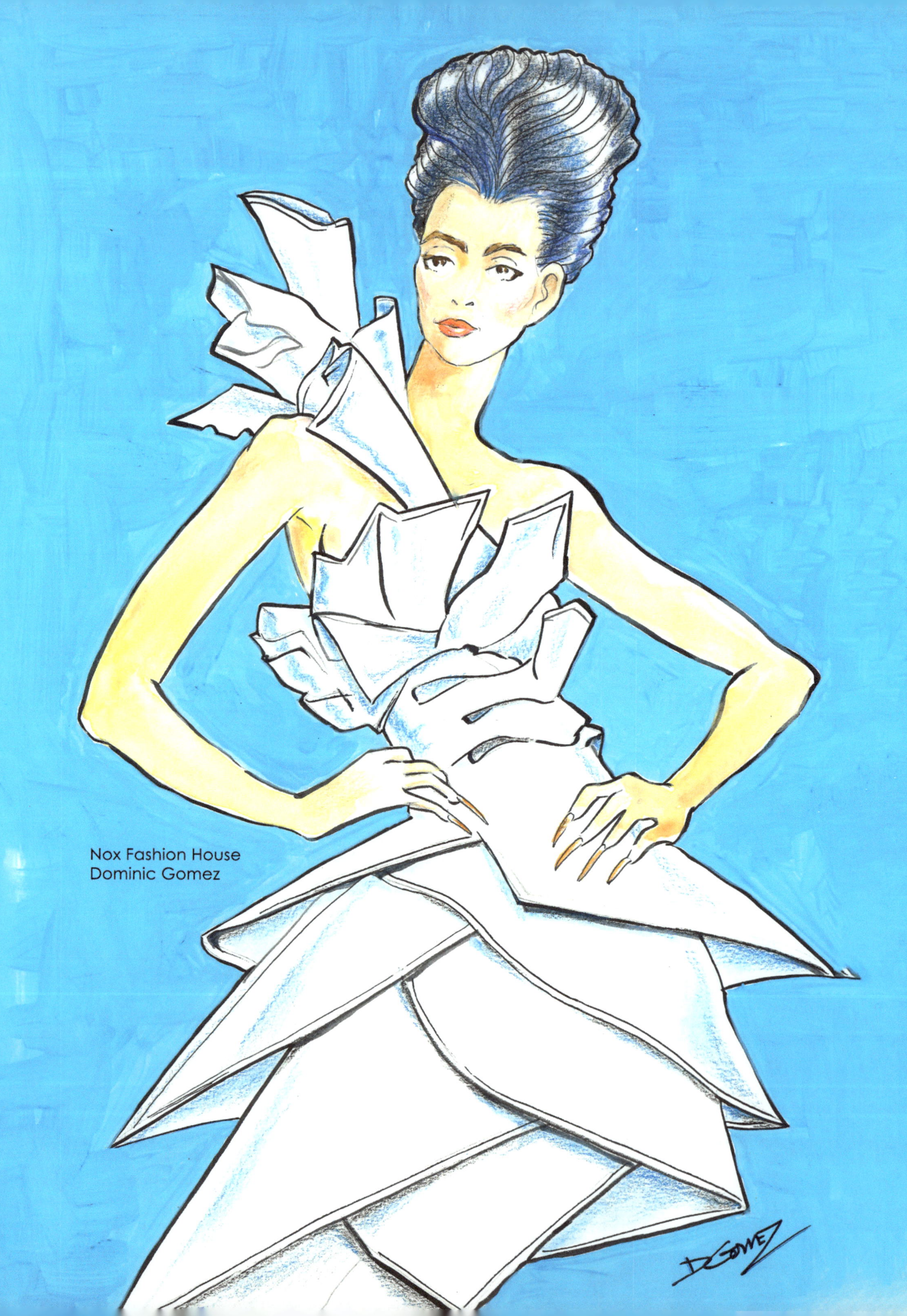

Nox Fashion House
Dominic Gomez

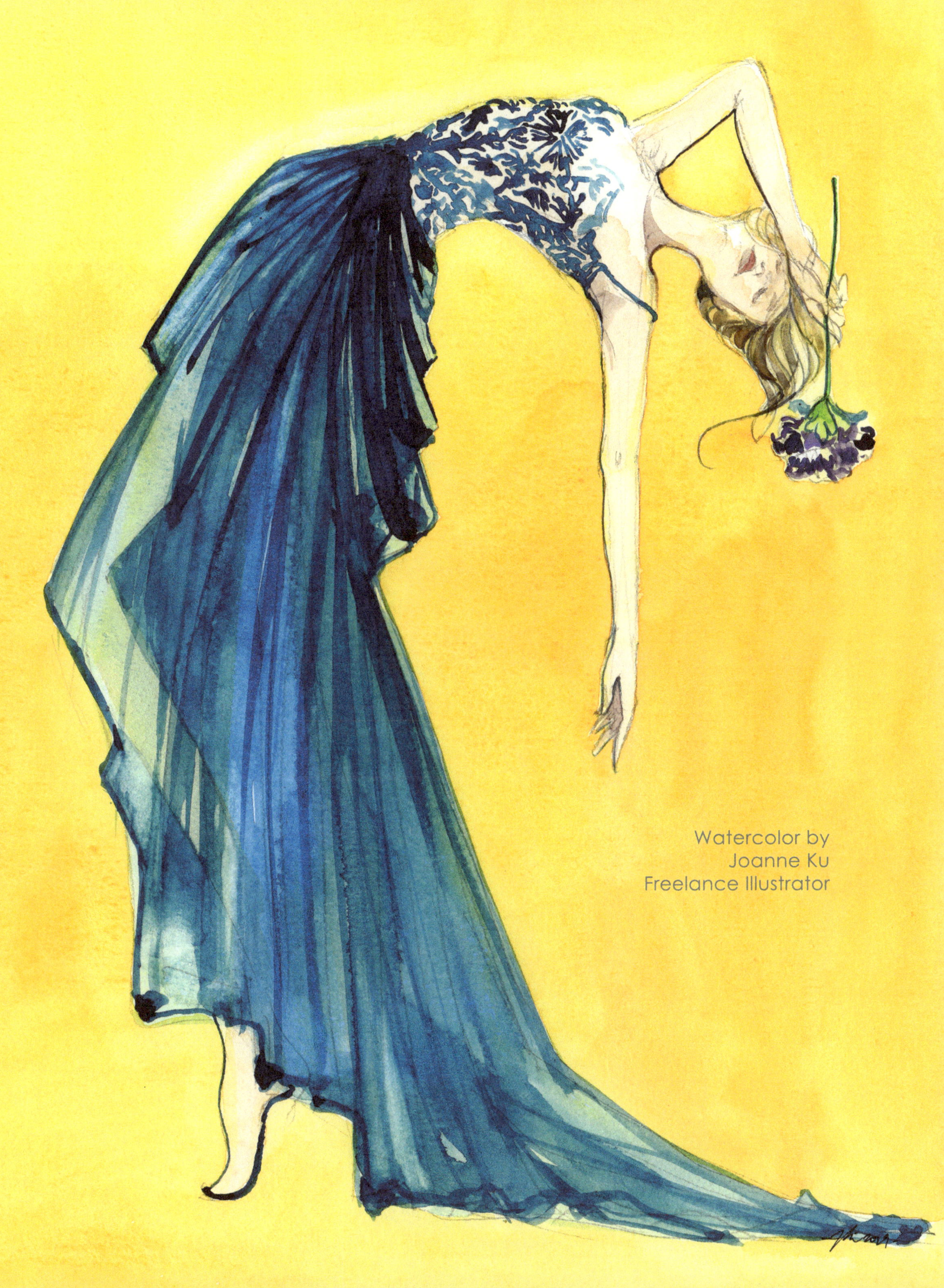
Watercolor by
Joanne Ku
Freelance Illustrator

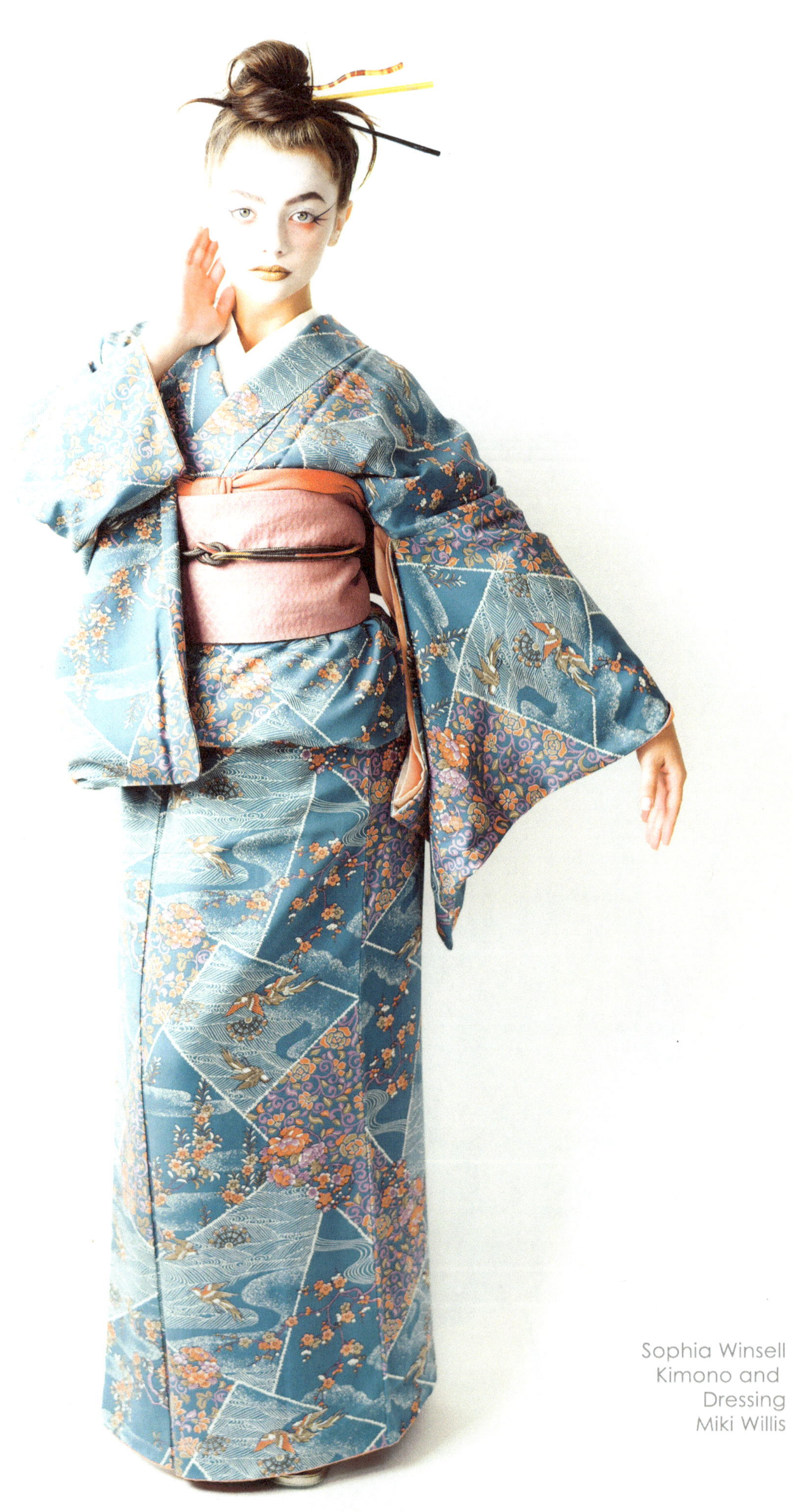

Sophia Winsell
Kimono and
Dressing
Miki Willis

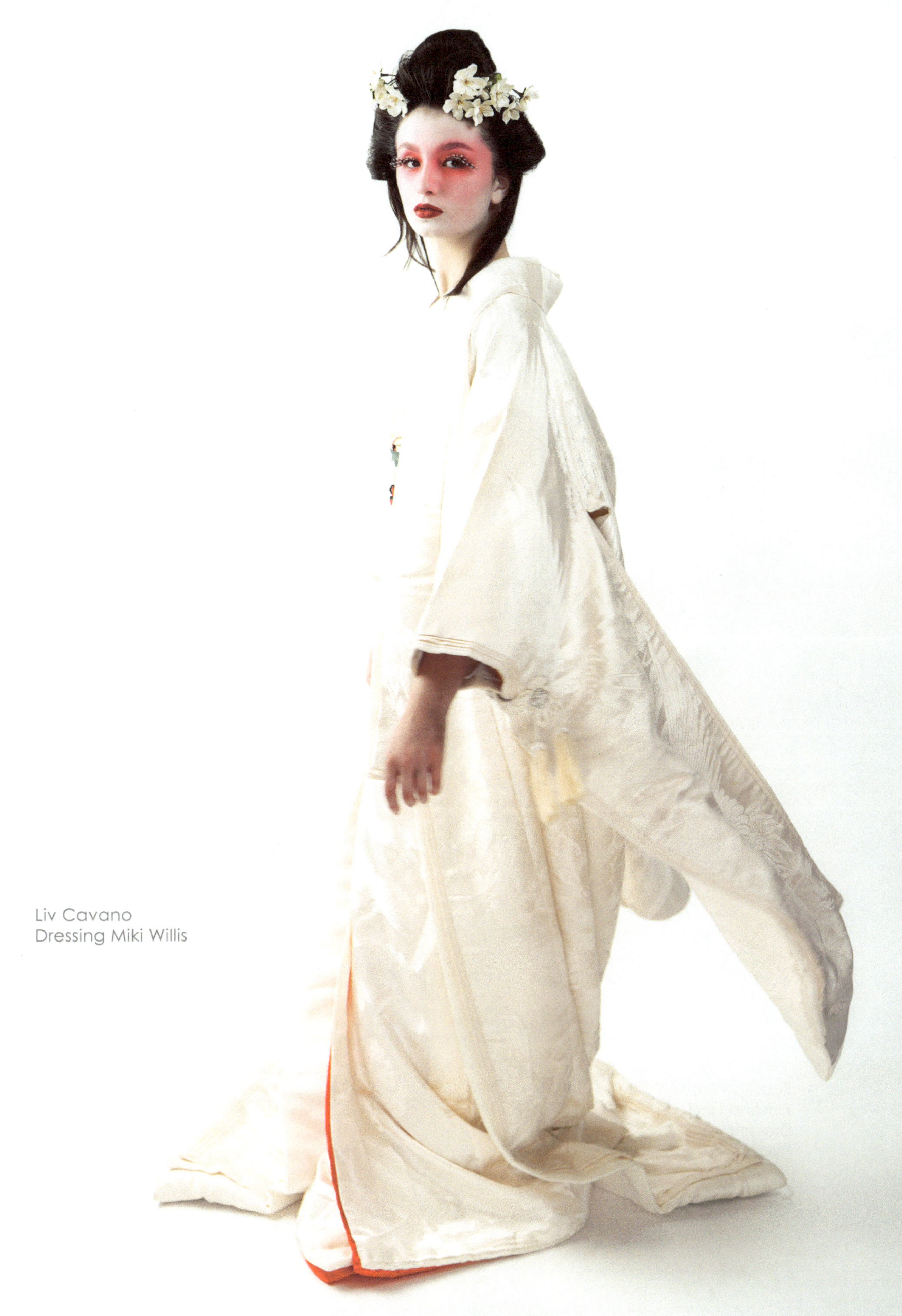

Liv Cavano
Dressing Miki Willis

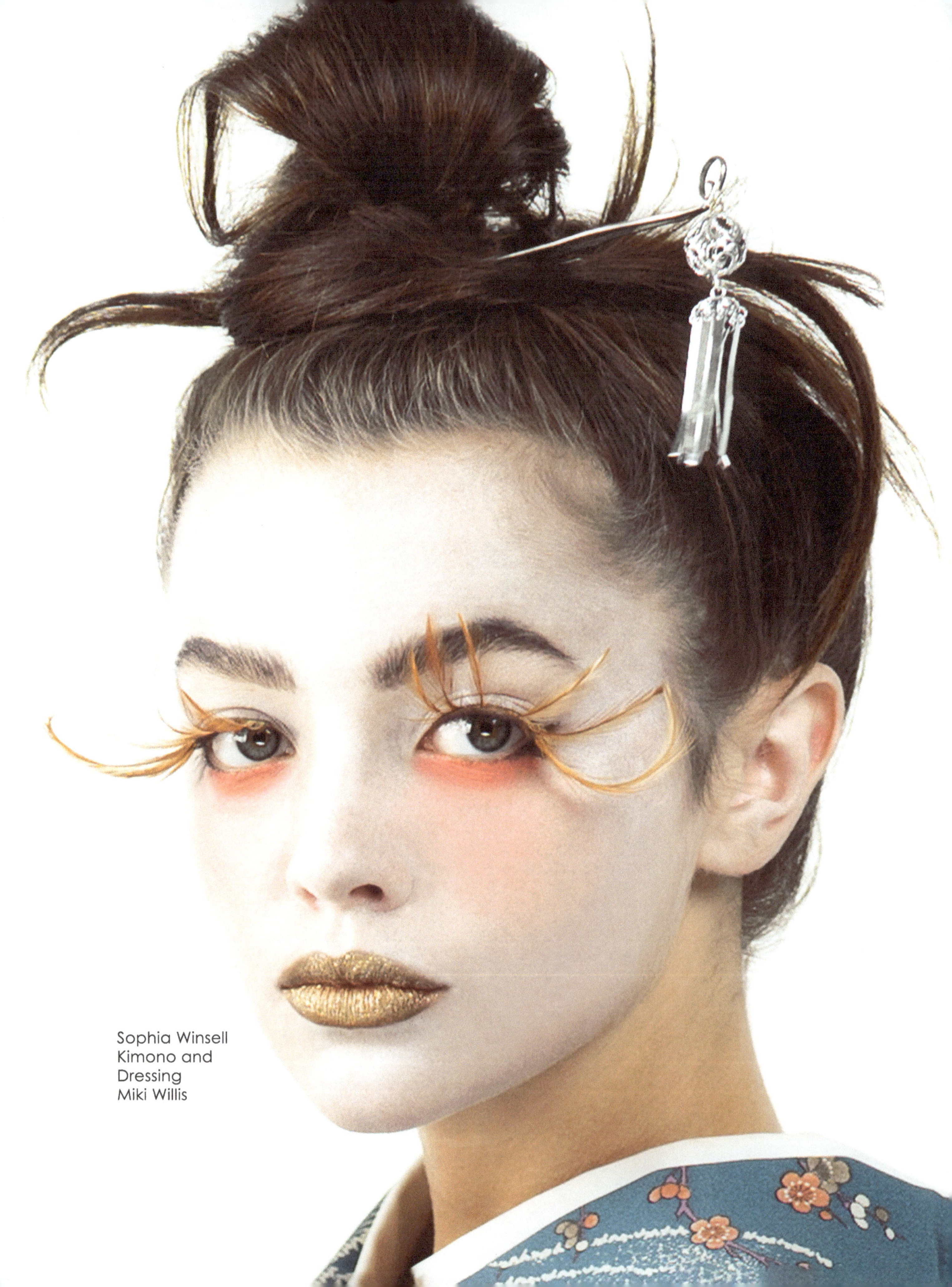

Sophia Winsell
Kimono and
Dressing
Miki Willis

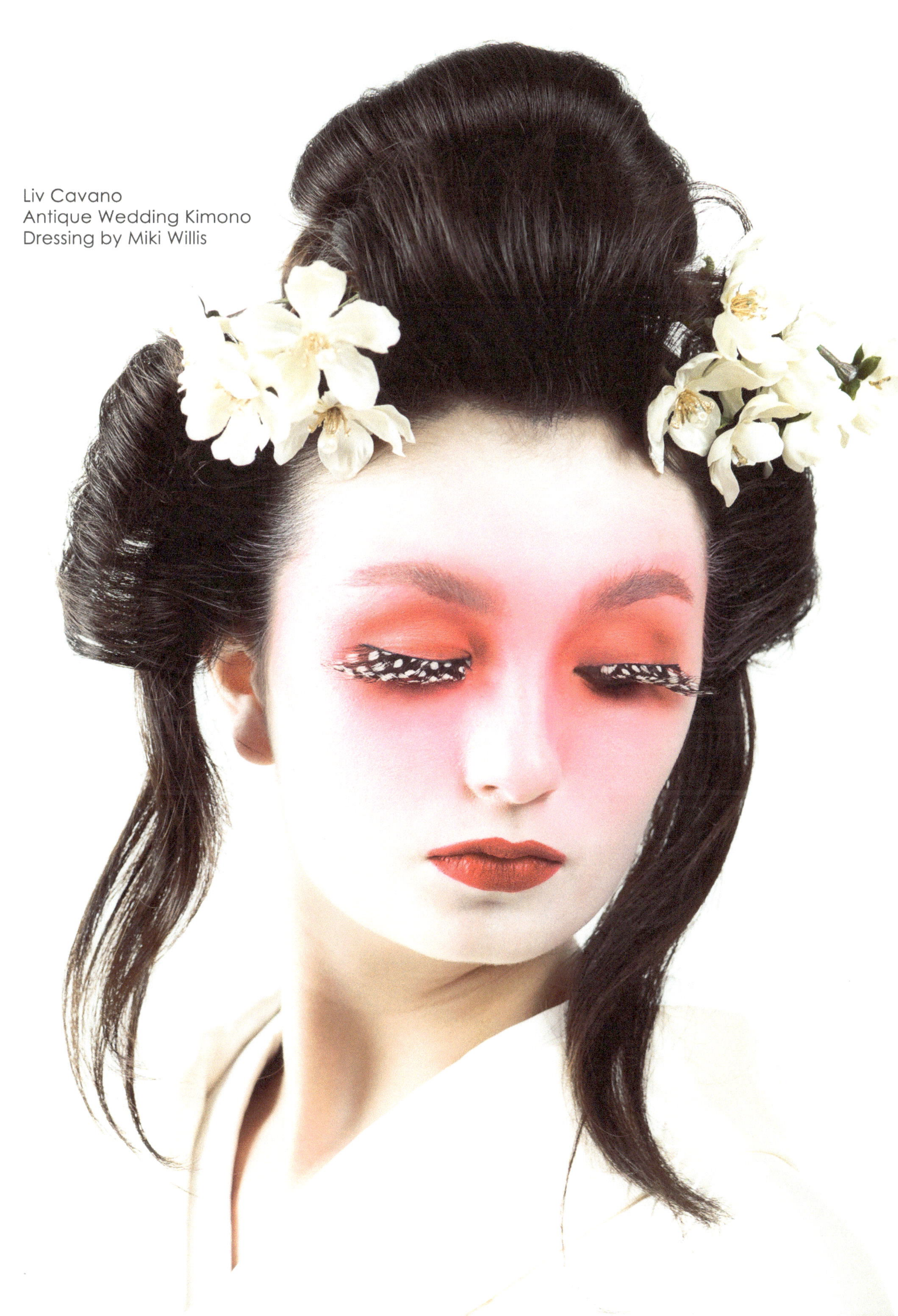

Liv Cavano
Antique Wedding Kimono
Dressing by Miki Willis

Liv Cavano
Antique Wedding Kimono
Dressing Miki Willis

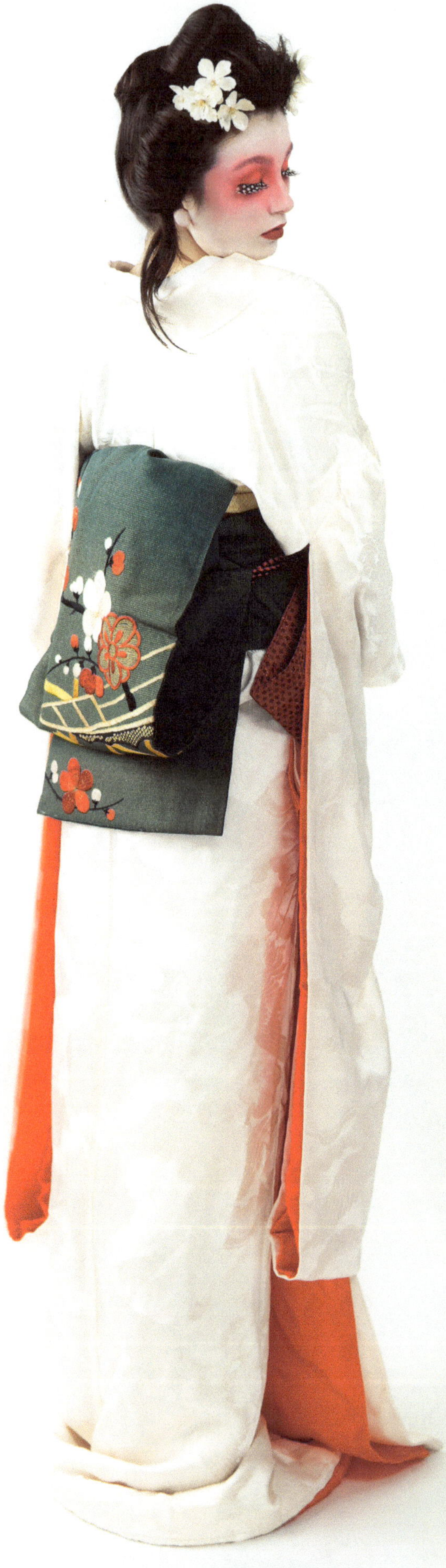

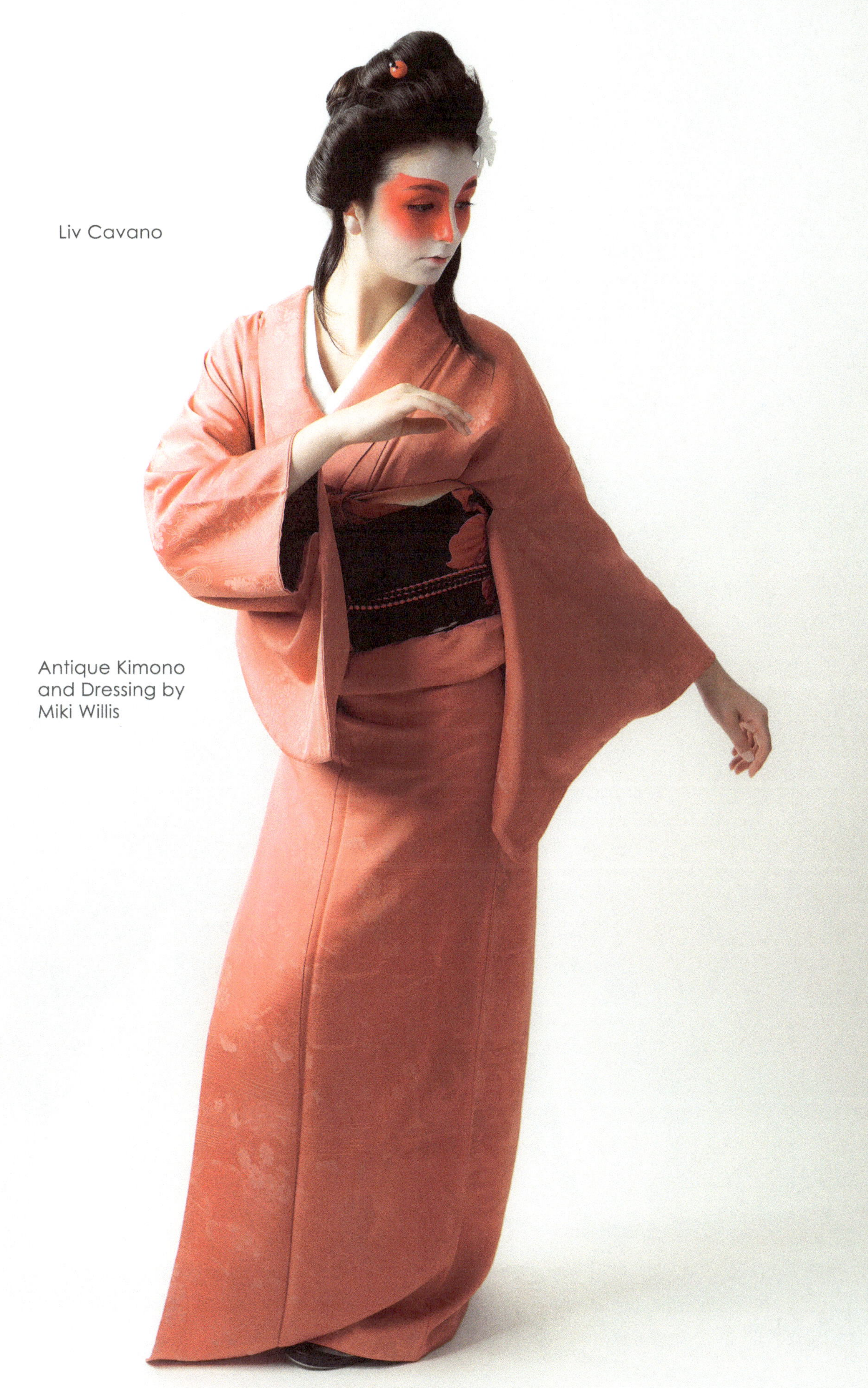

Liv Cavano

Antique Kimono
and Dressing by
Miki Willis

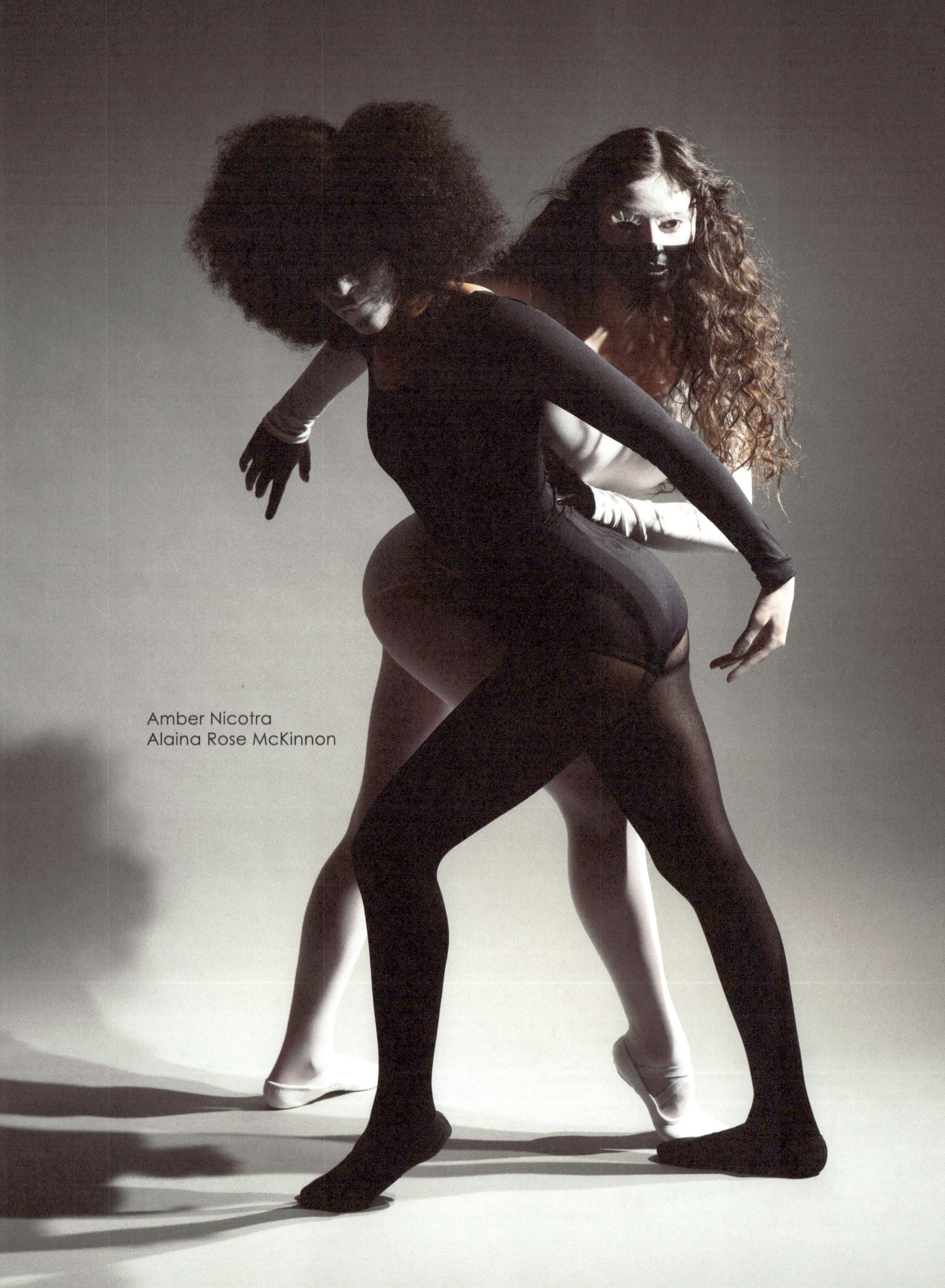

Amber Nicotra
Alaina Rose McKinnon

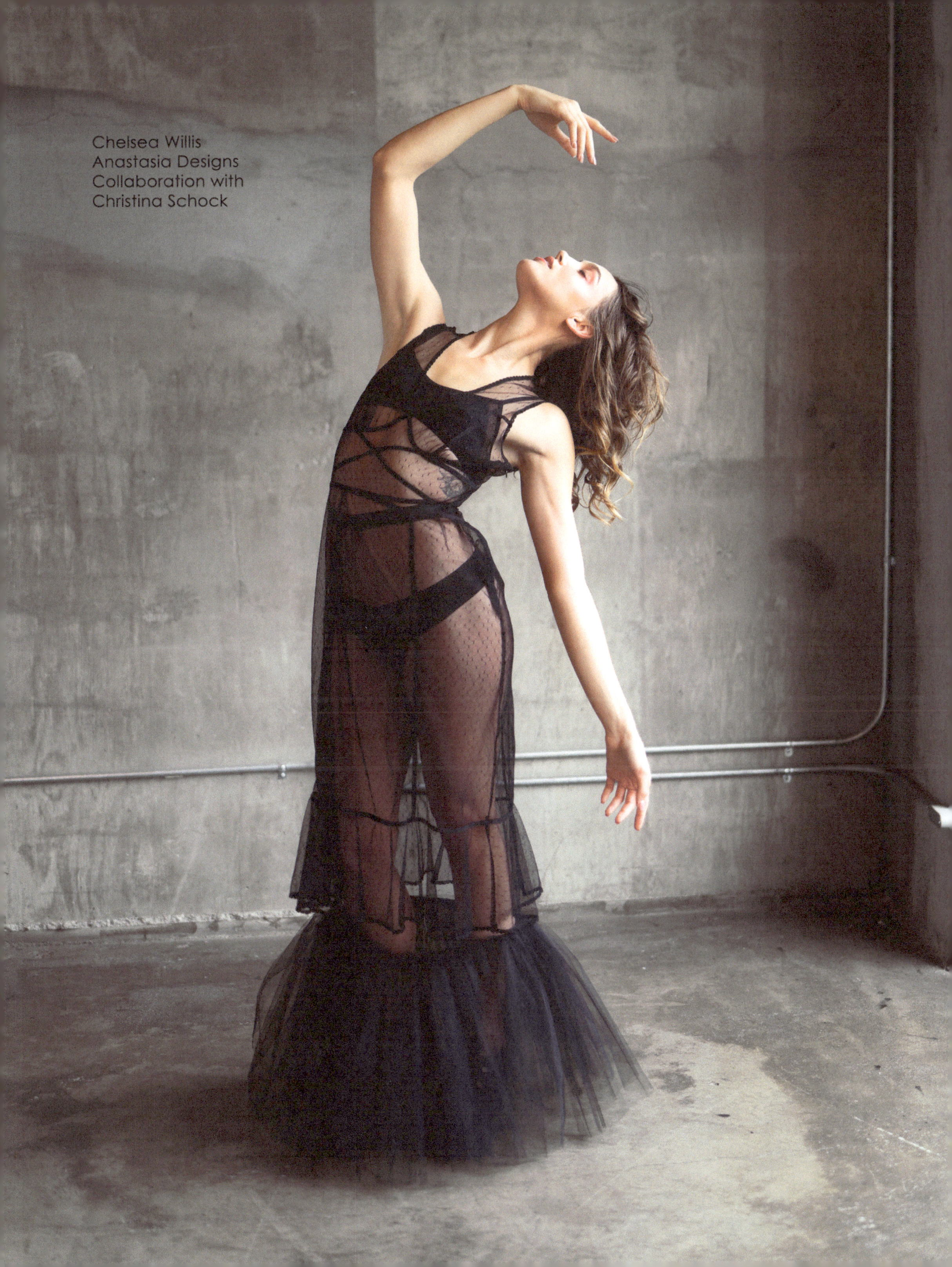

Chelsea Willis
Anastasia Designs
Collaboration with
Christina Schock

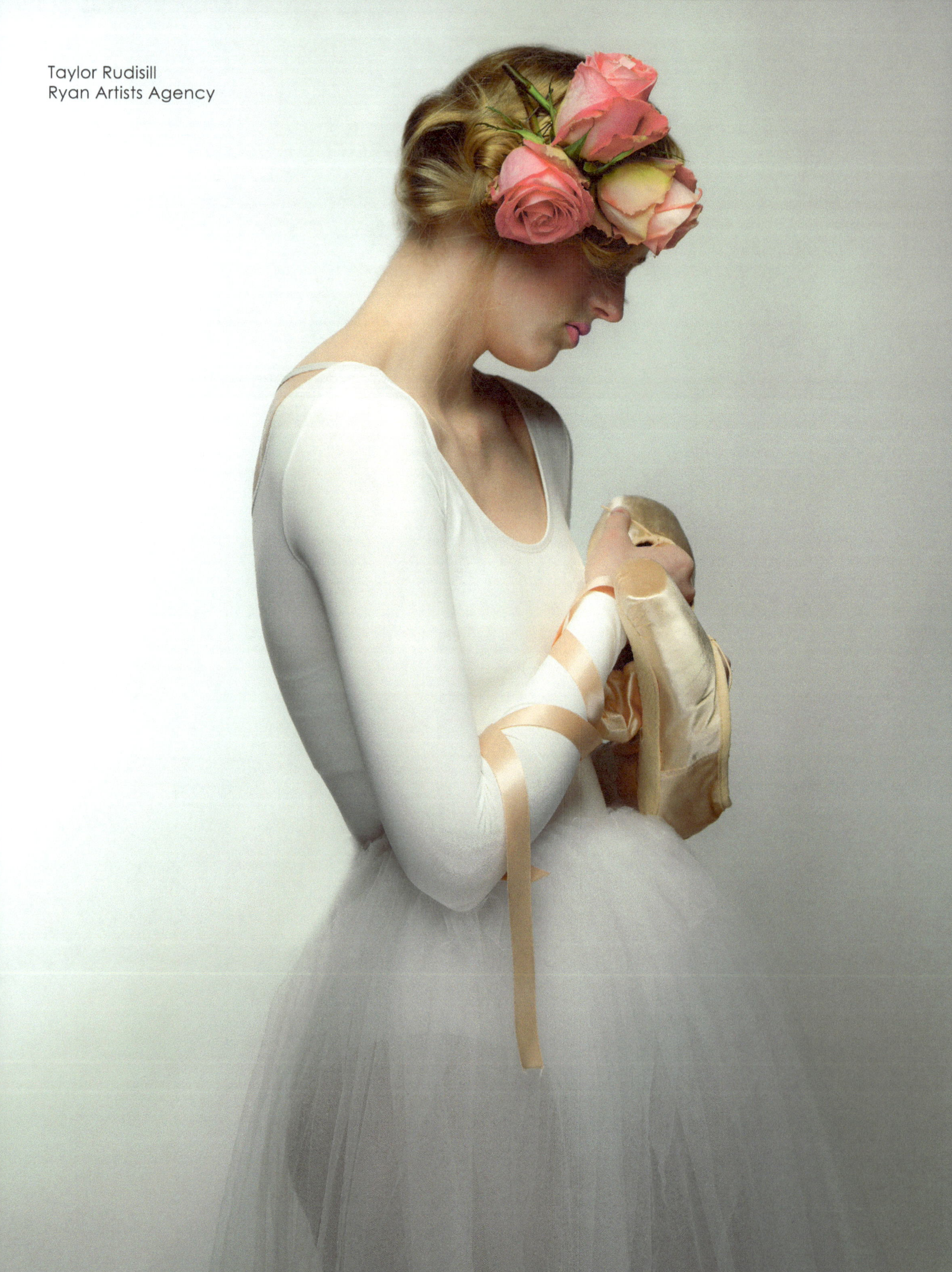
Taylor Rudisill
Ryan Artists Agency

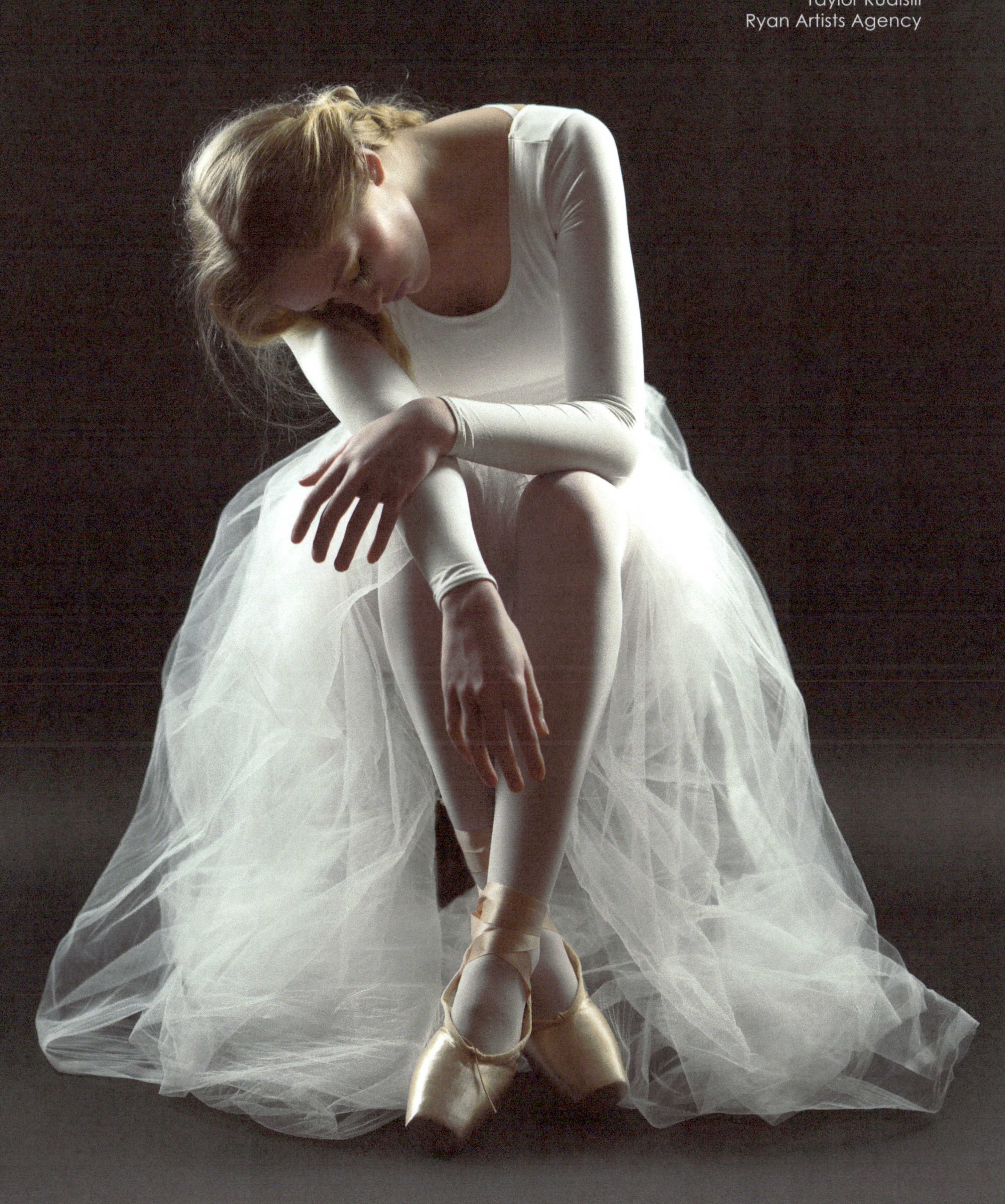
Taylor Rudisill
Ryan Artists Agency

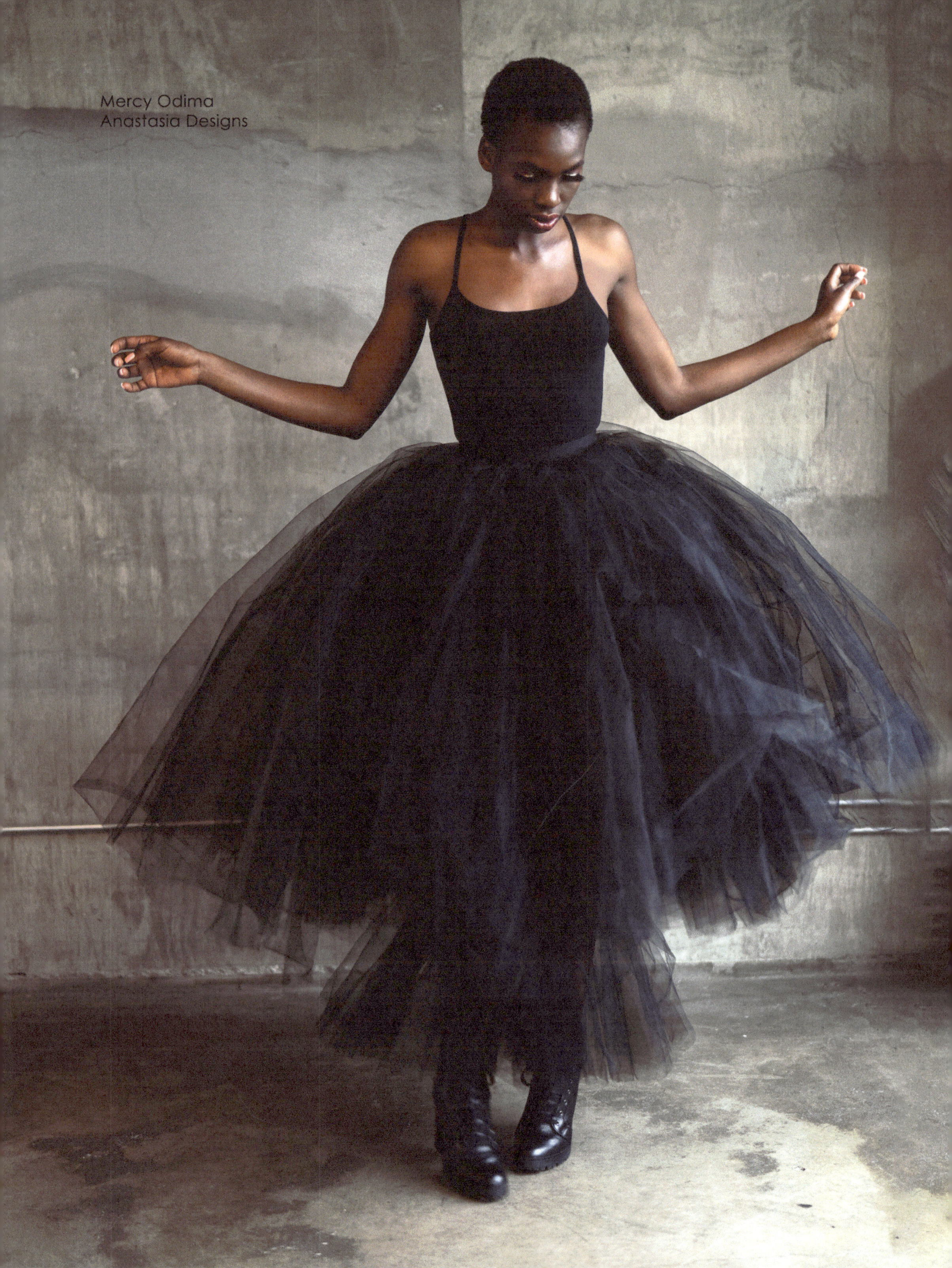

Mercy Odima
Anastasia Designs

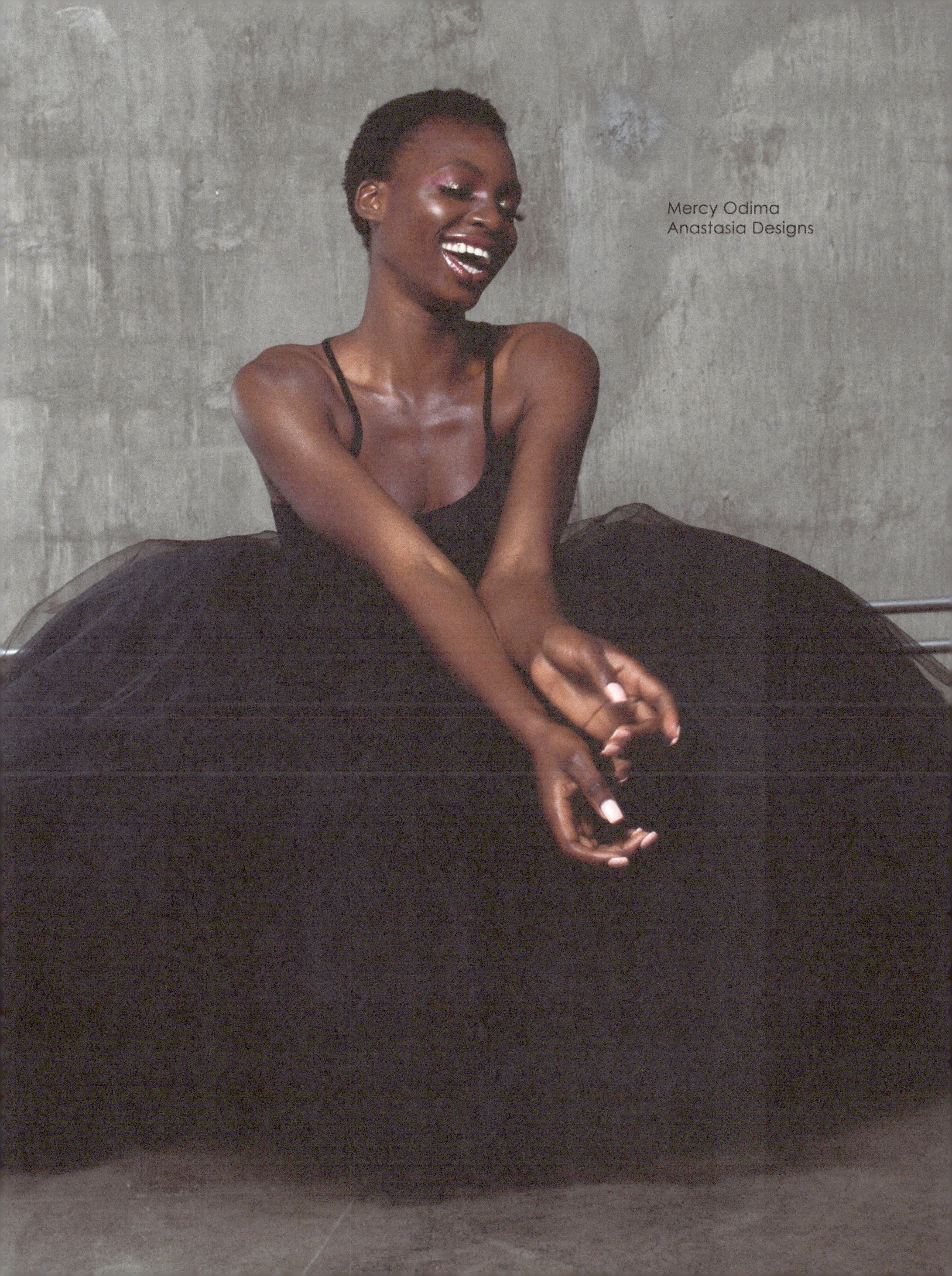
Mercy Odima
Anastasia Designs

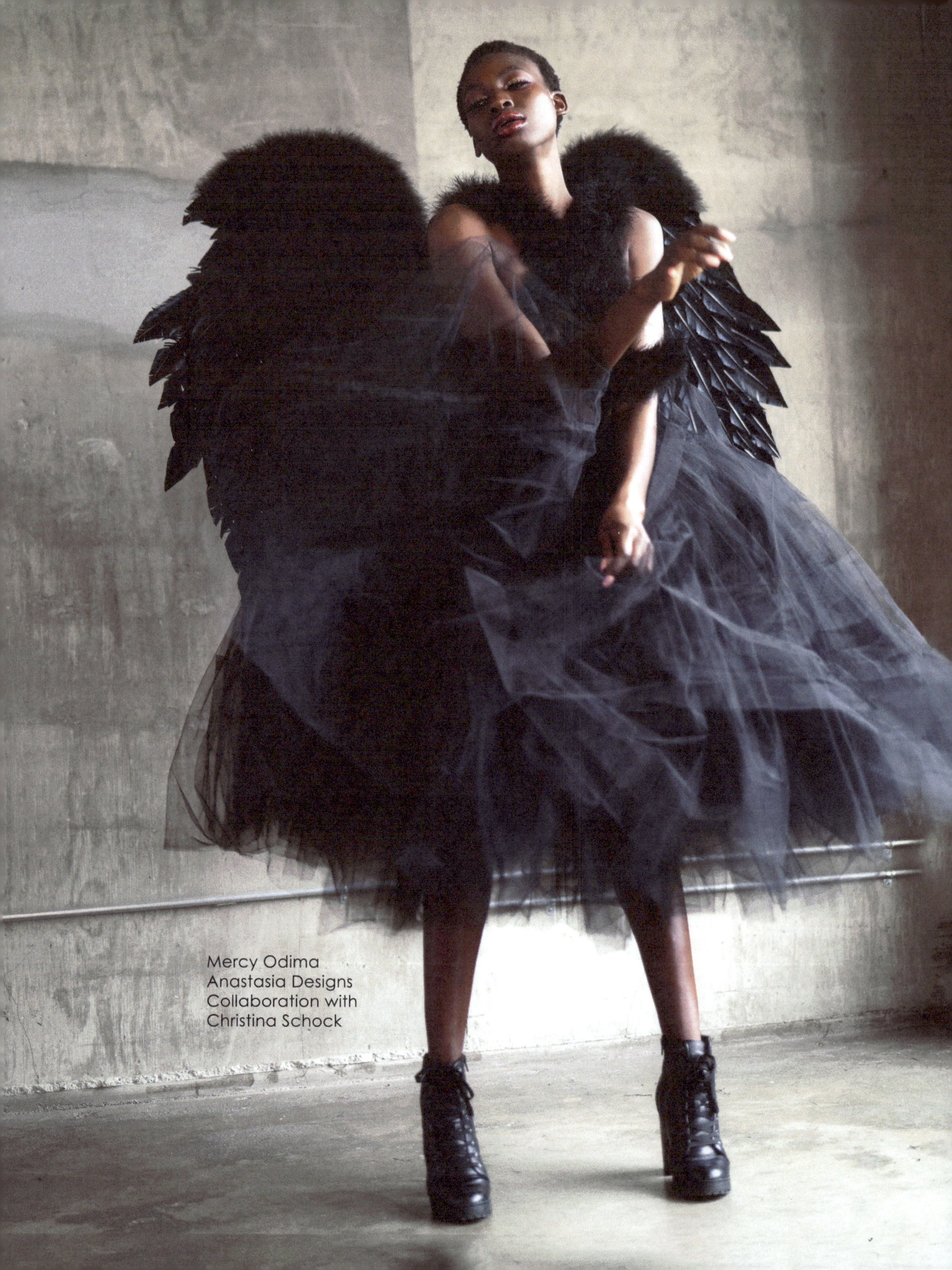
Mercy Odima
Anastasia Designs
Collaboration with
Christina Schock

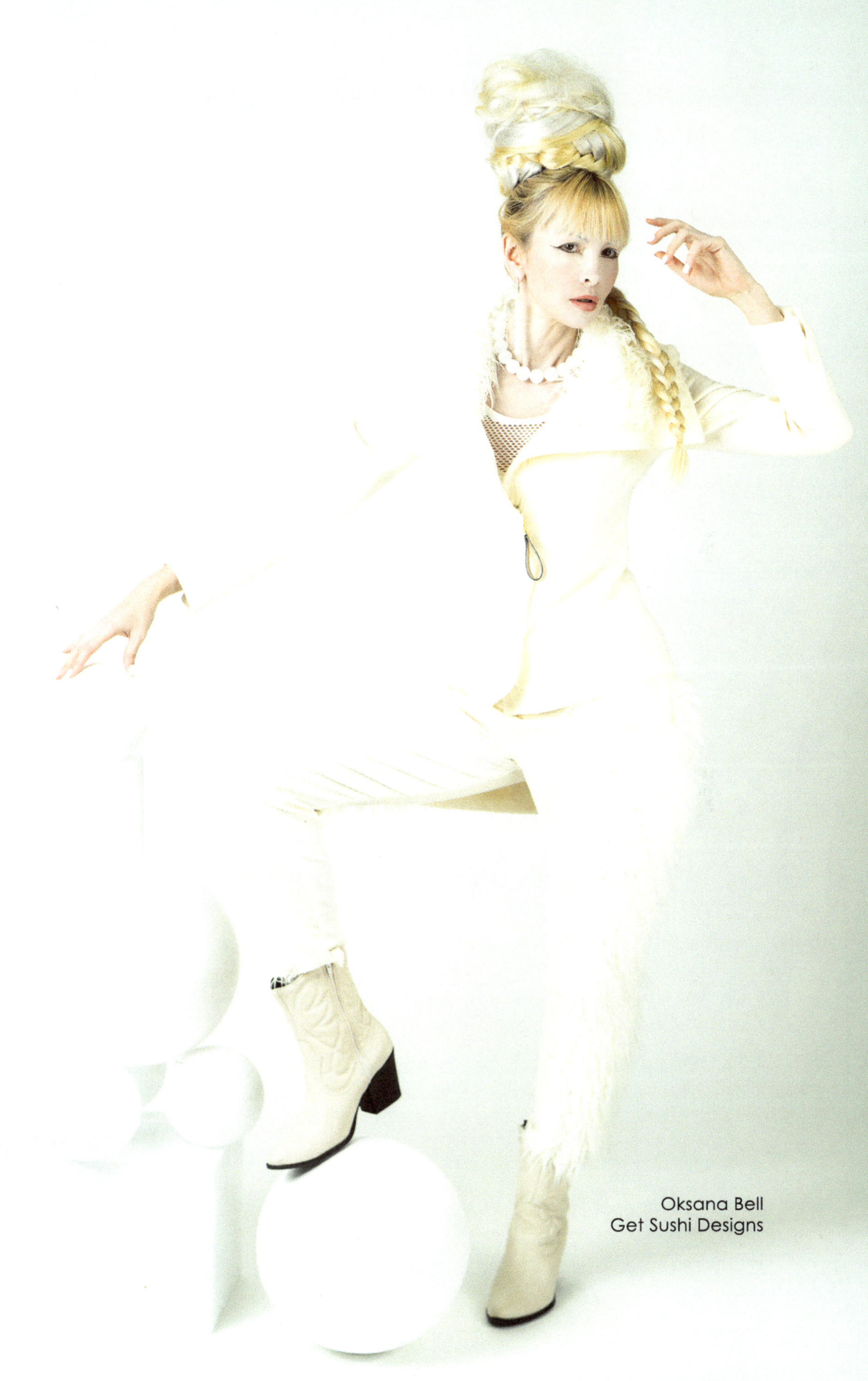

Oksana Bell
Get Sushi Designs

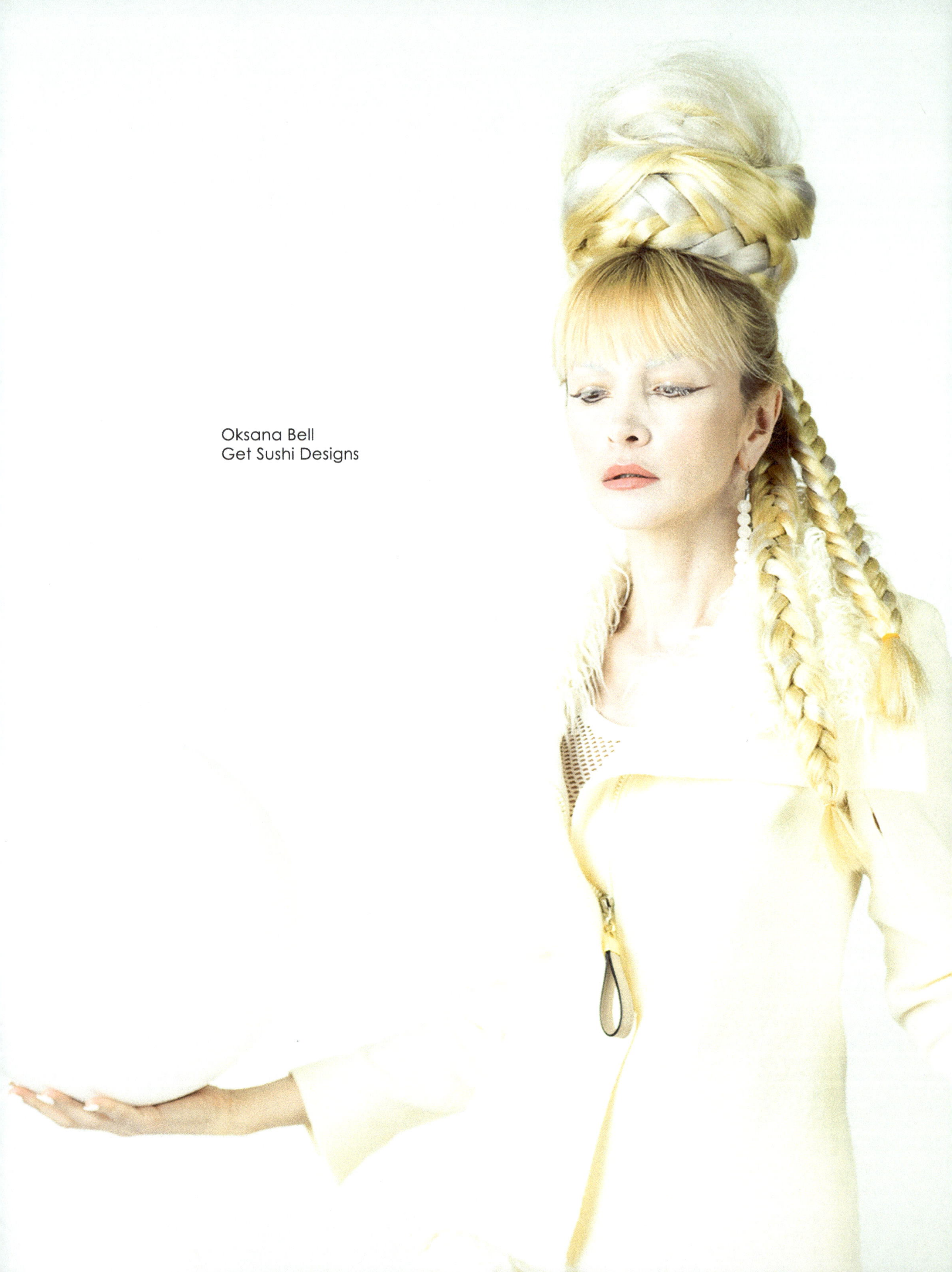
Oksana Bell
Get Sushi Designs

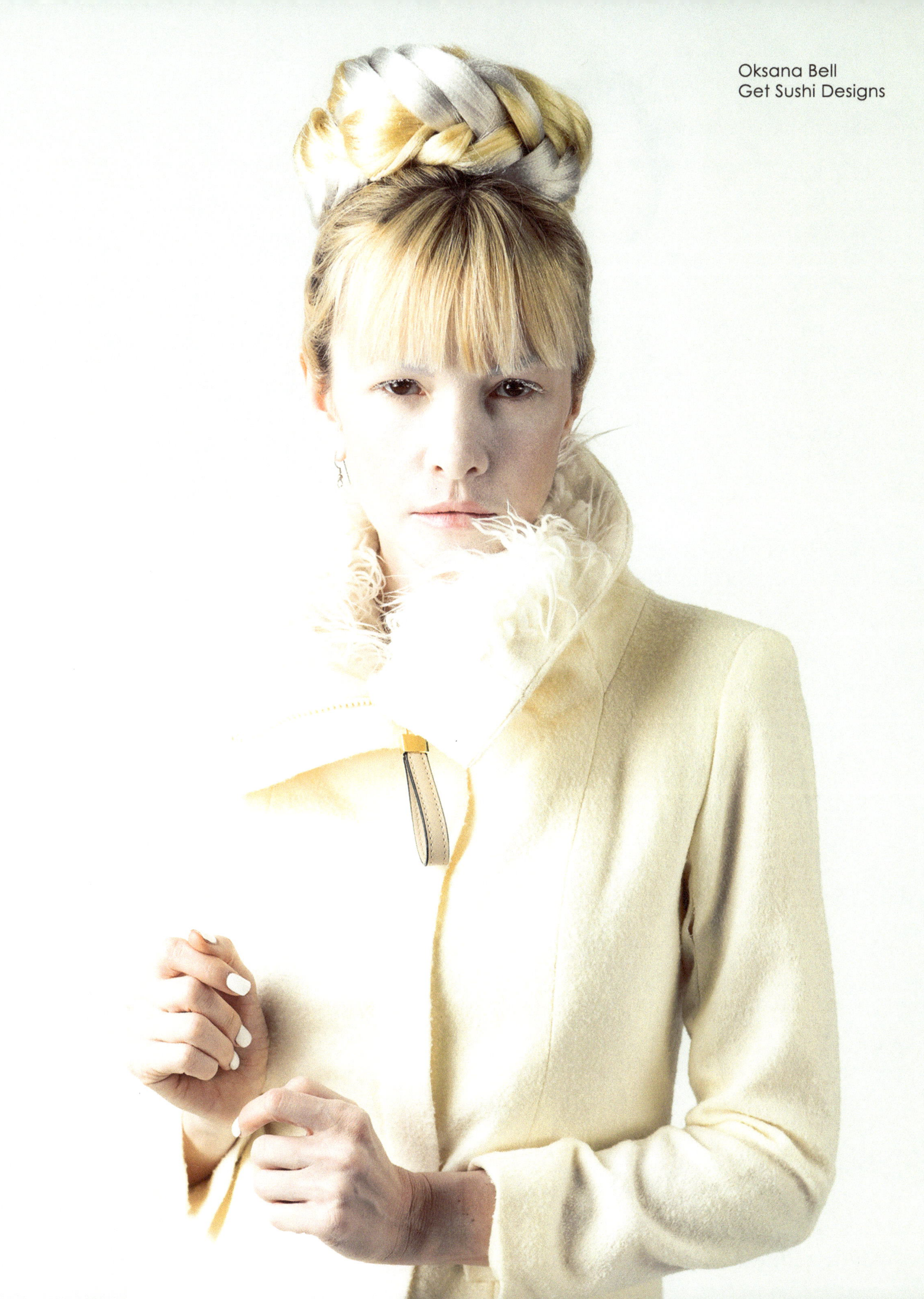

Oksana Bell
Get Sushi Designs

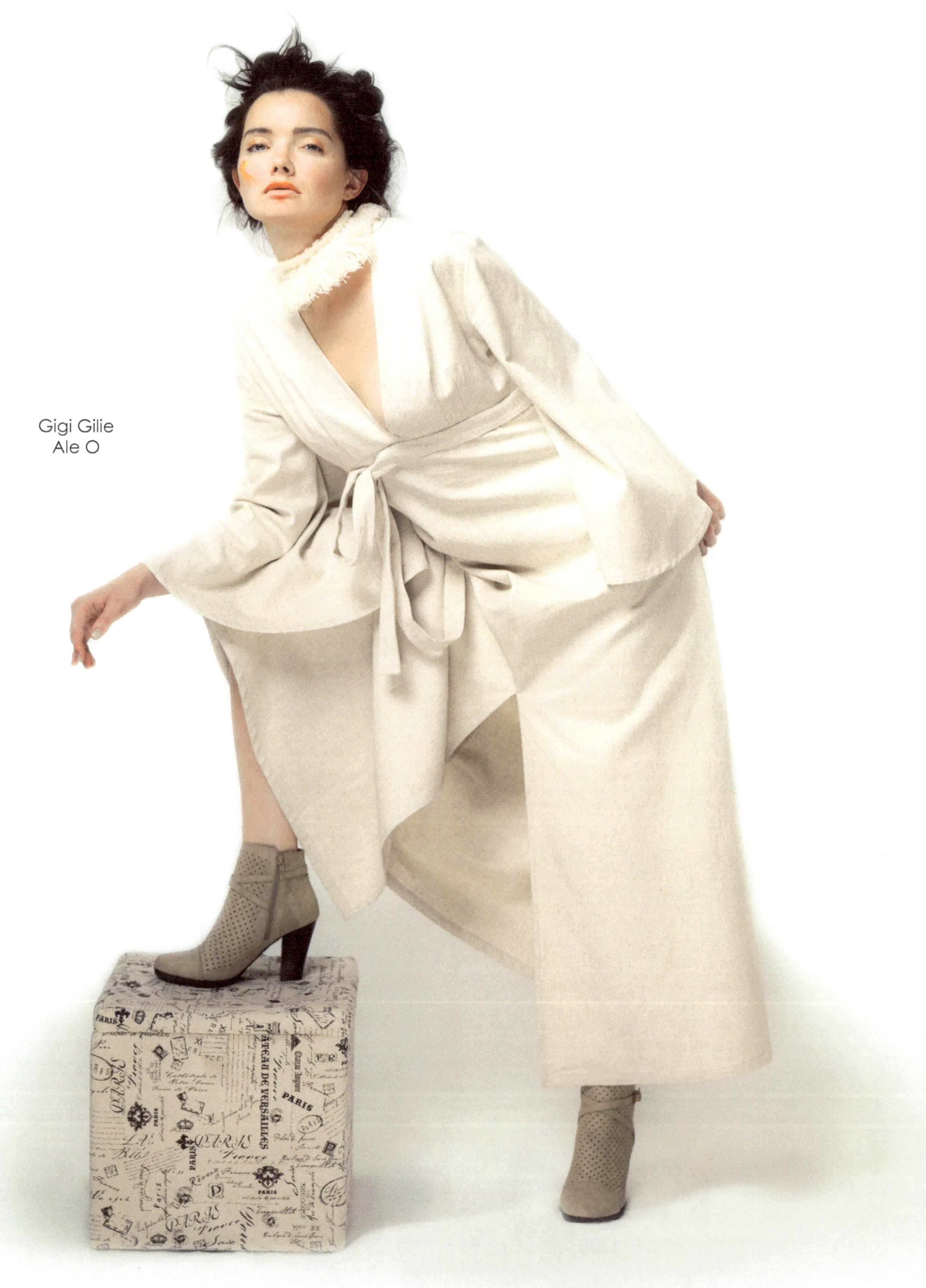

Gigi Gilie
Ale O

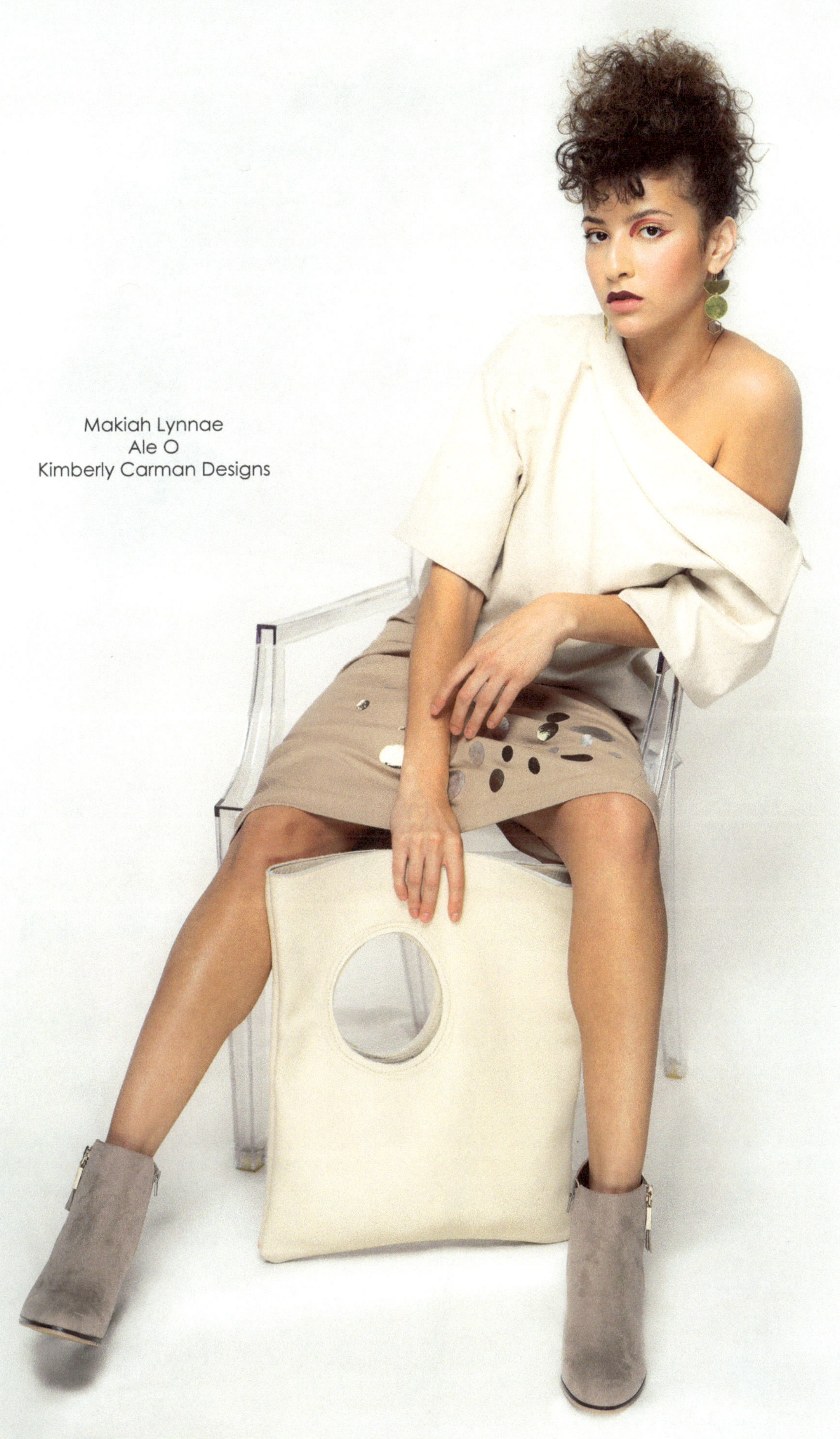

Makiah Lynnae
Ale O
Kimberly Carman Designs

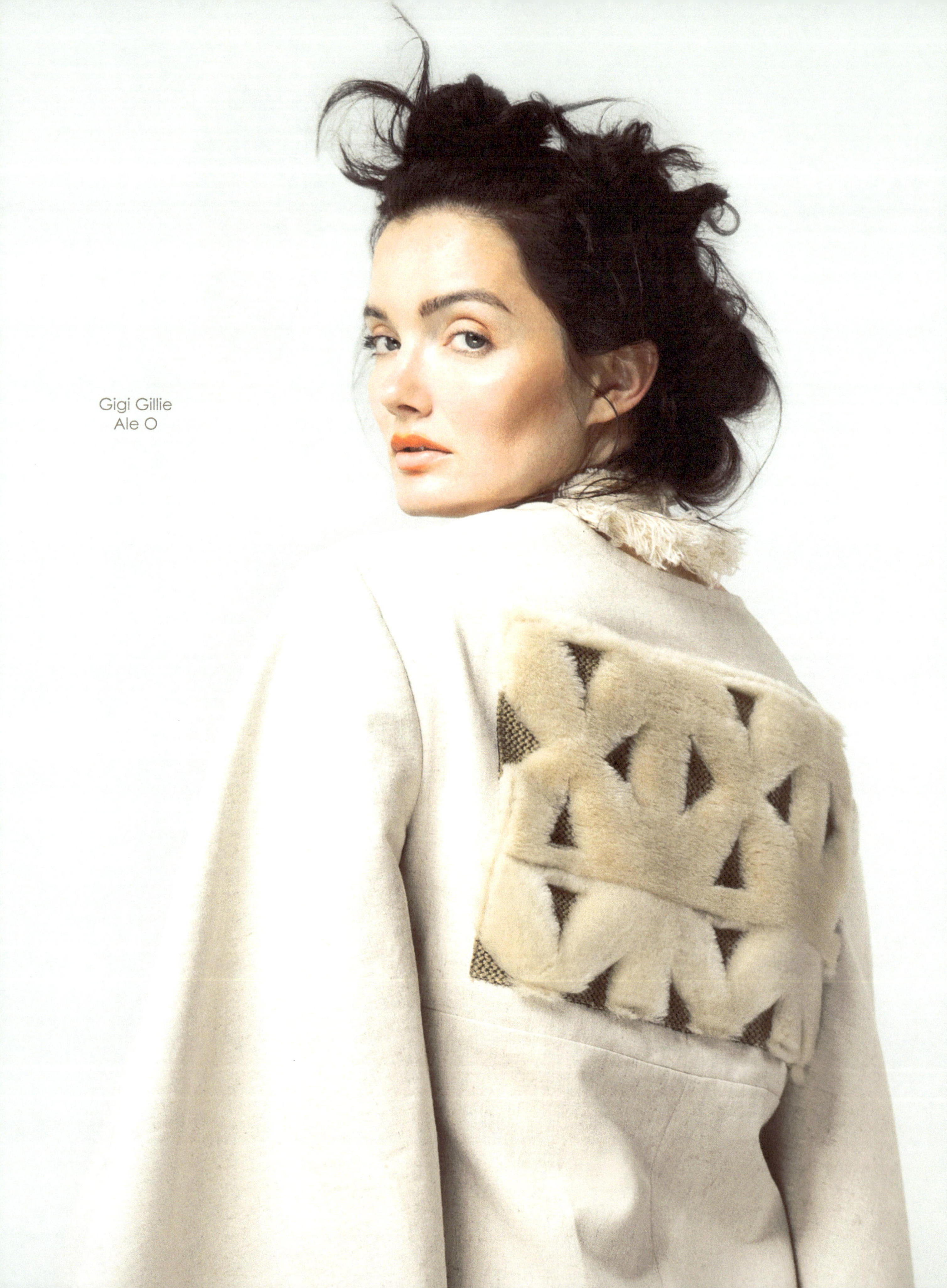

Gigi Gillie
Ale O

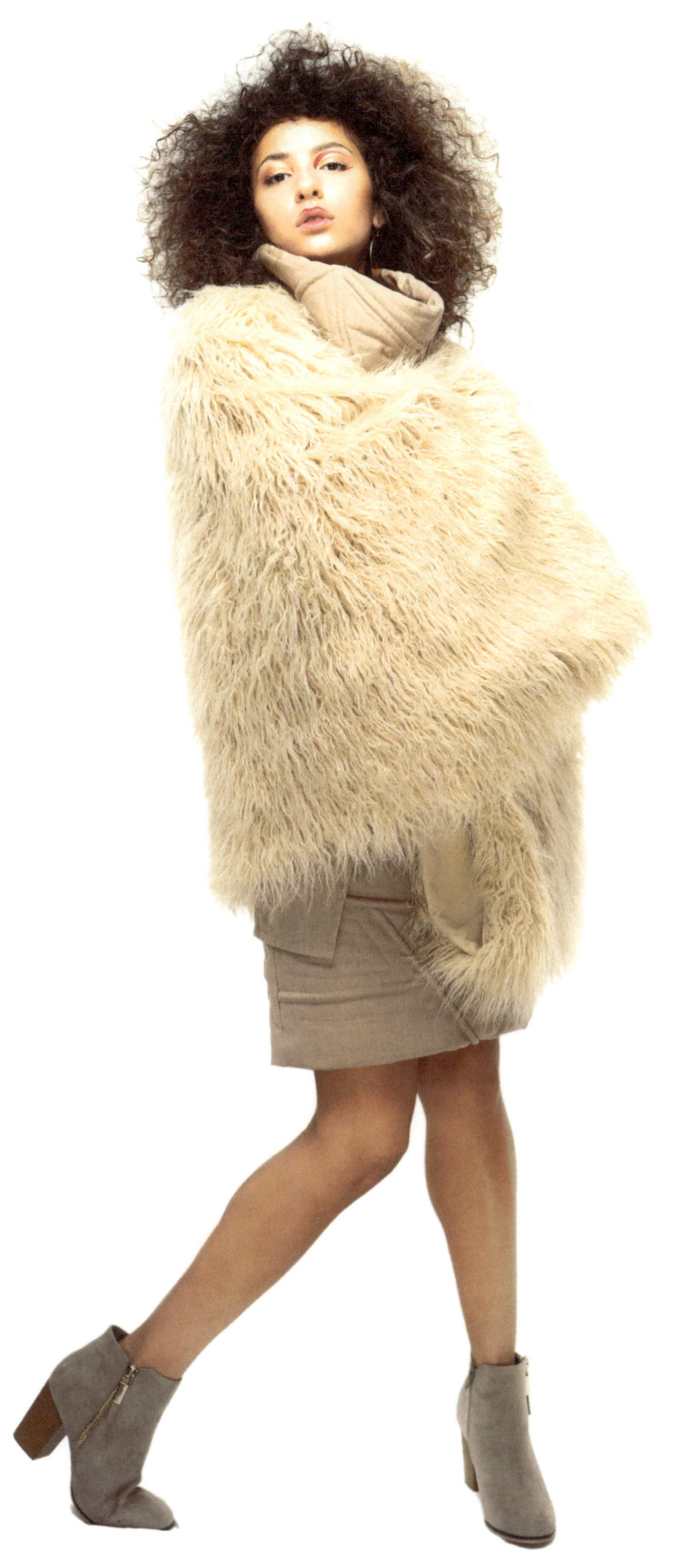

Makiah Lynnae
Ale O

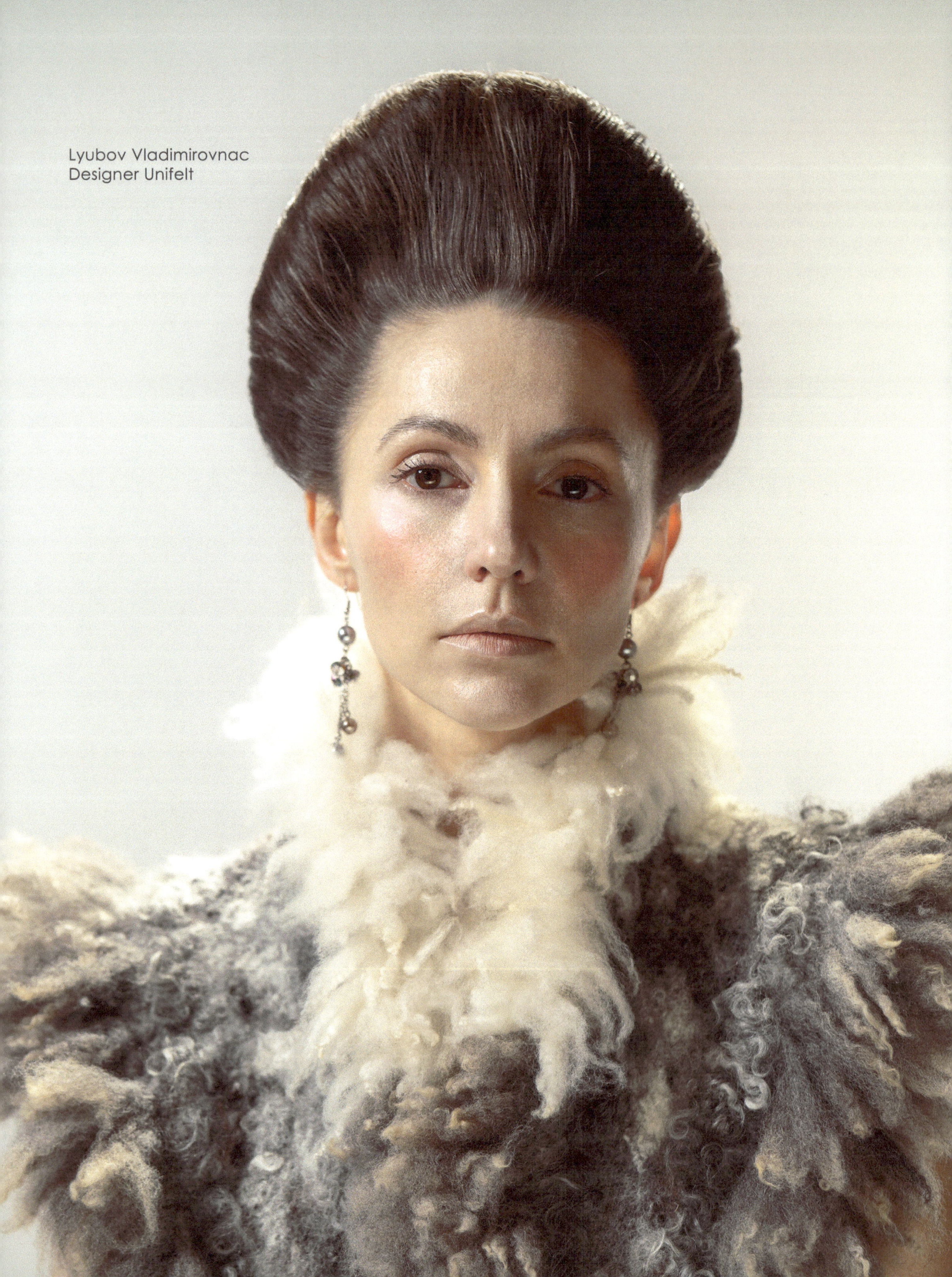

Lyubov Vladimirovnac
Designer Unifelt

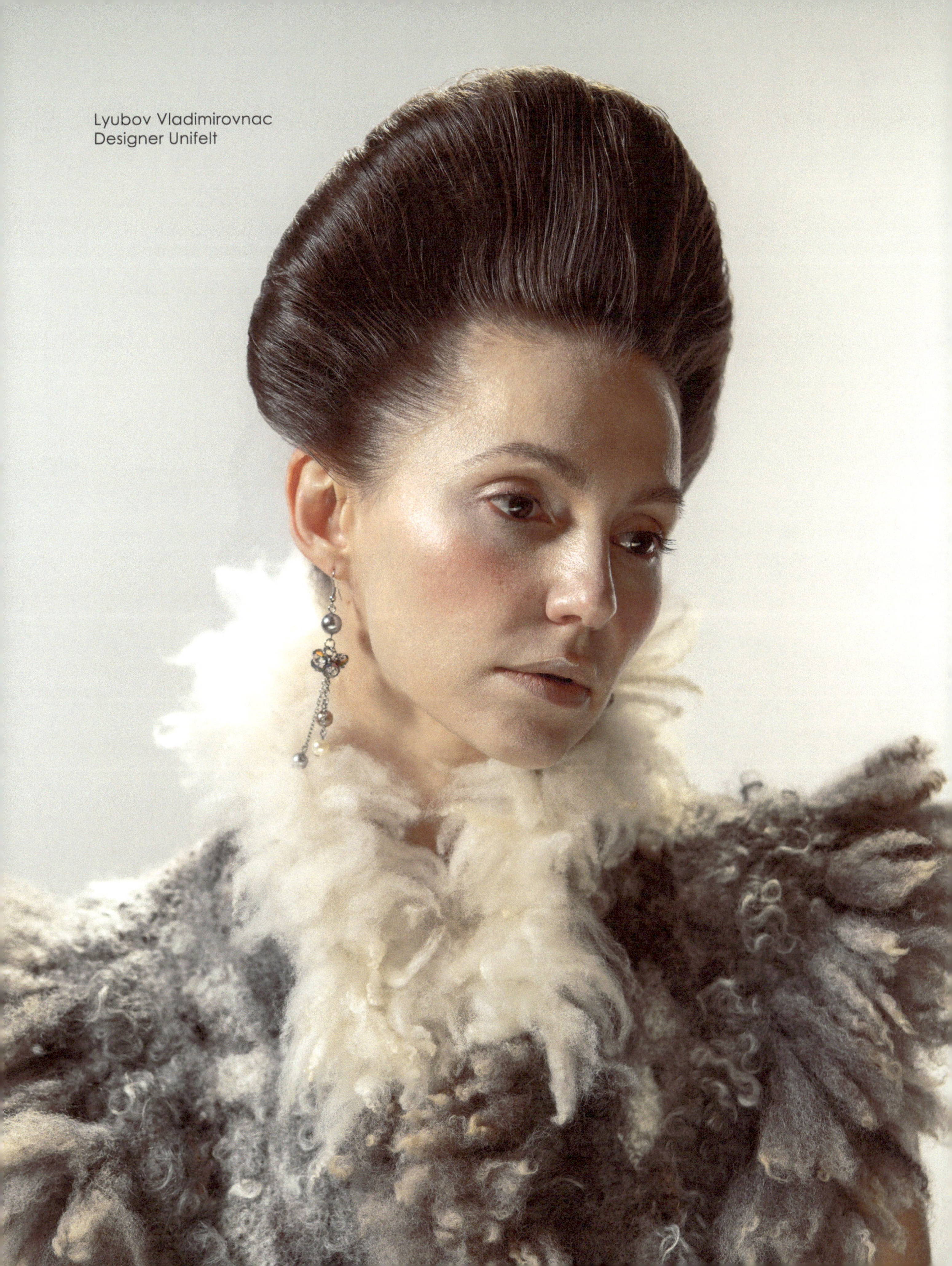
Lyubov Vladimirovnac
Designer Unifelt

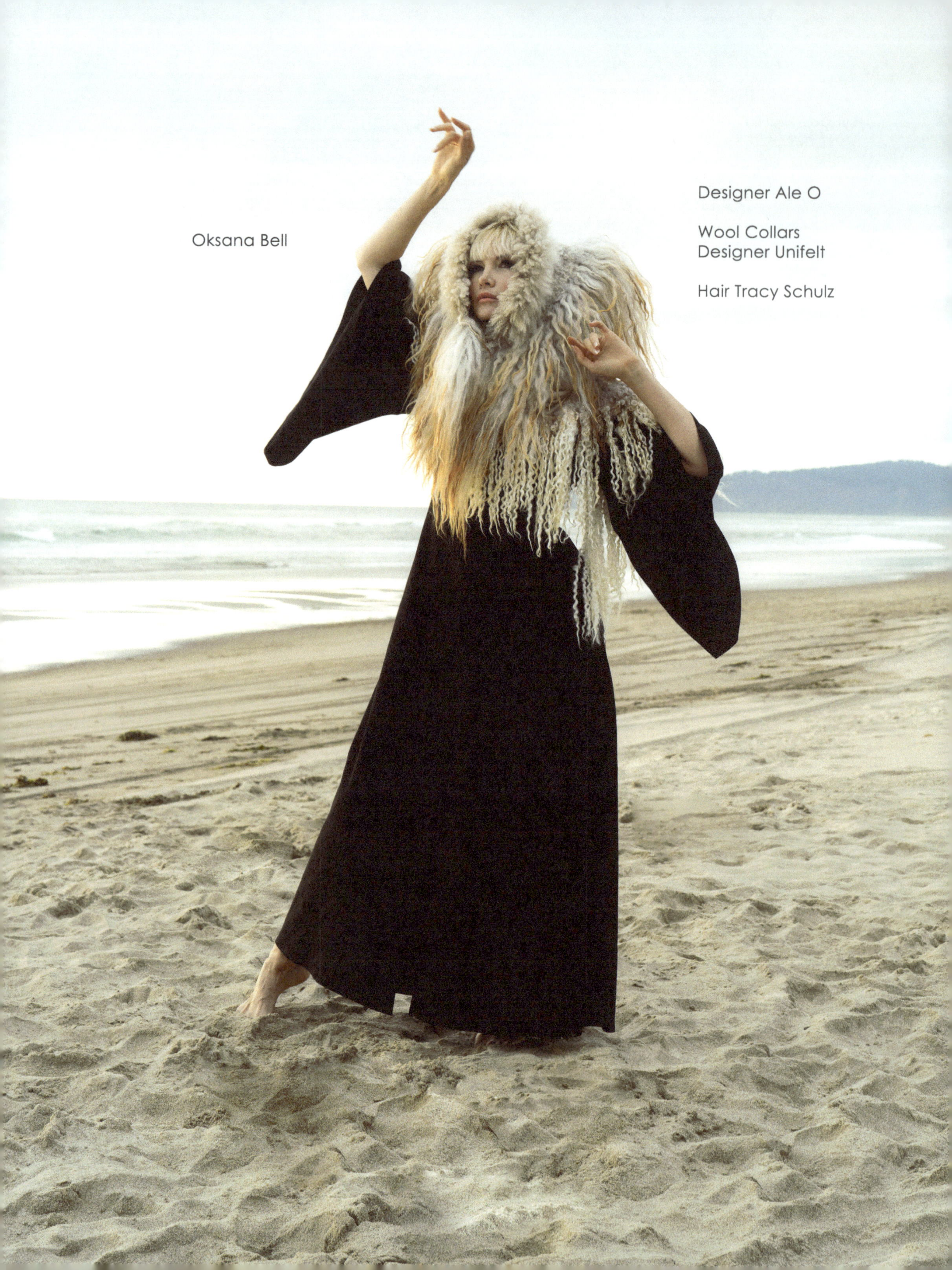
Oksana Bell

Designer Ale O

Wool Collars
Designer Unifelt

Hair Tracy Schulz

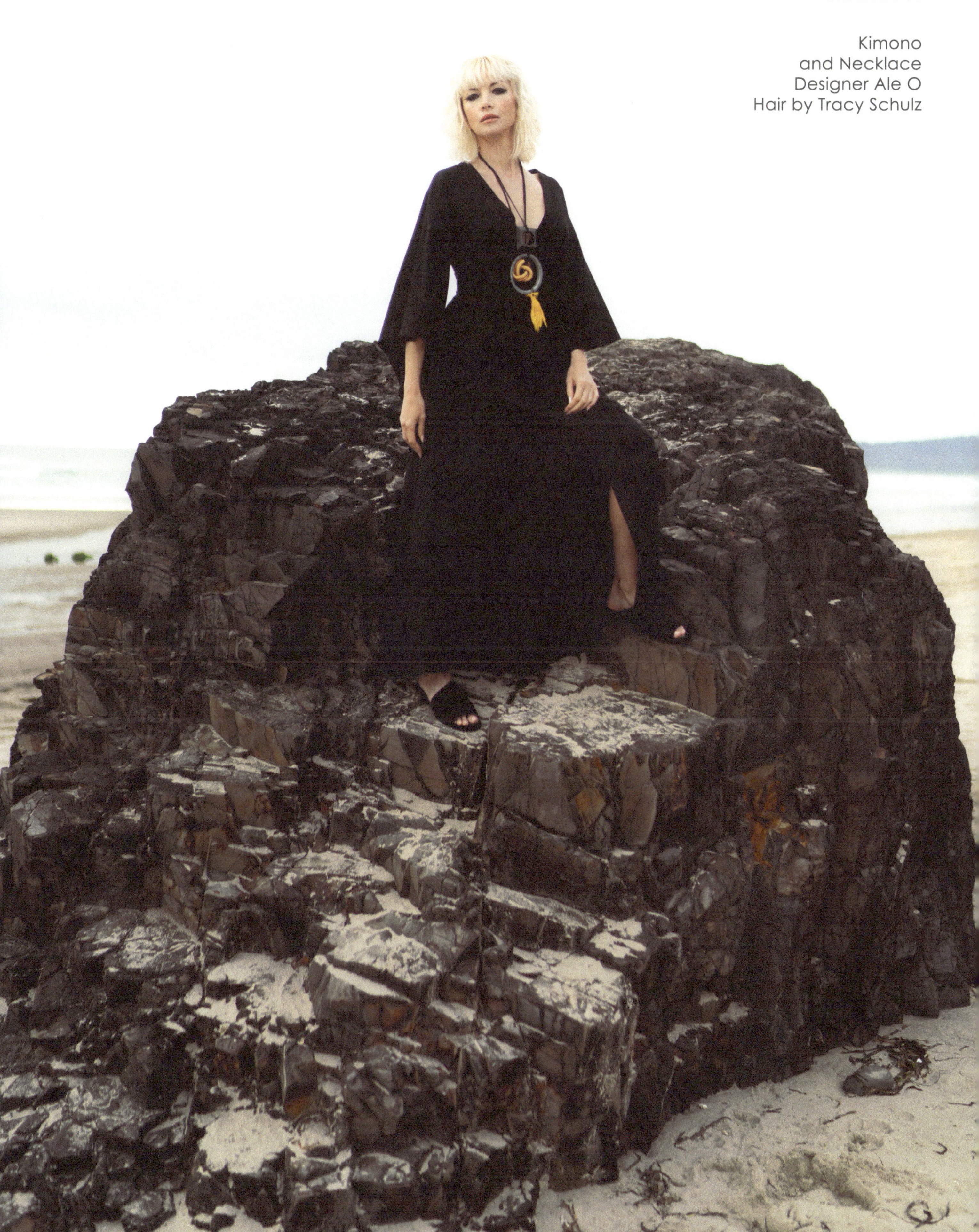

Oksana Bell

Kimono
and Necklace
Designer Ale O
Hair by Tracy Schulz

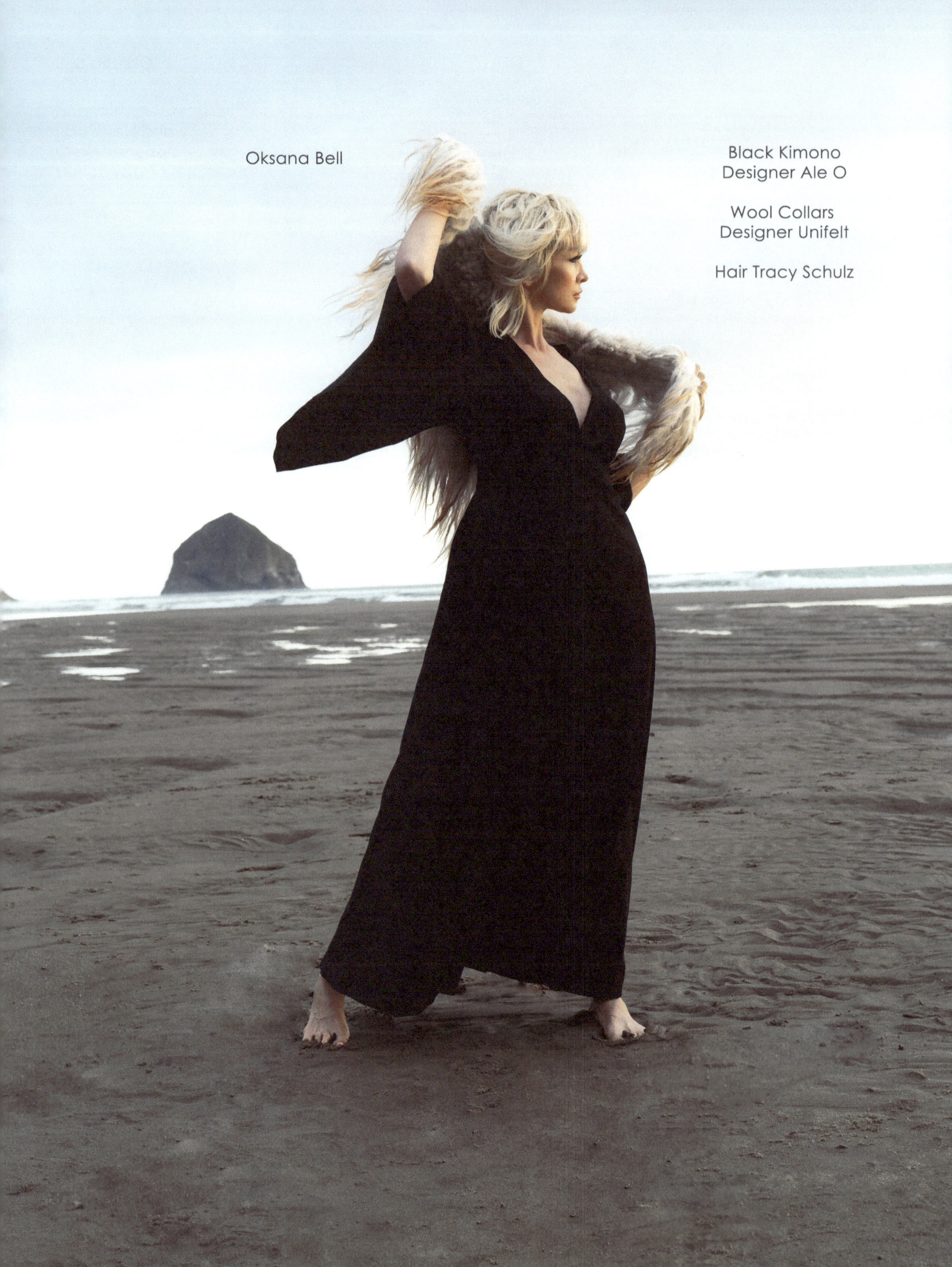

Oksana Bell

Black Kimono
Designer Ale O

Wool Collars
Designer Unifelt

Hair Tracy Schulz

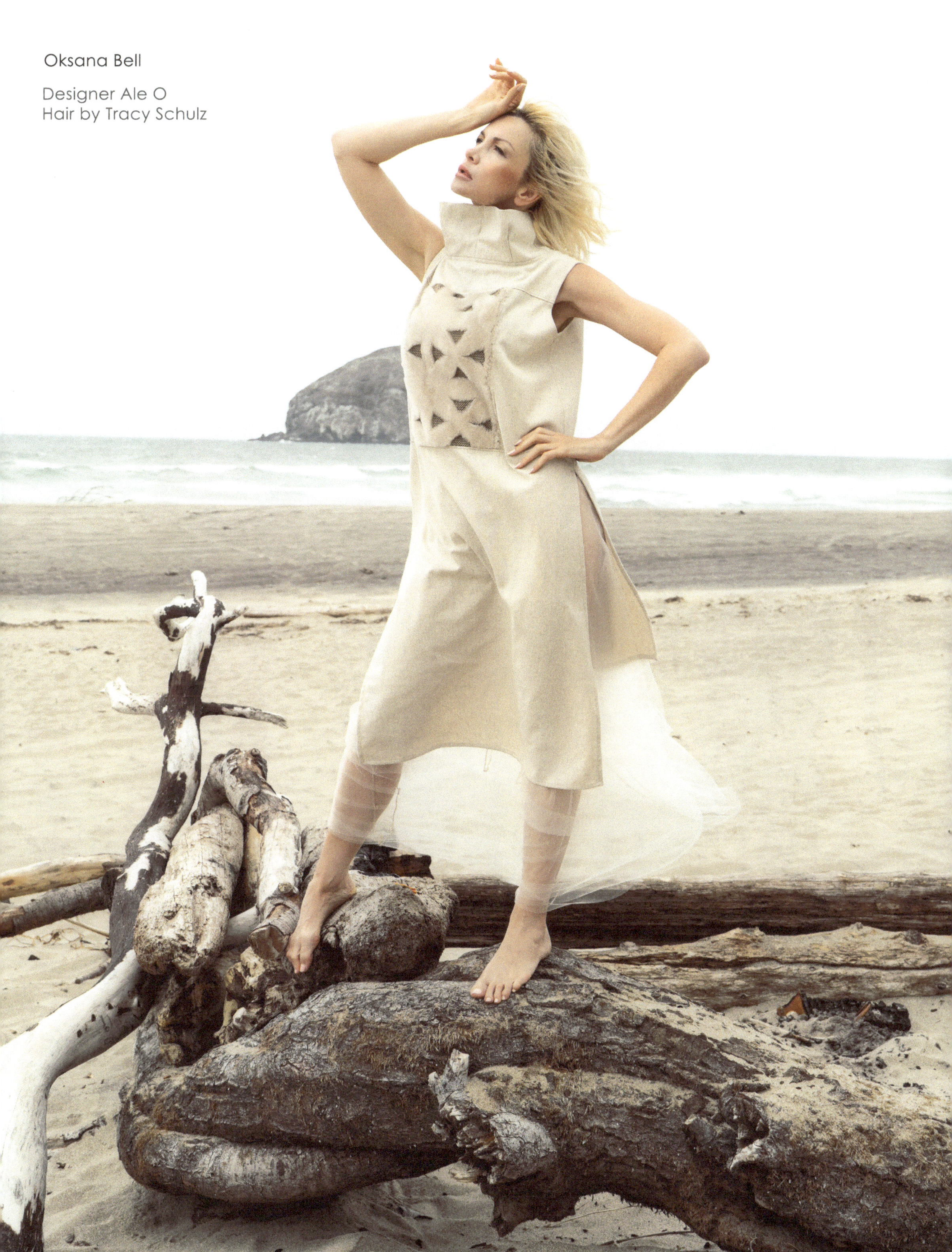

Oksana Bell

Designer Ale O
Hair by Tracy Schulz

Grace McGowan
Oksana Bell
Amber Nicotra
Mikyla Bordner

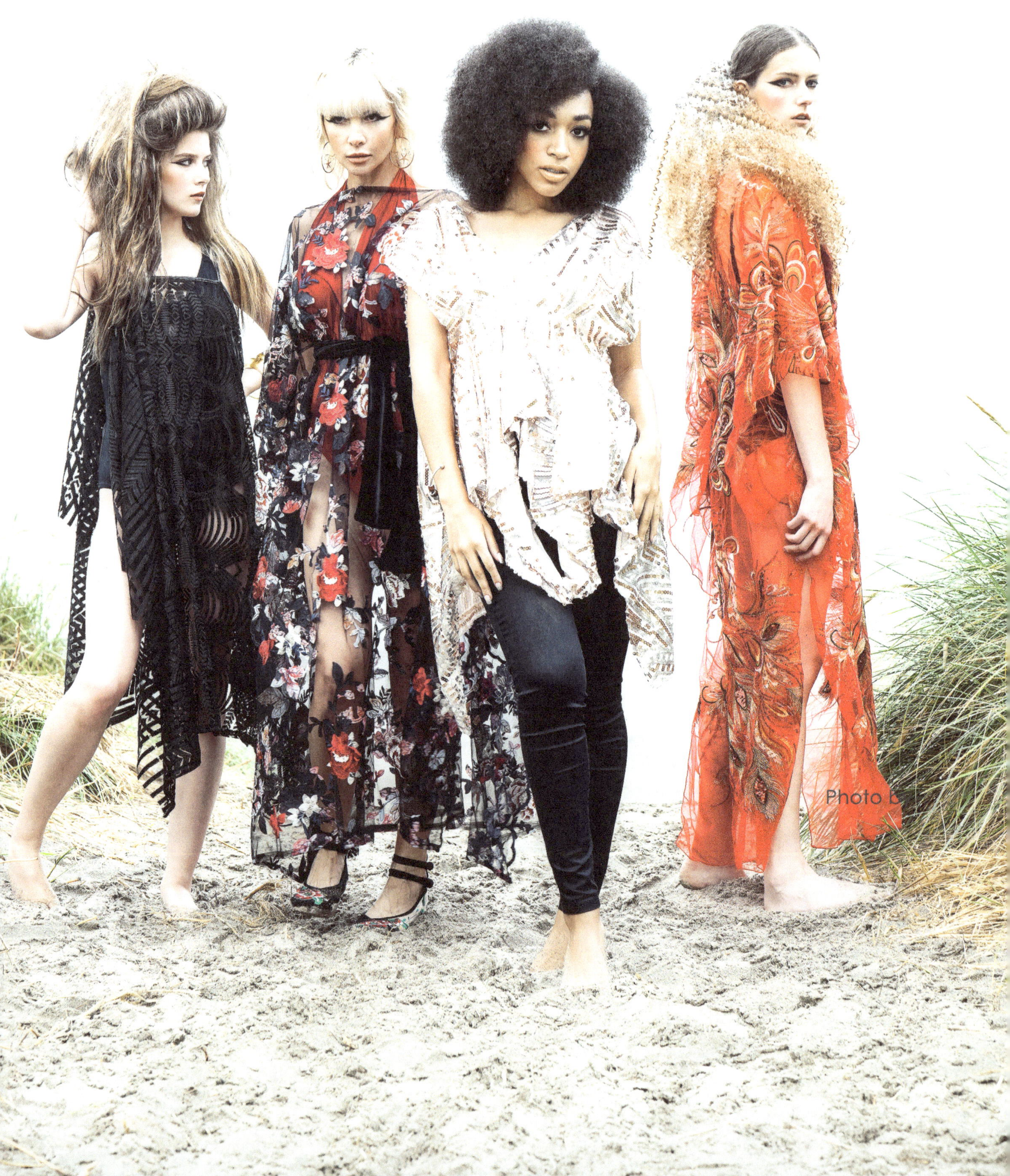

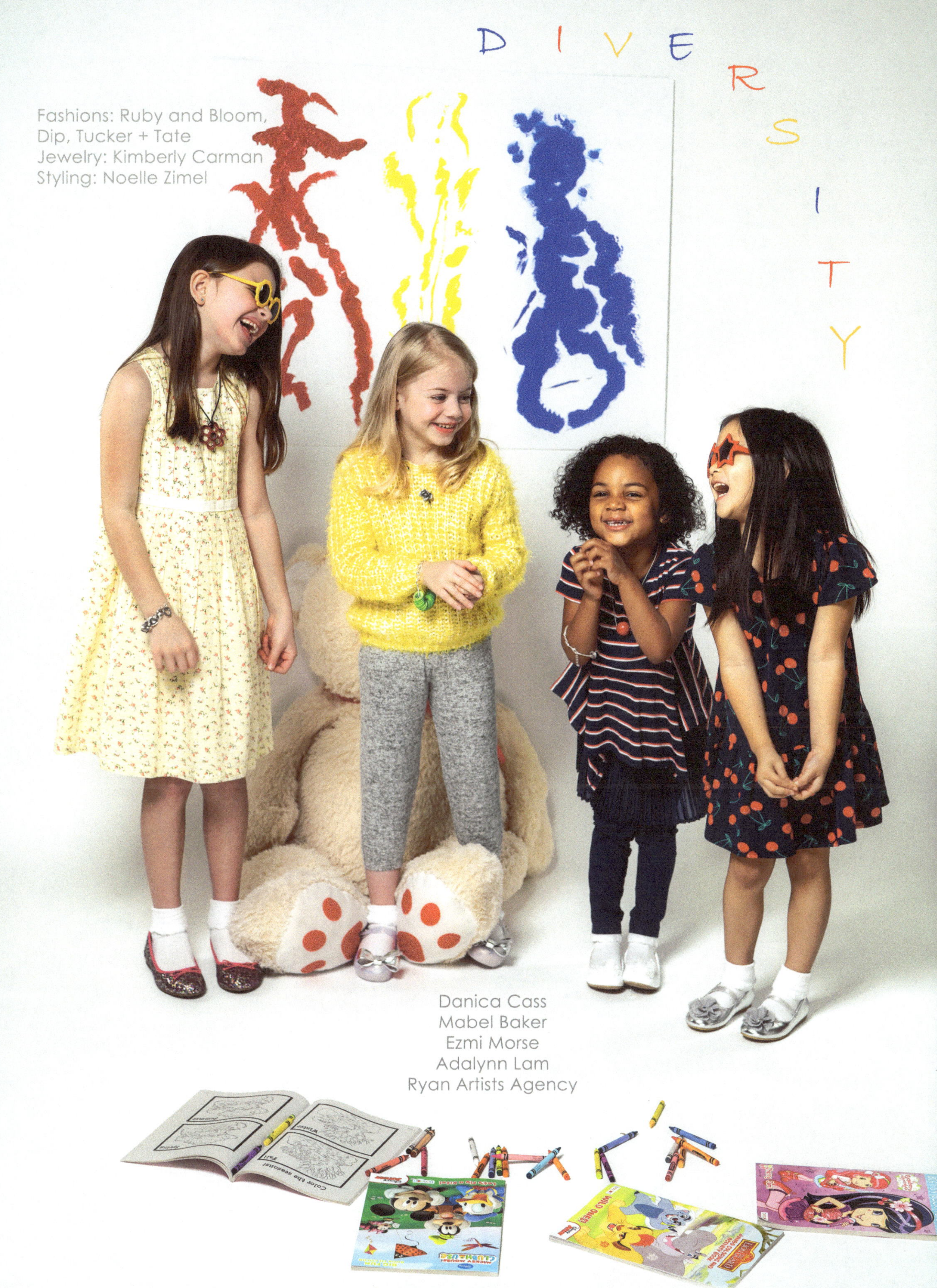

DIVERSITY
Fashions: Ruby and Bloom,
Dip, Tucker + Tate
Jewelry: Kimberly Carman
Styling: Noelle Zime!
Danica Cass
Mabel Baker
Ezmi Morse
Adalynn Lam
Ryan Artists Agency

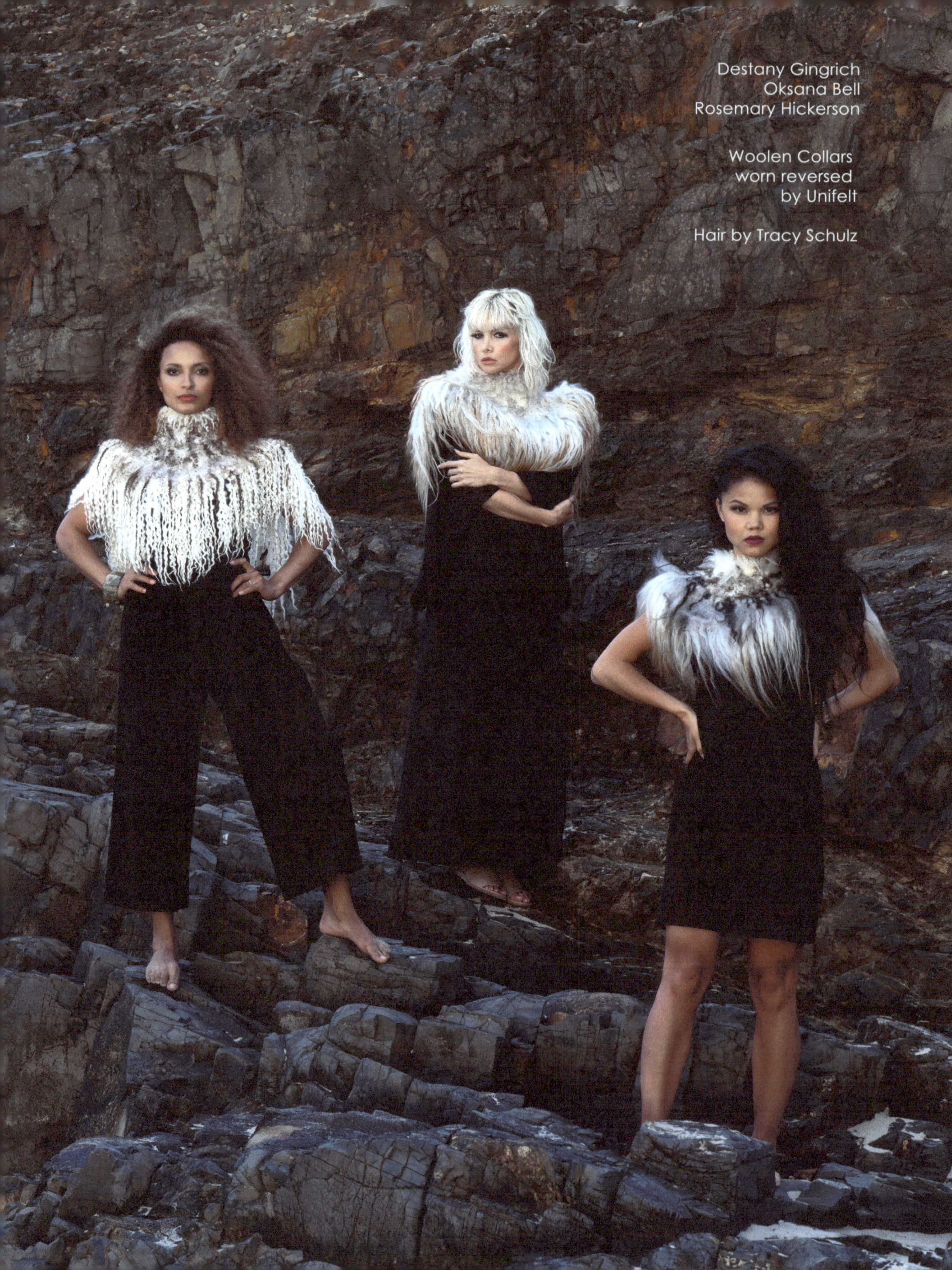

Destany Gingrich
Oksana Bell
Rosemary Hickerson

Woolen Collars
worn reversed
by Unifelt

Hair by Tracy Schulz

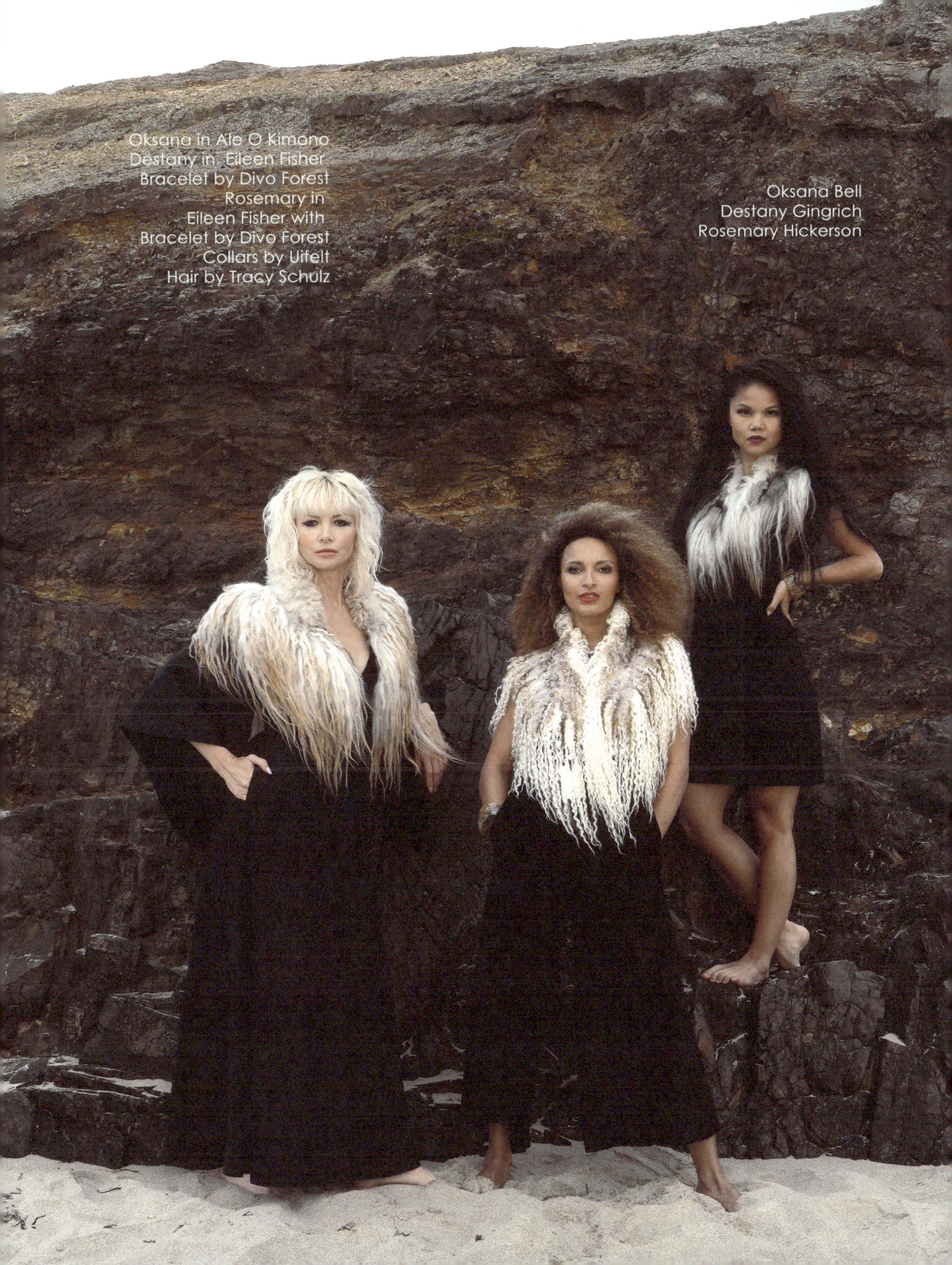

Oksana in Ale O Kimono
Destany in Eileen Fisher
Bracelet by Divo Forest
Rosemary in
Eileen Fisher with
Bracelet by Divo Forest
Collars by Uifelt
Hair by Tracy Schulz

Oksana Bell
Destany Gingrich
Rosemary Hickerson

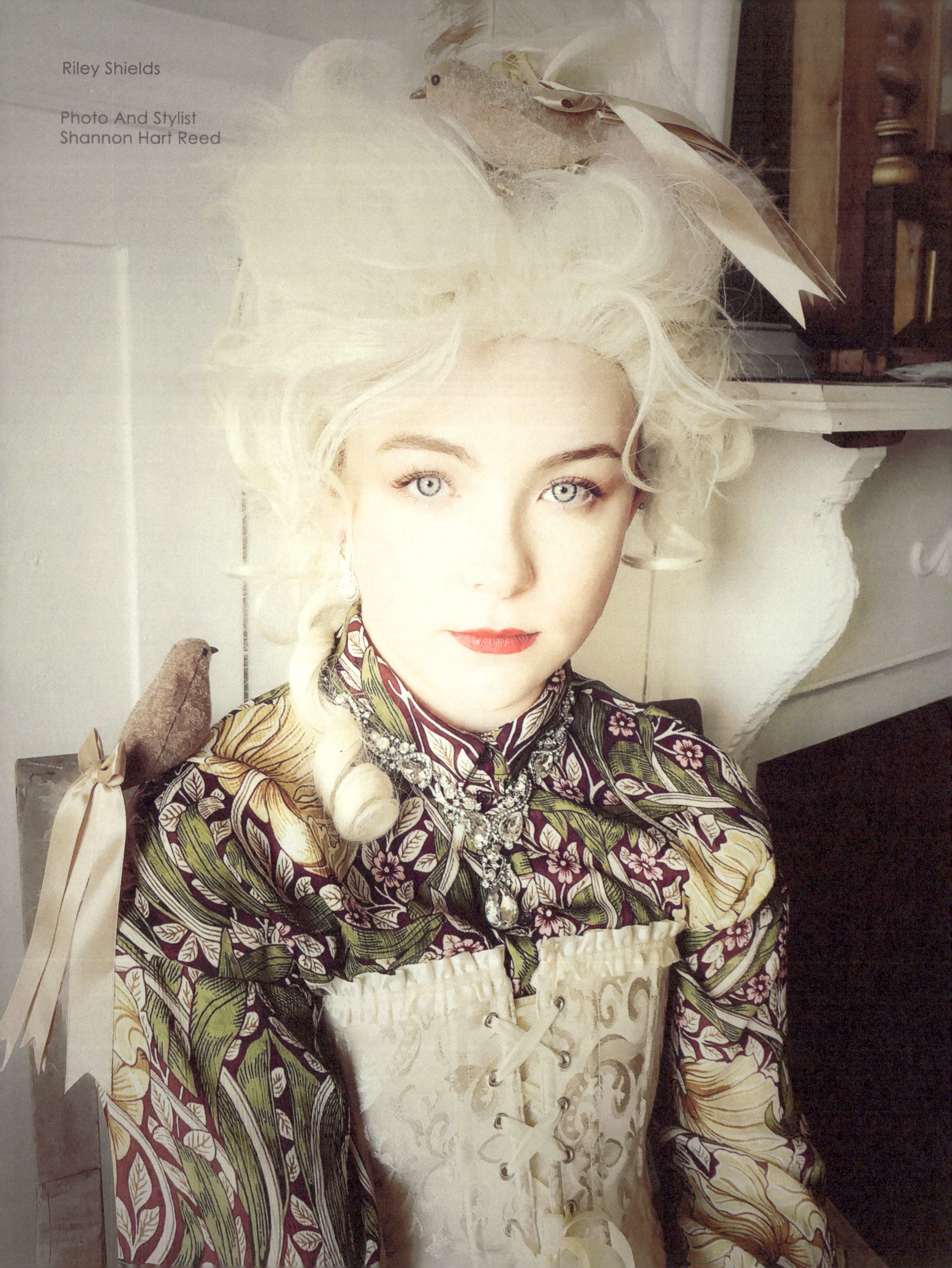

Riley Shields

Photo And Stylist
Shannon Hart Reed

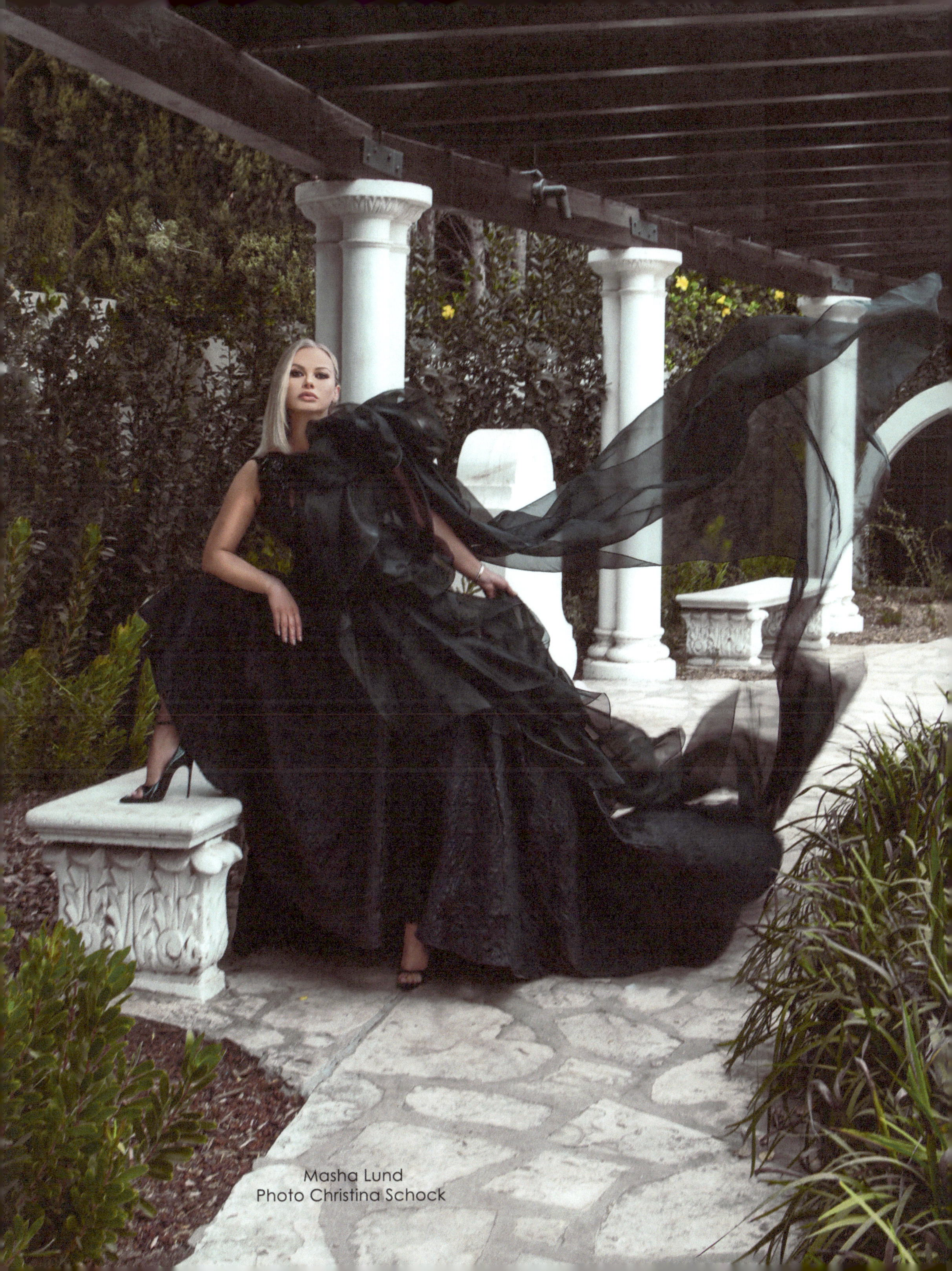

Masha Lund
Photo Christina Schock

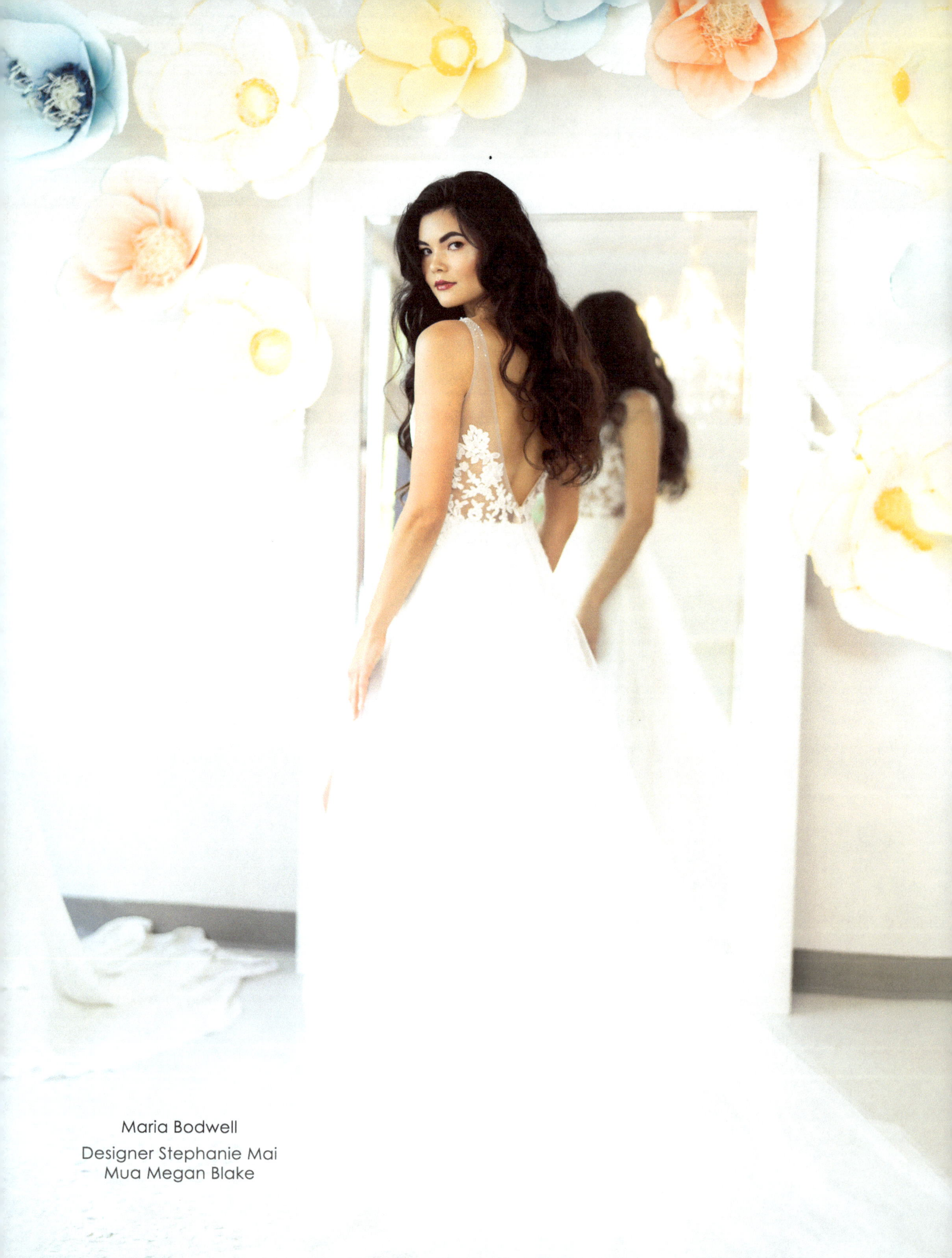

Maria Bodwell
Designer Stephanie Mai
Mua Megan Blake

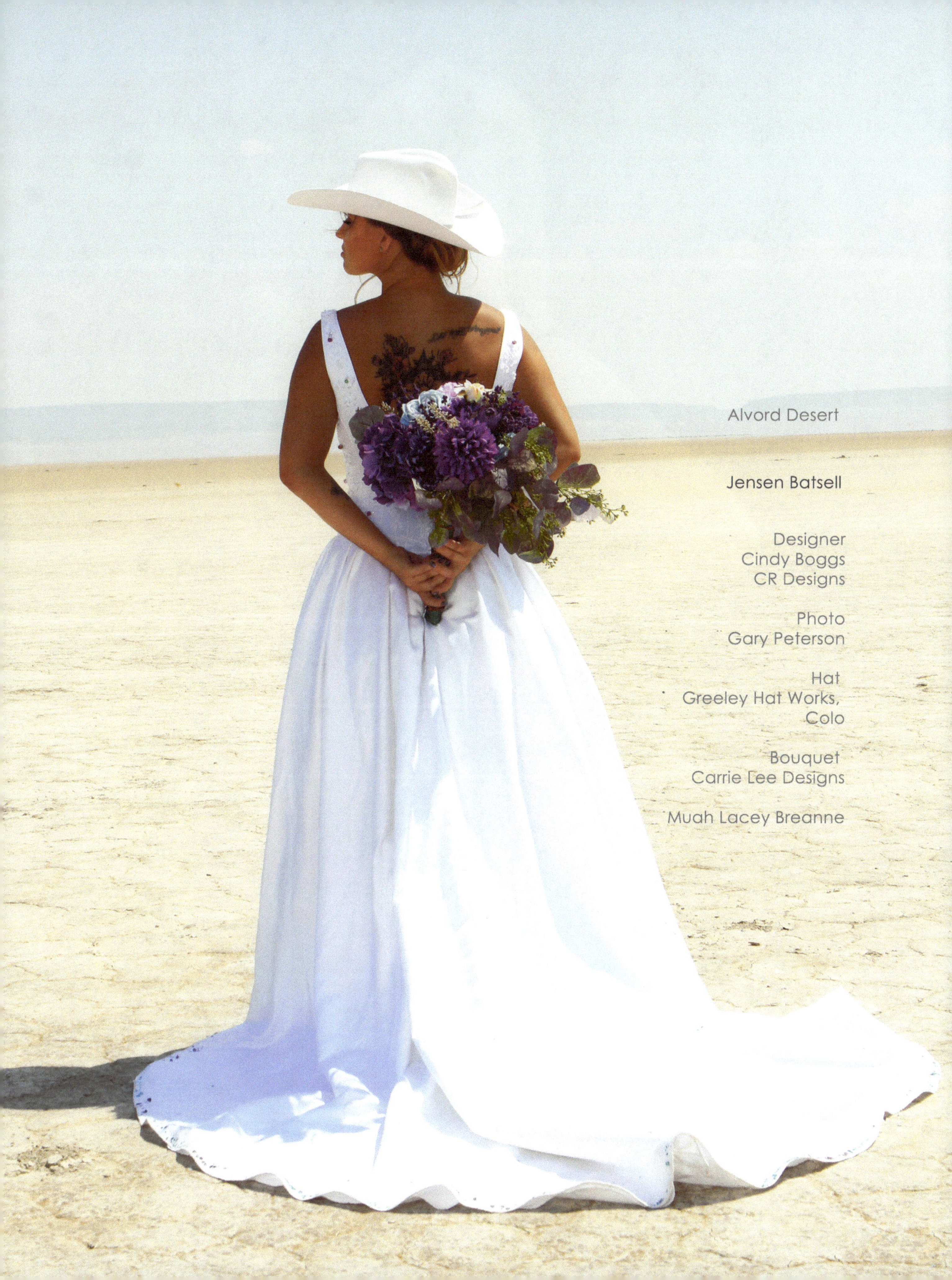

Alvord Desert

Jensen Batsell

Designer
Cindy Boggs
CR Designs

Photo
Gary Peterson

Hat
Greeley Hat Works,
Colo

Bouquet
Carrie Lee Designs

Muah Lacey Breanne

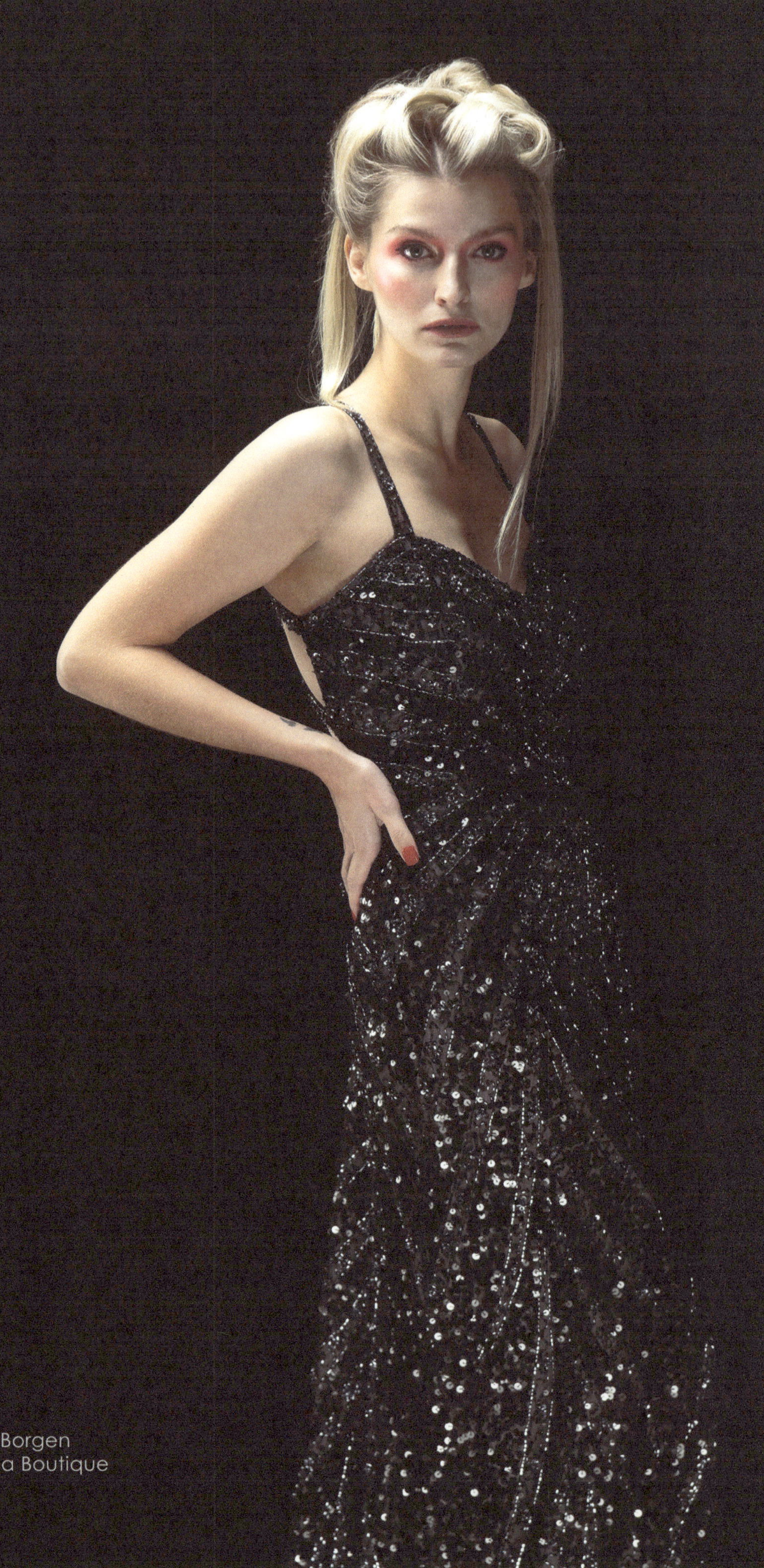

Kayla Borgen
Velonia Boutique

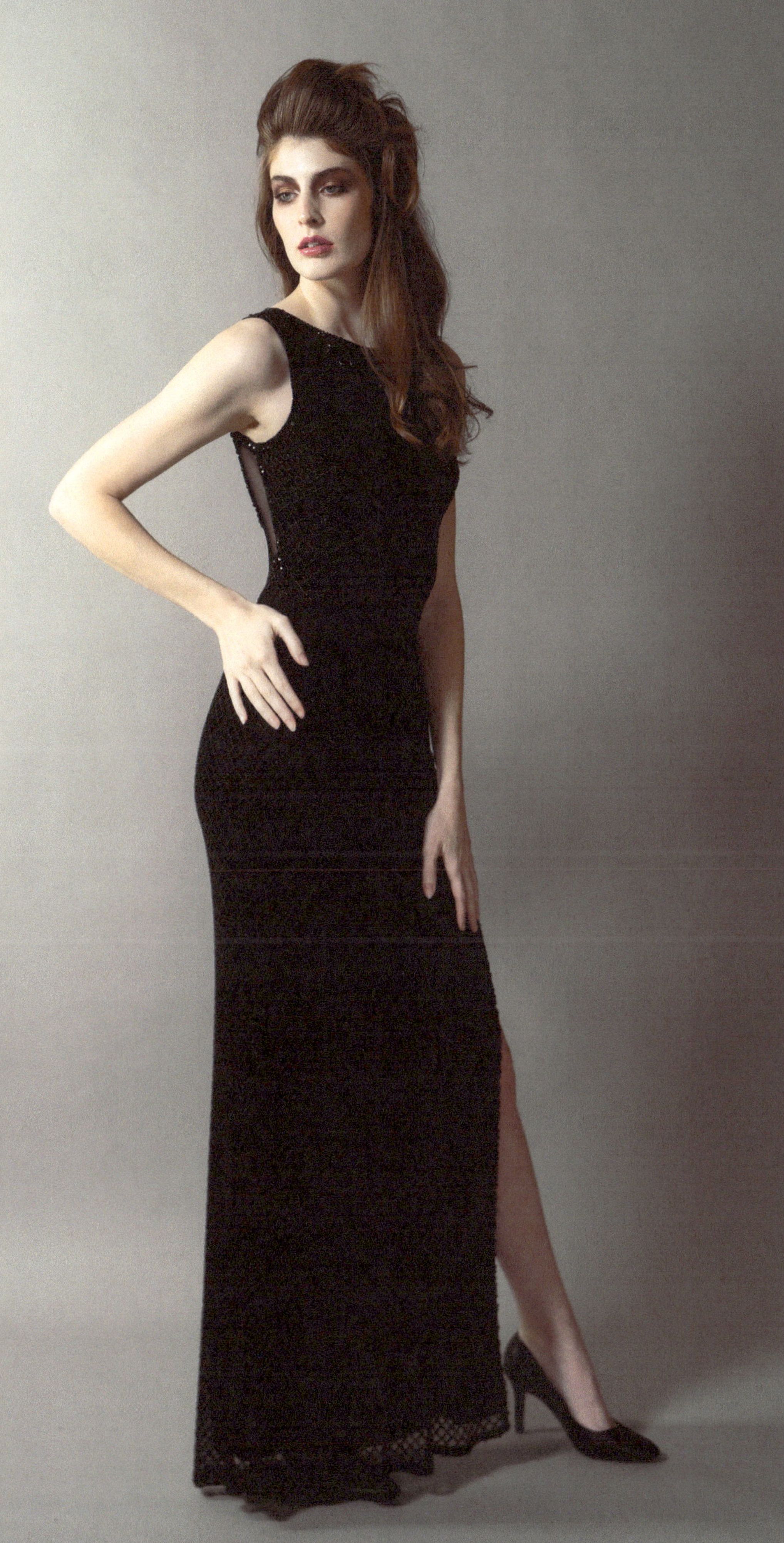

Amy Evans
Velonia Boutique

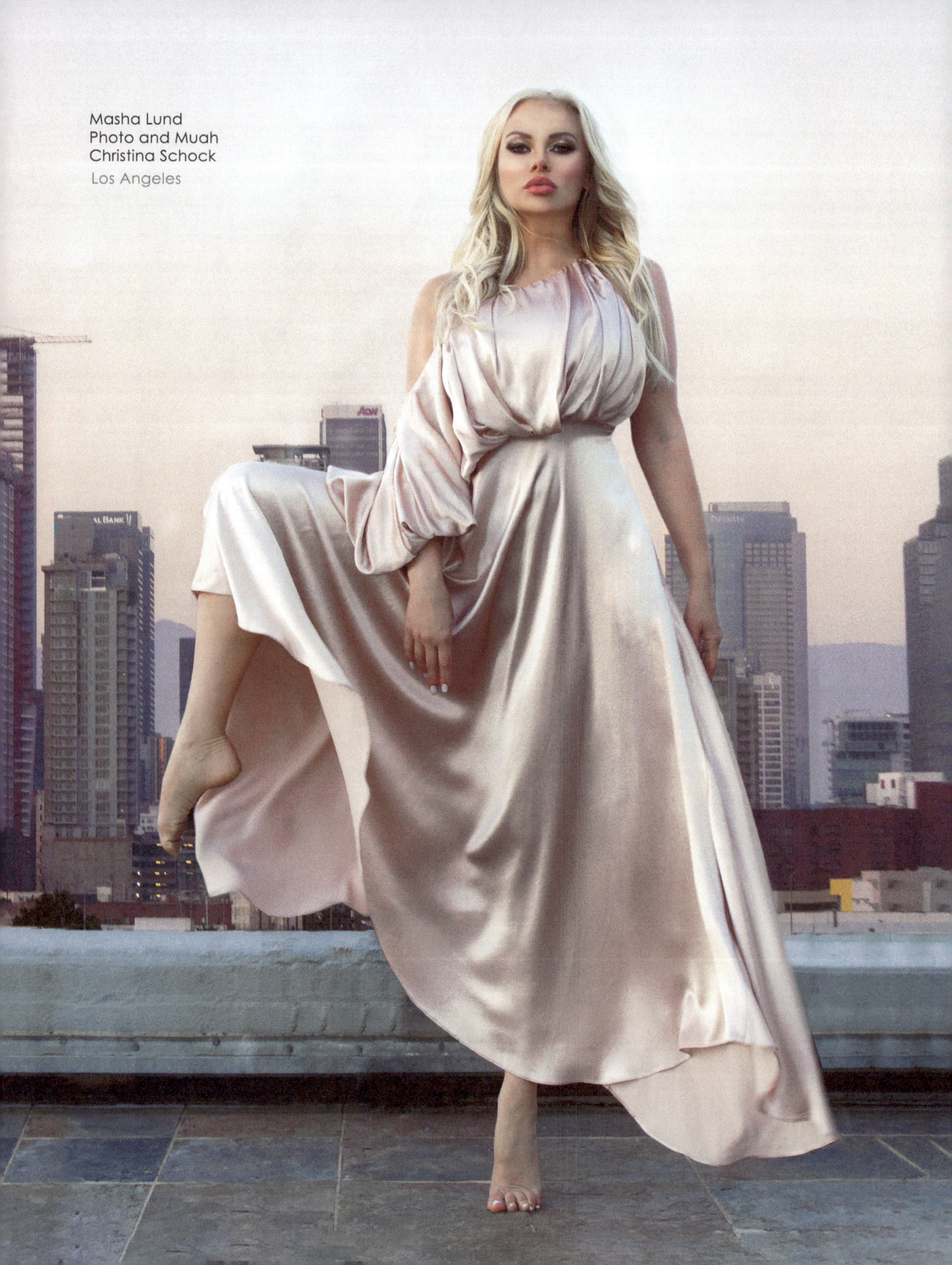
Masha Lund
Photo and Muah
Christina Schock
Los Angeles

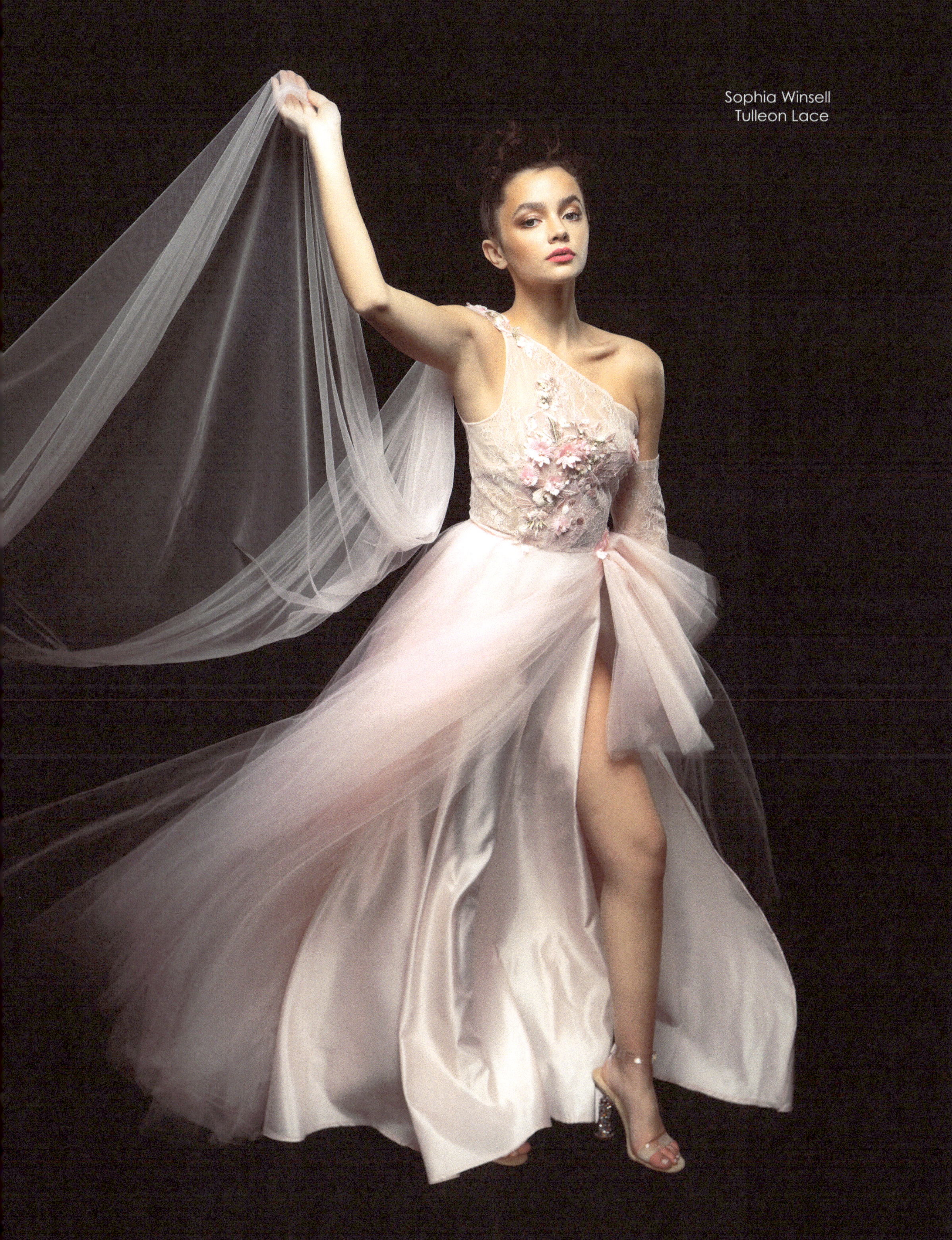
Sophia Winsell
Tulleon Lace

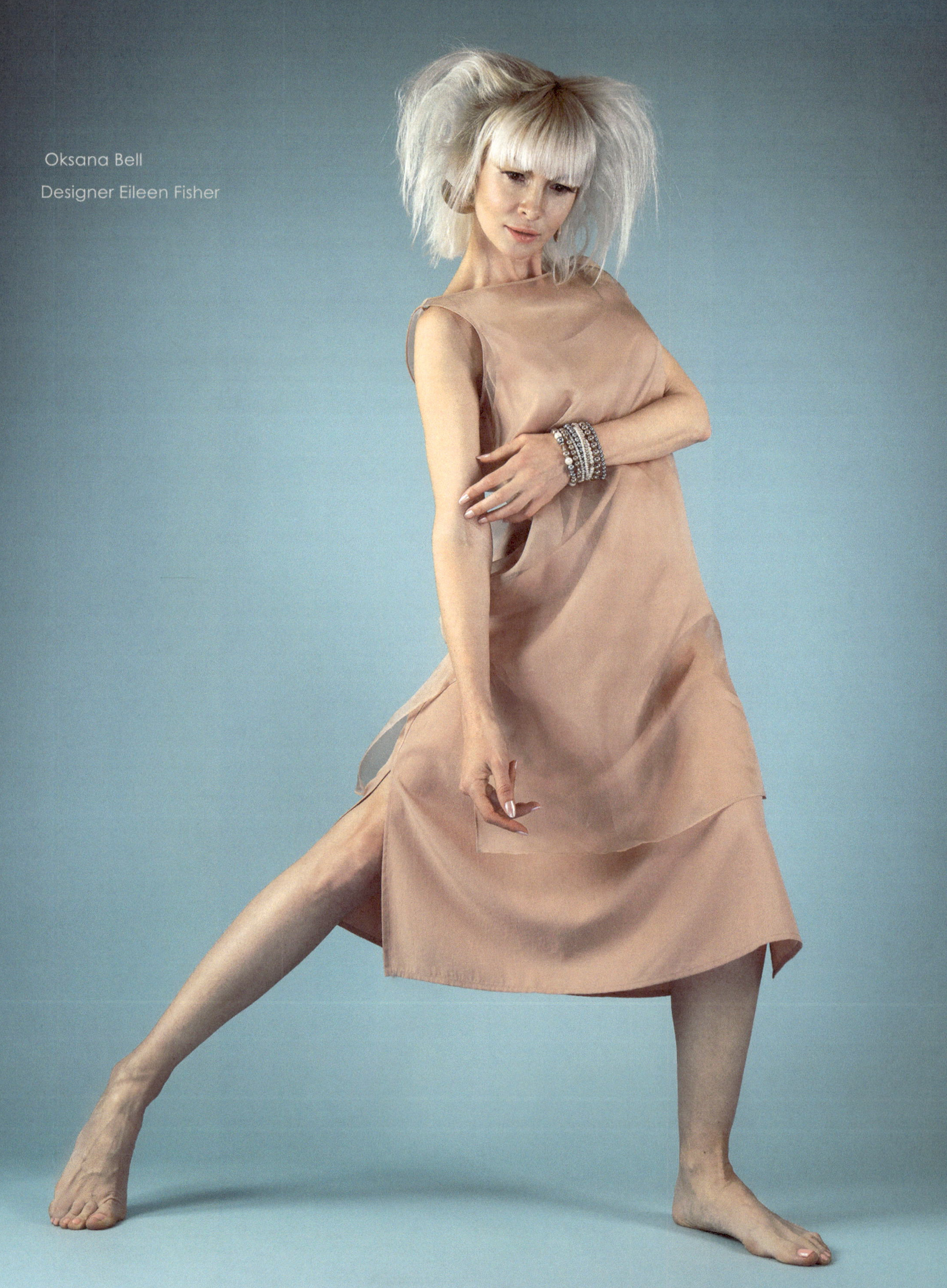
Oksana Bell
Designer Eileen Fisher

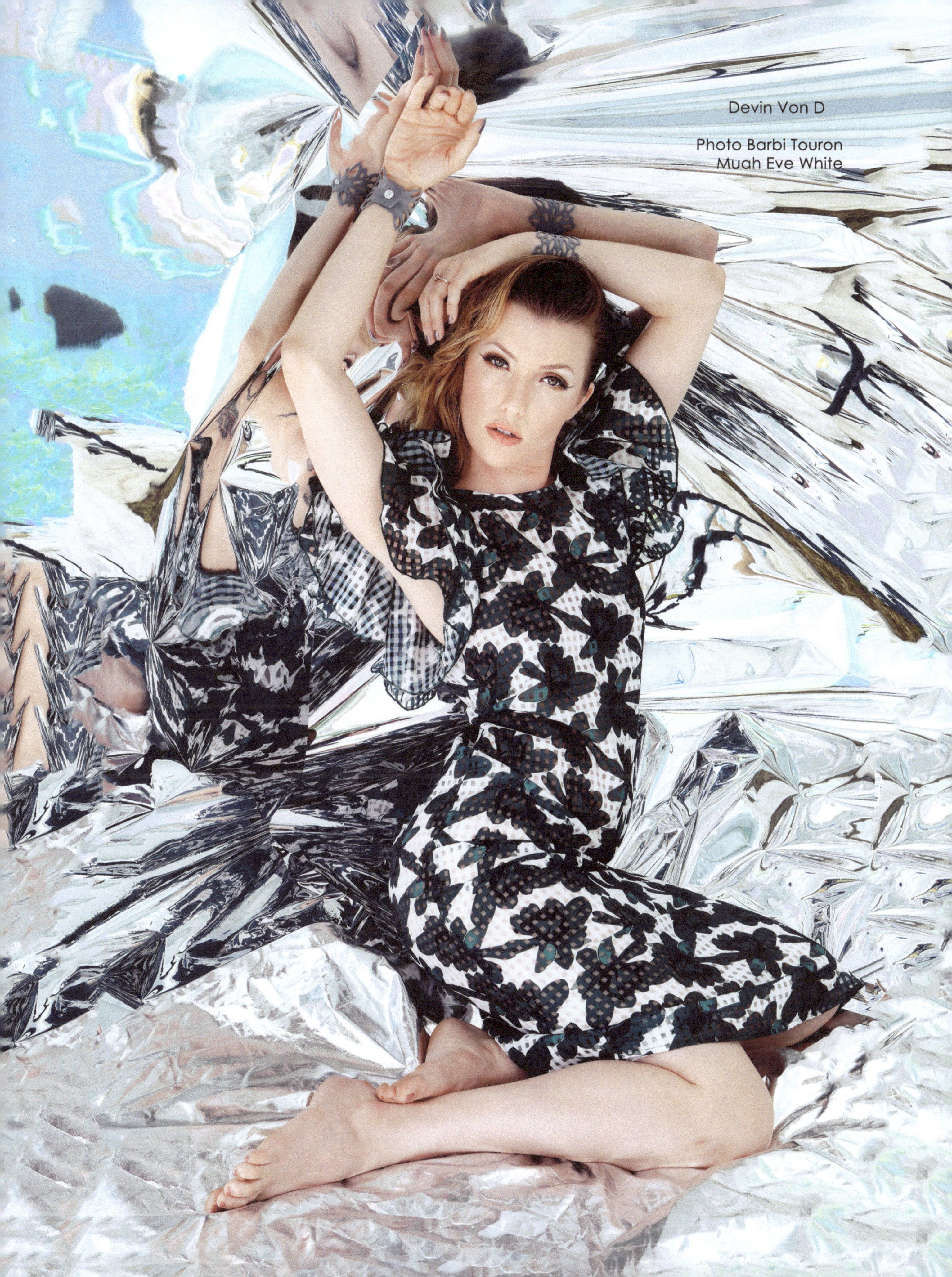
Devin Von D

Photo Barbi Touron
Muah Eve White

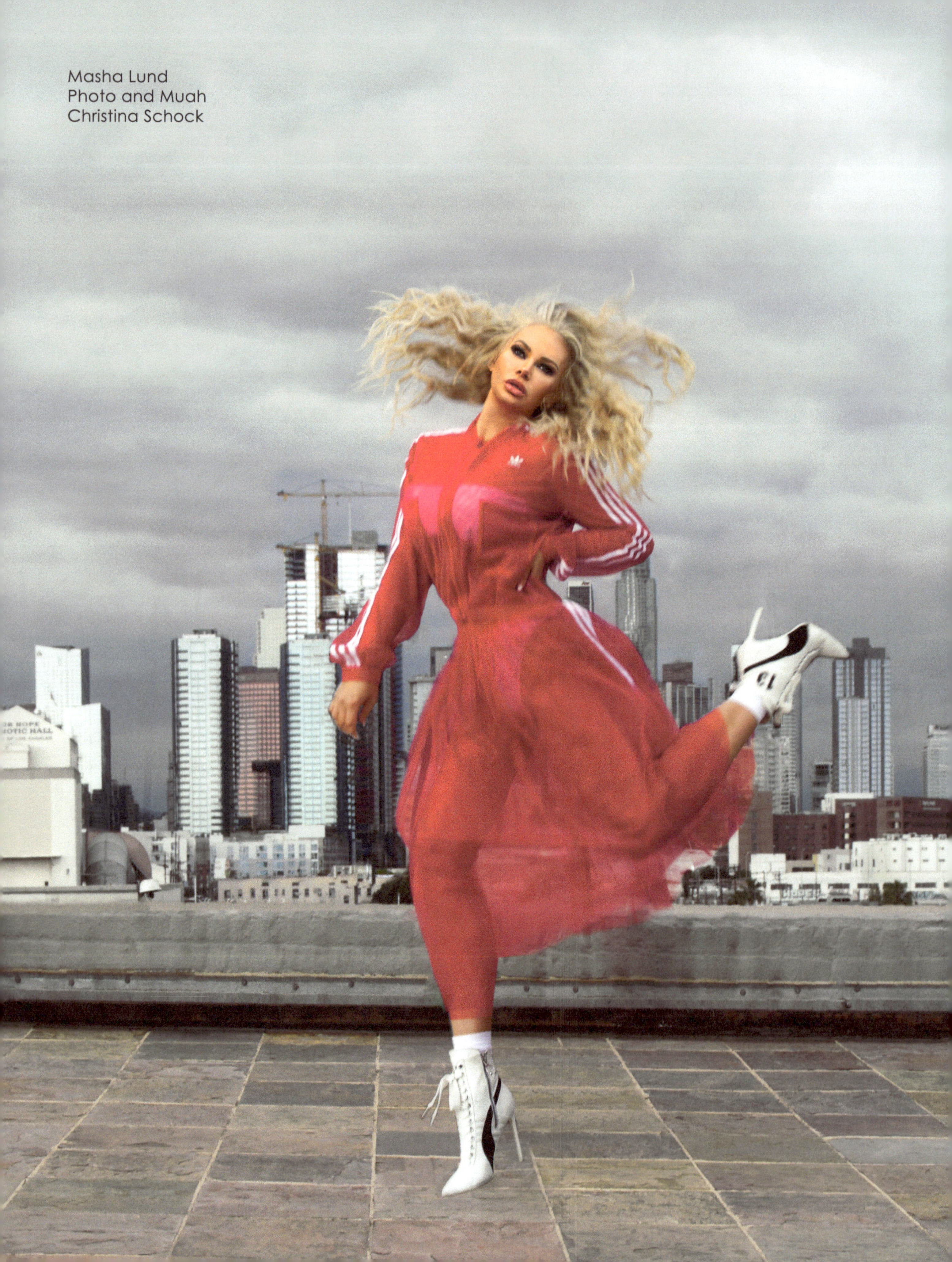

Masha Lund
Photo and Muah
Christina Schock

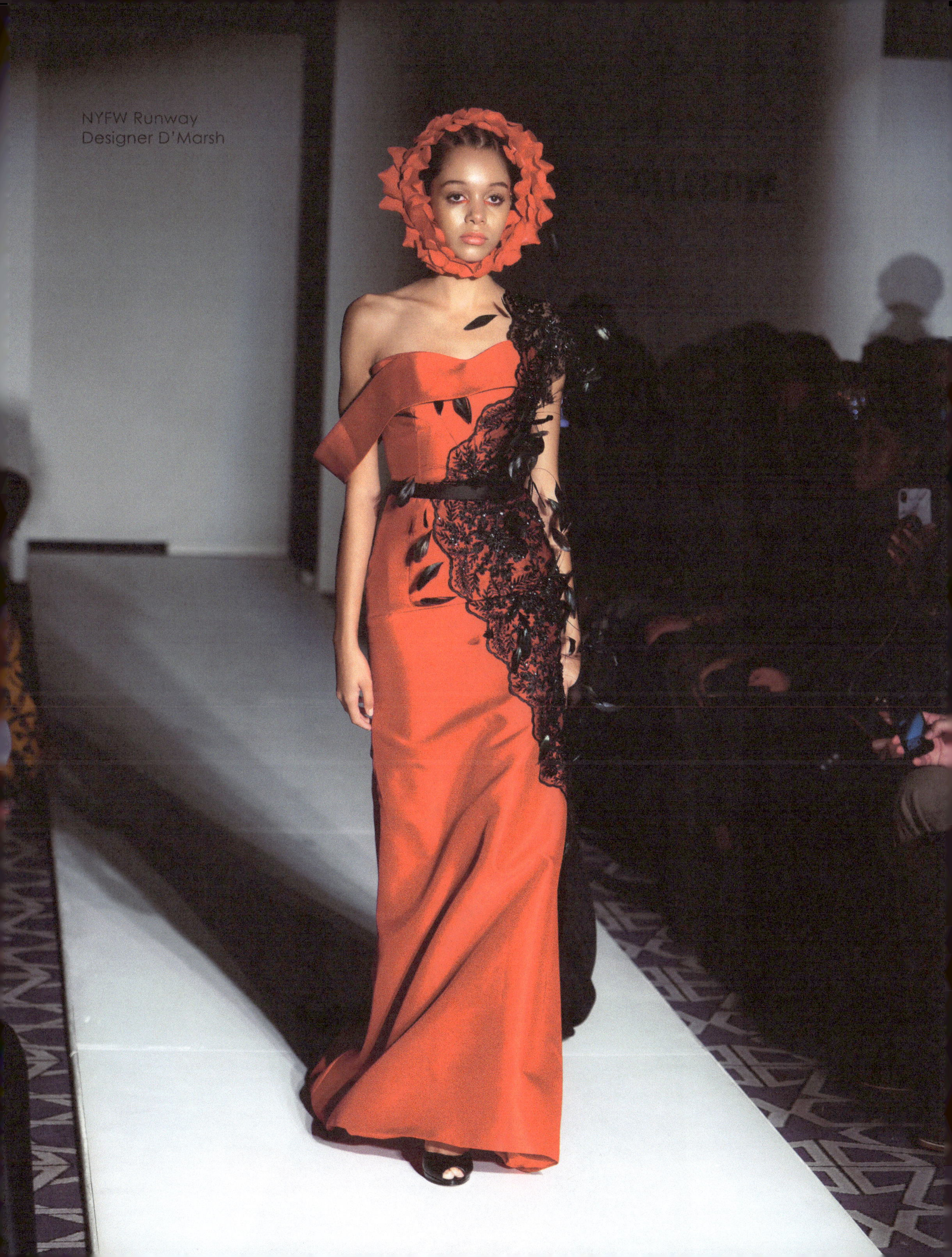
NYFW Runway
Designer D'Marsh

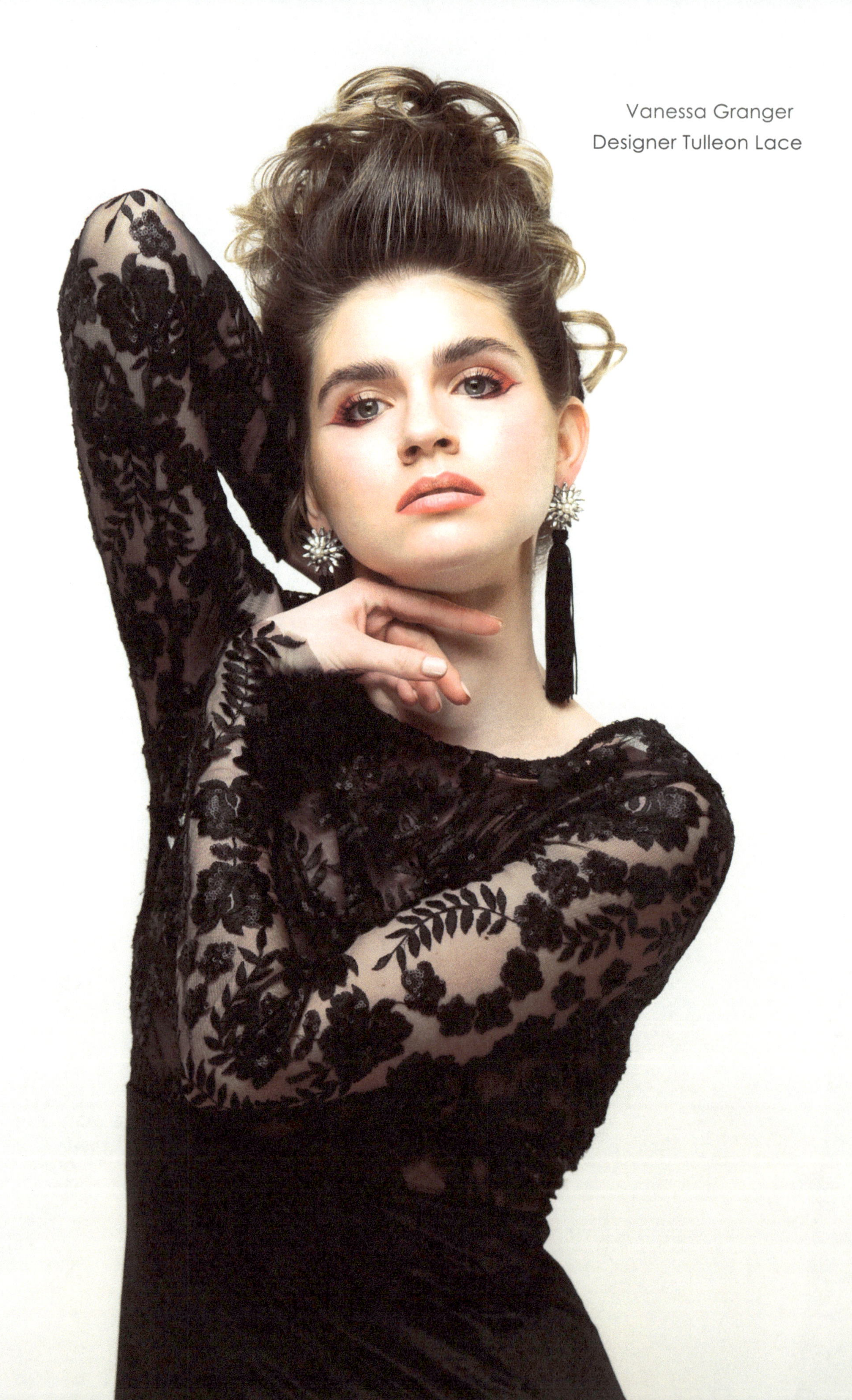
Vanessa Granger
Designer Tulleon Lace

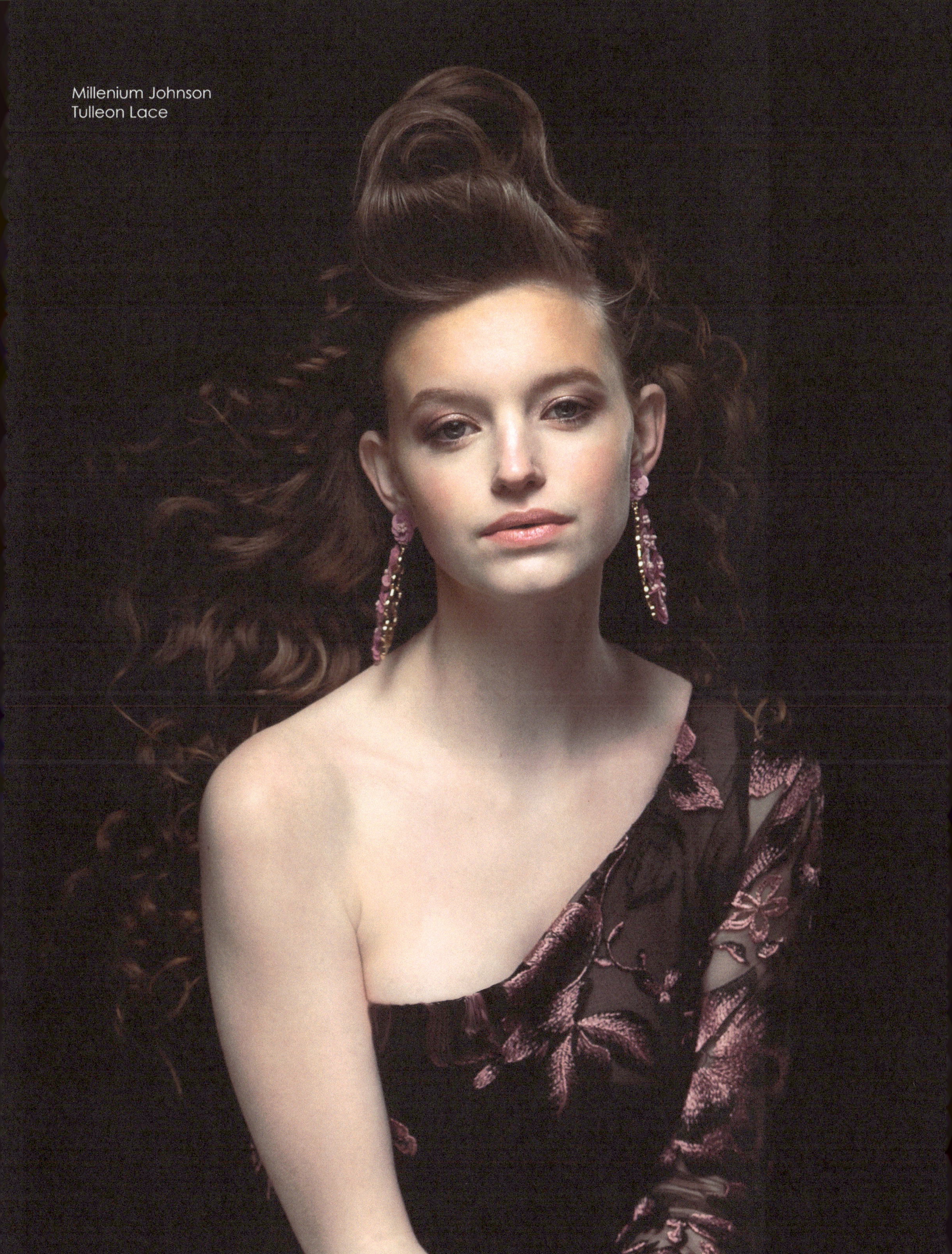

Millenium Johnson
Tulleon Lace

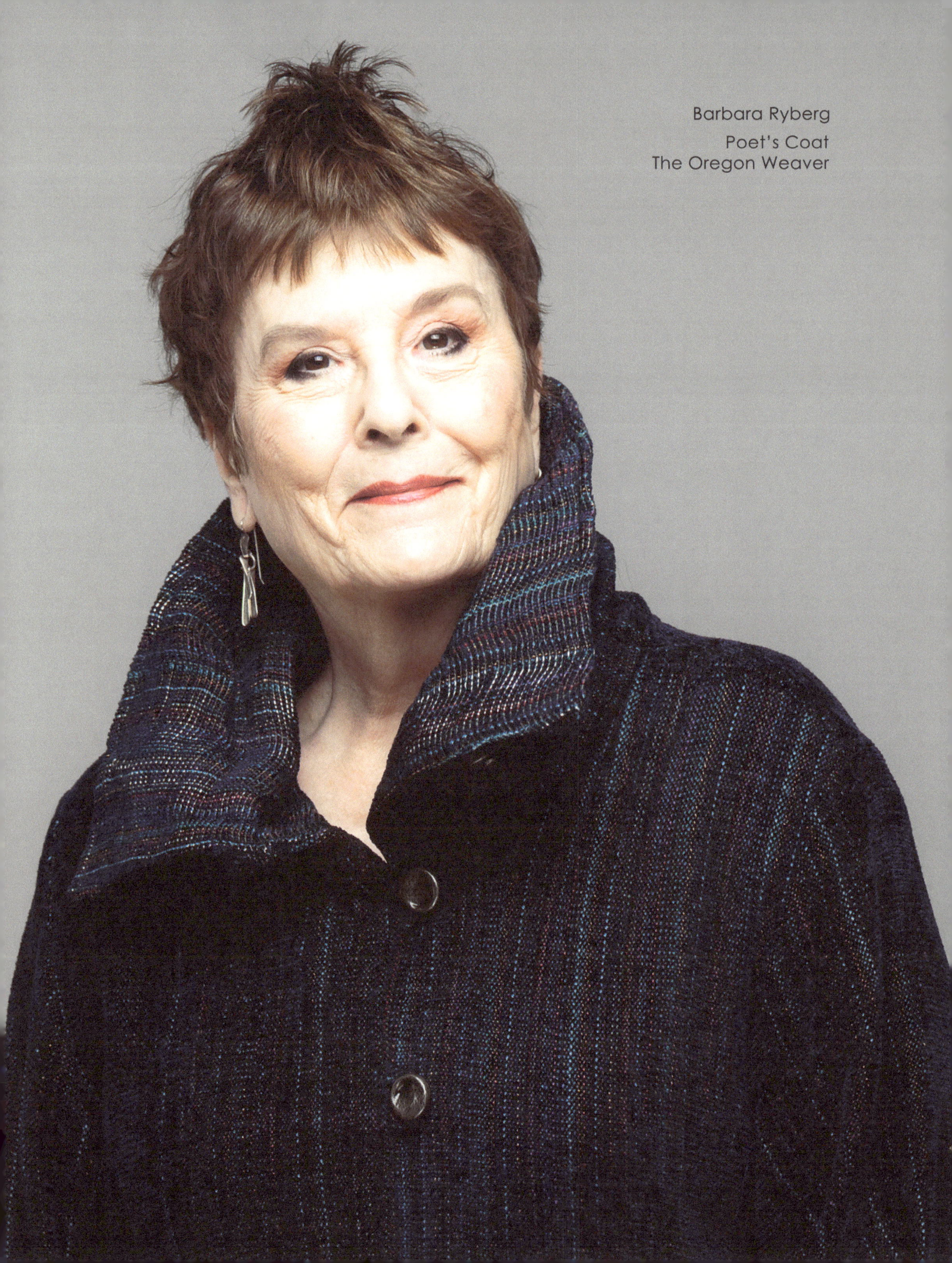

Barbara Ryberg
Poet's Coat
The Oregon Weaver

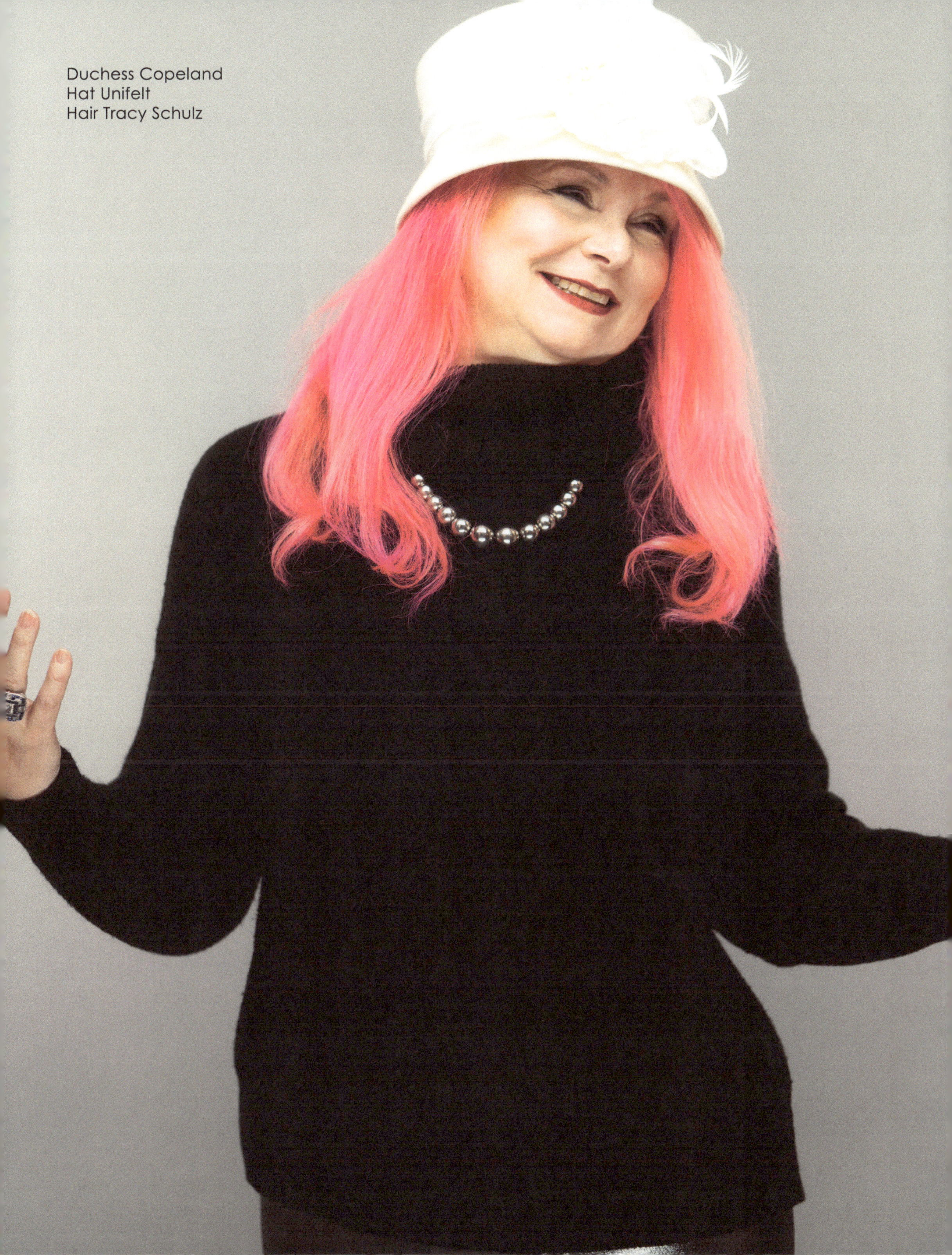

Duchess Copeland
Hat Unifelt
Hair Tracy Schulz

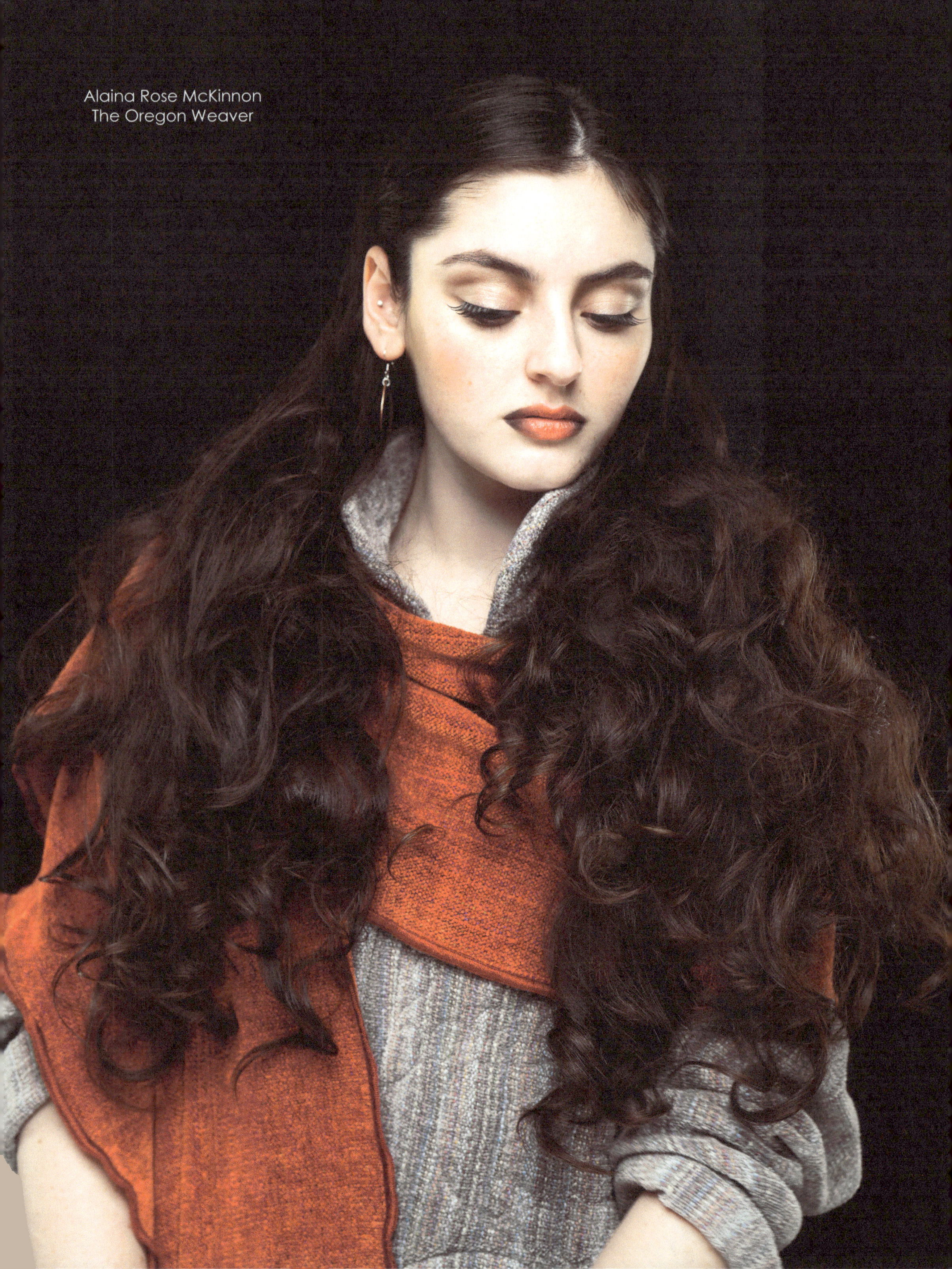

Alaina Rose McKinnon
The Oregon Weaver

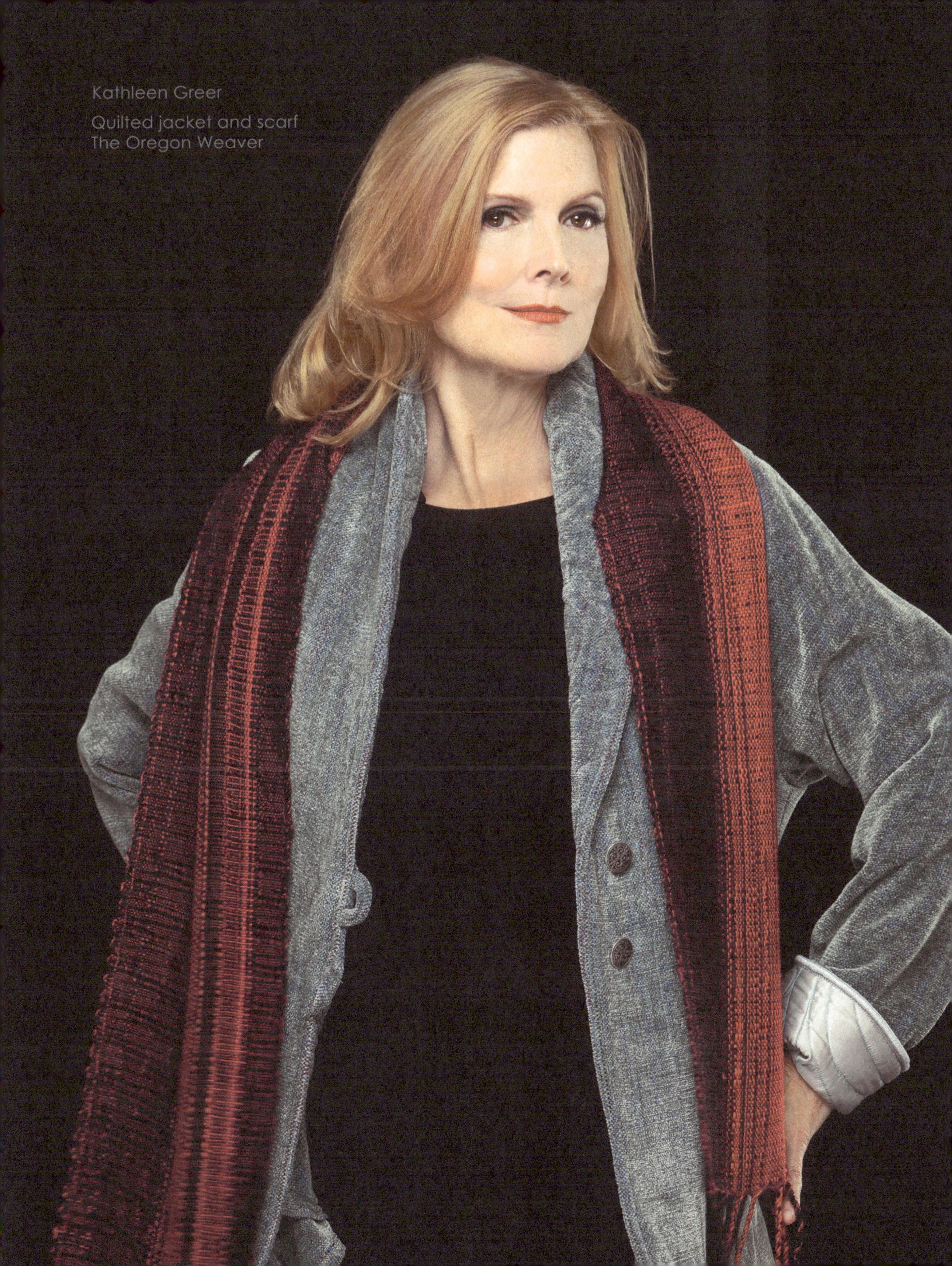
Kathleen Greer
Quilted jacket and scarf
The Oregon Weaver

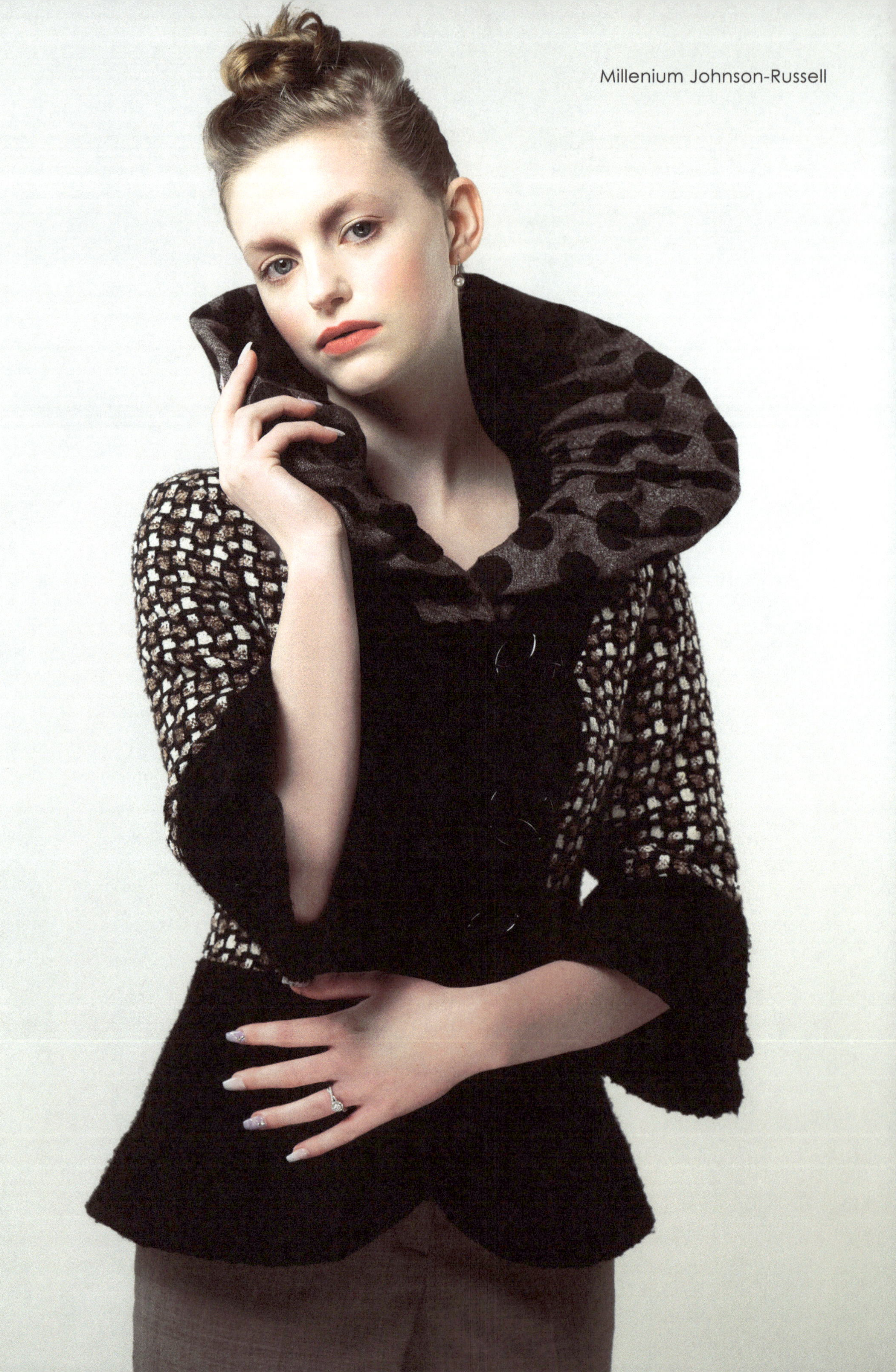
Millenium Johnson-Russell

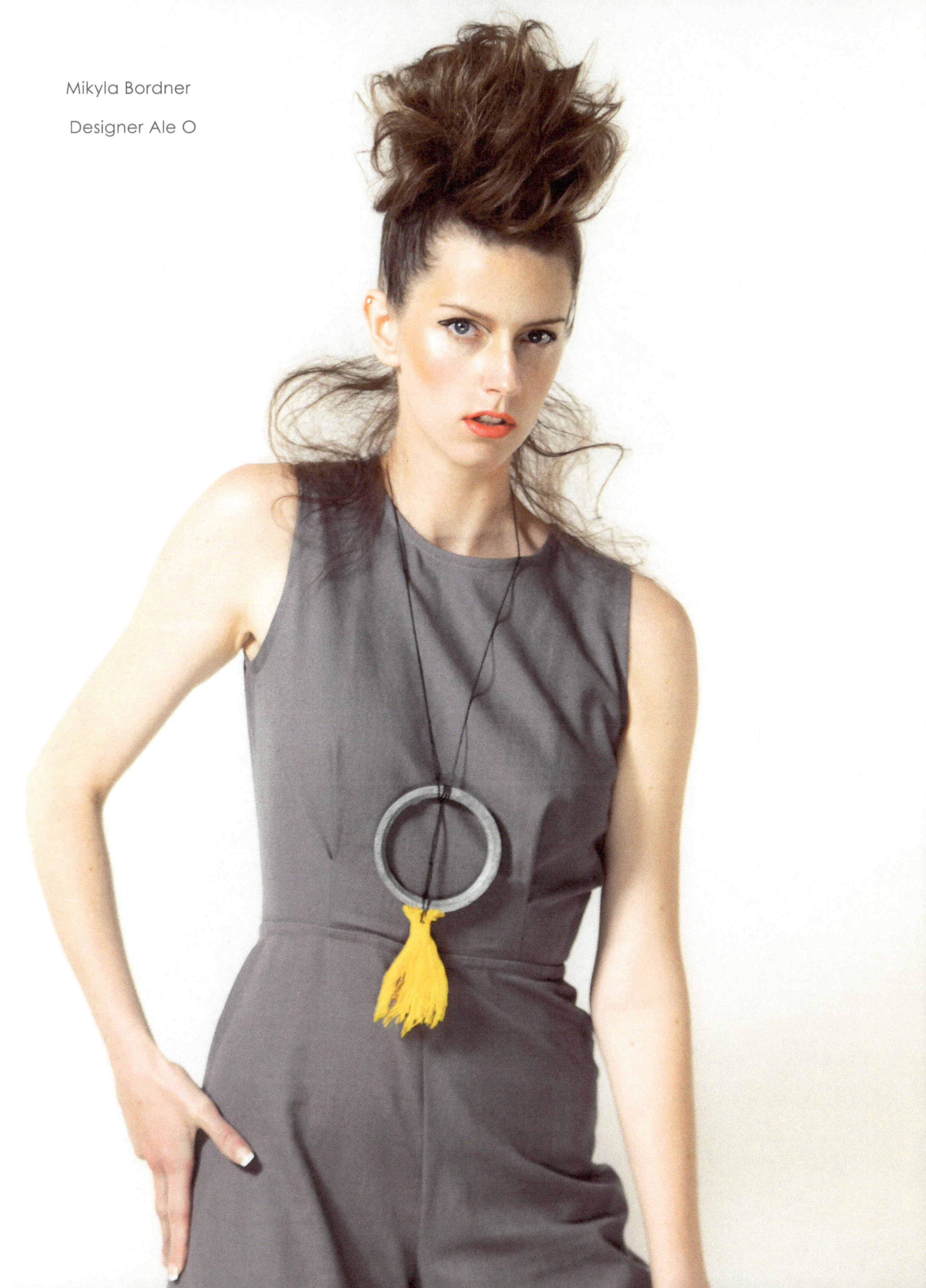

Mikyla Bordner
Designer Ale O

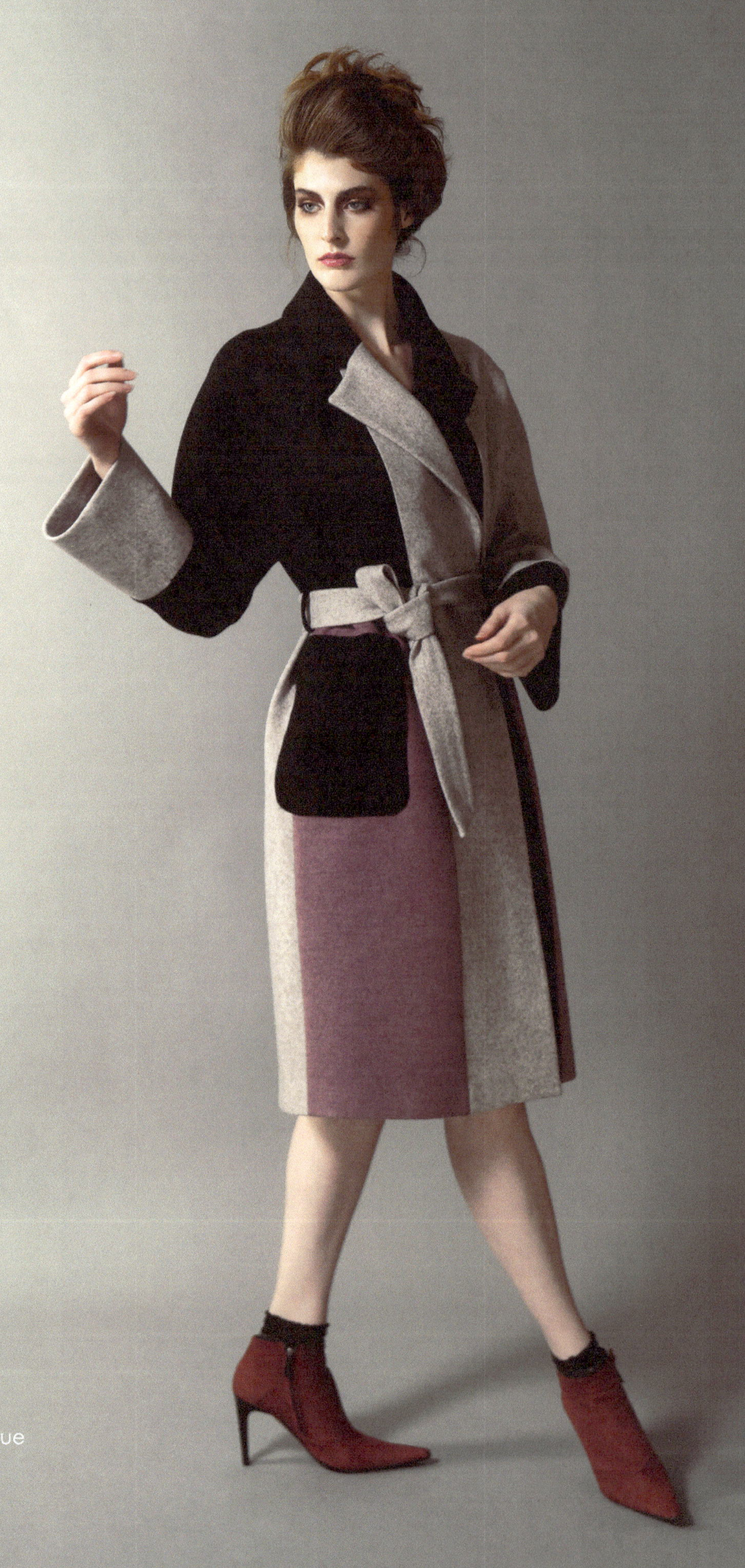

Amy Evans
Velonia Boutique

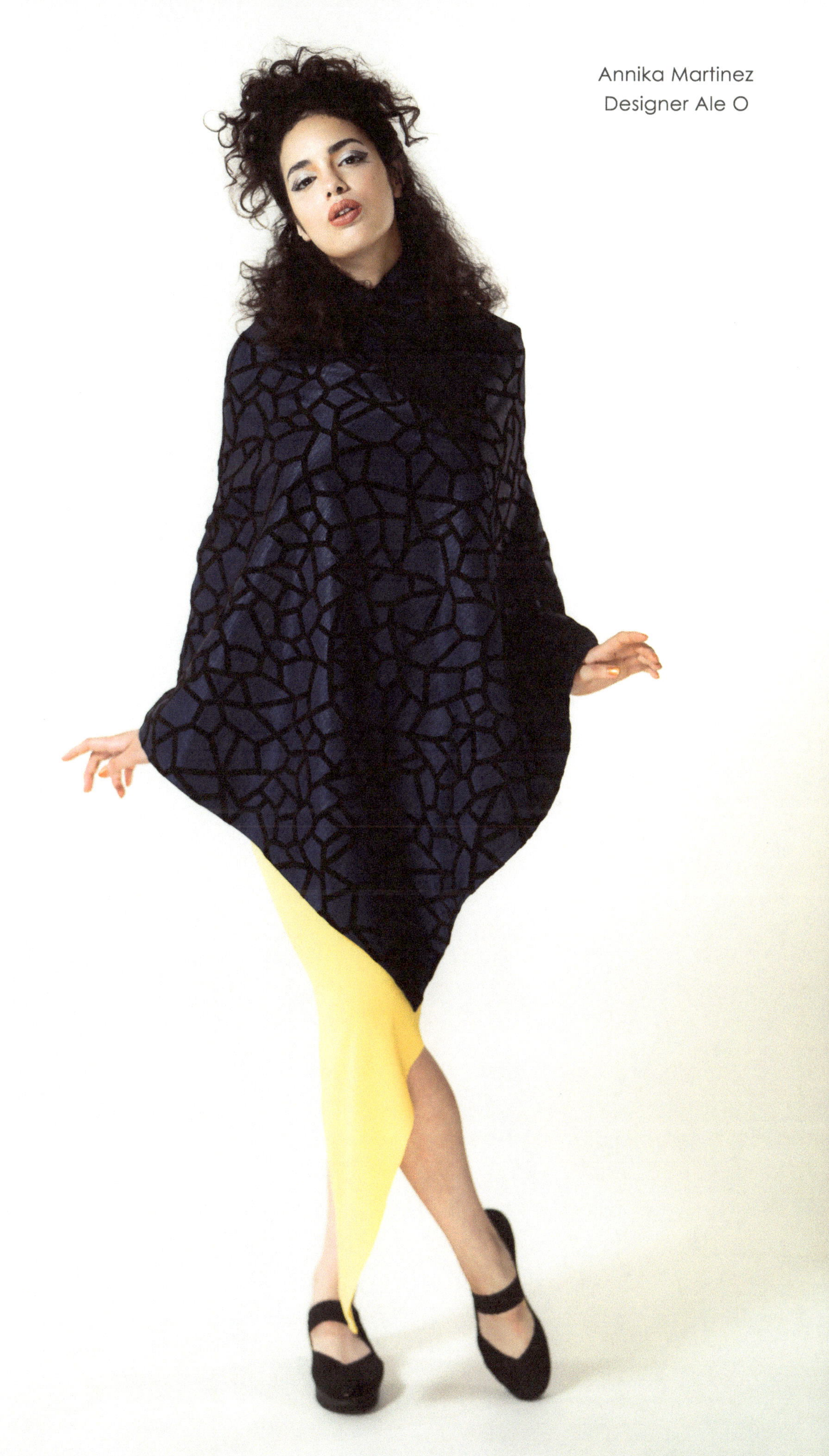

Annika Martinez
Designer Ale O

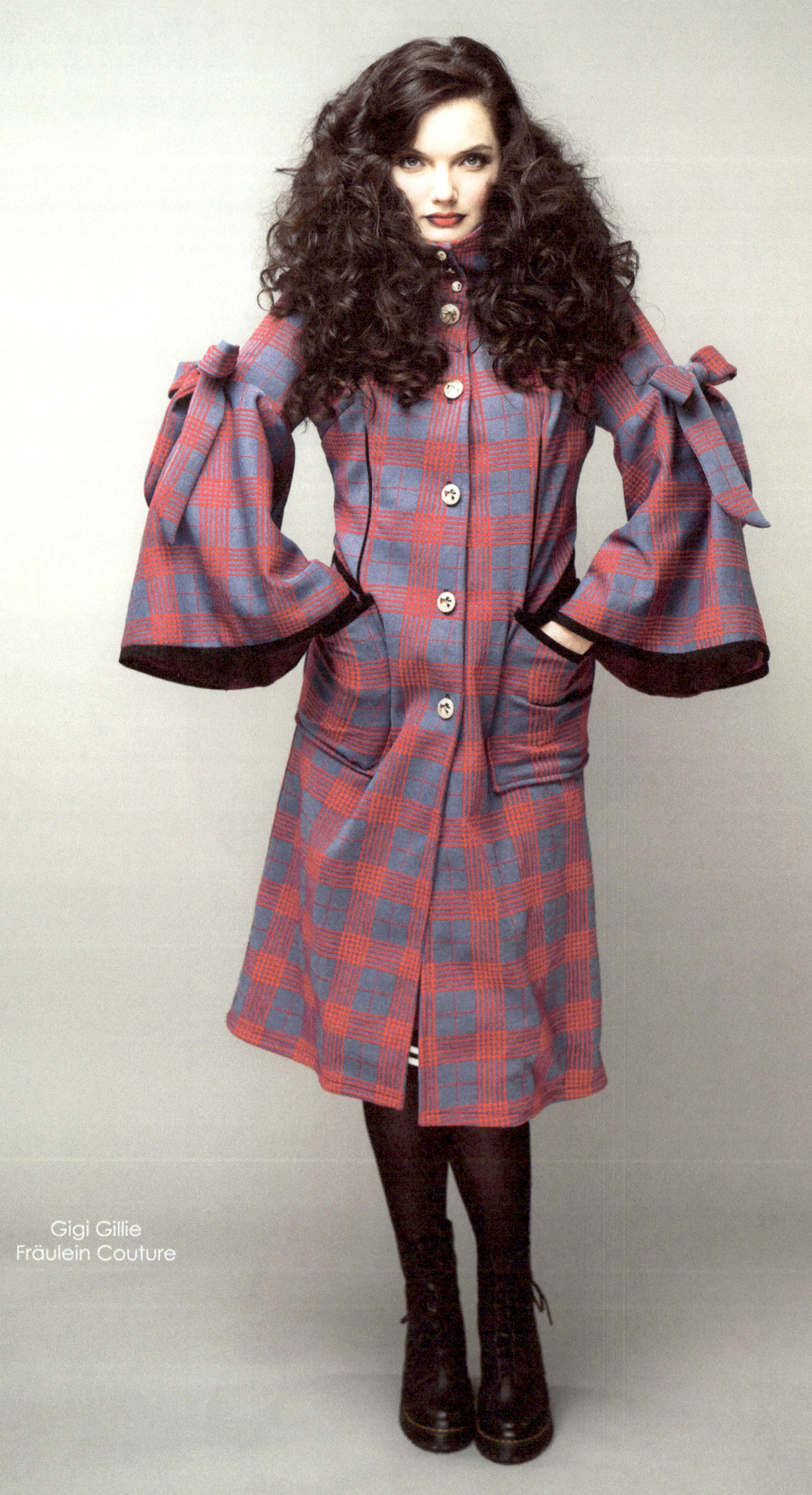

Gigi Gillie
Fräulein Couture

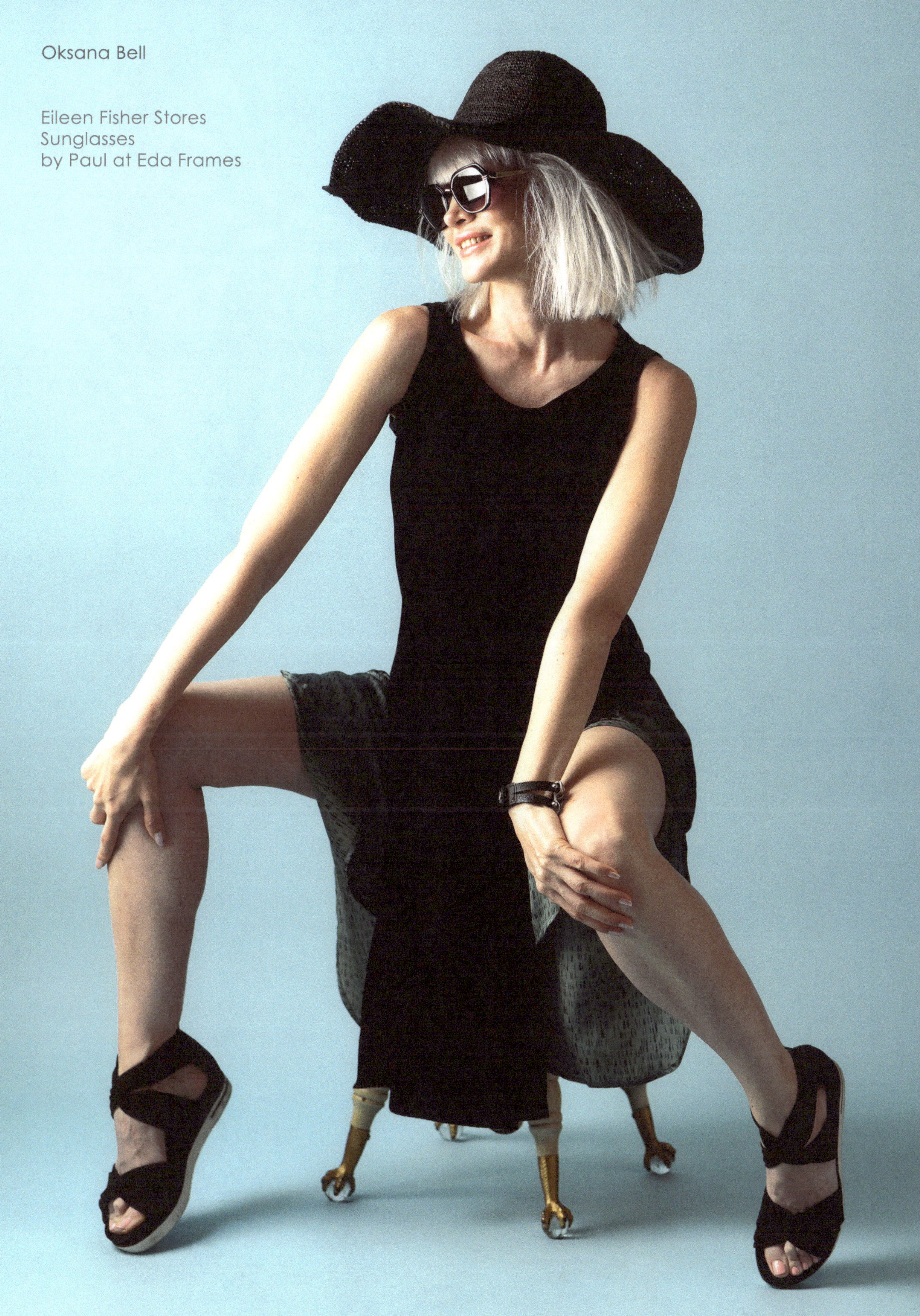

Oksana Bell

Eileen Fisher Stores
Sunglasses
by Paul at Eda Frames

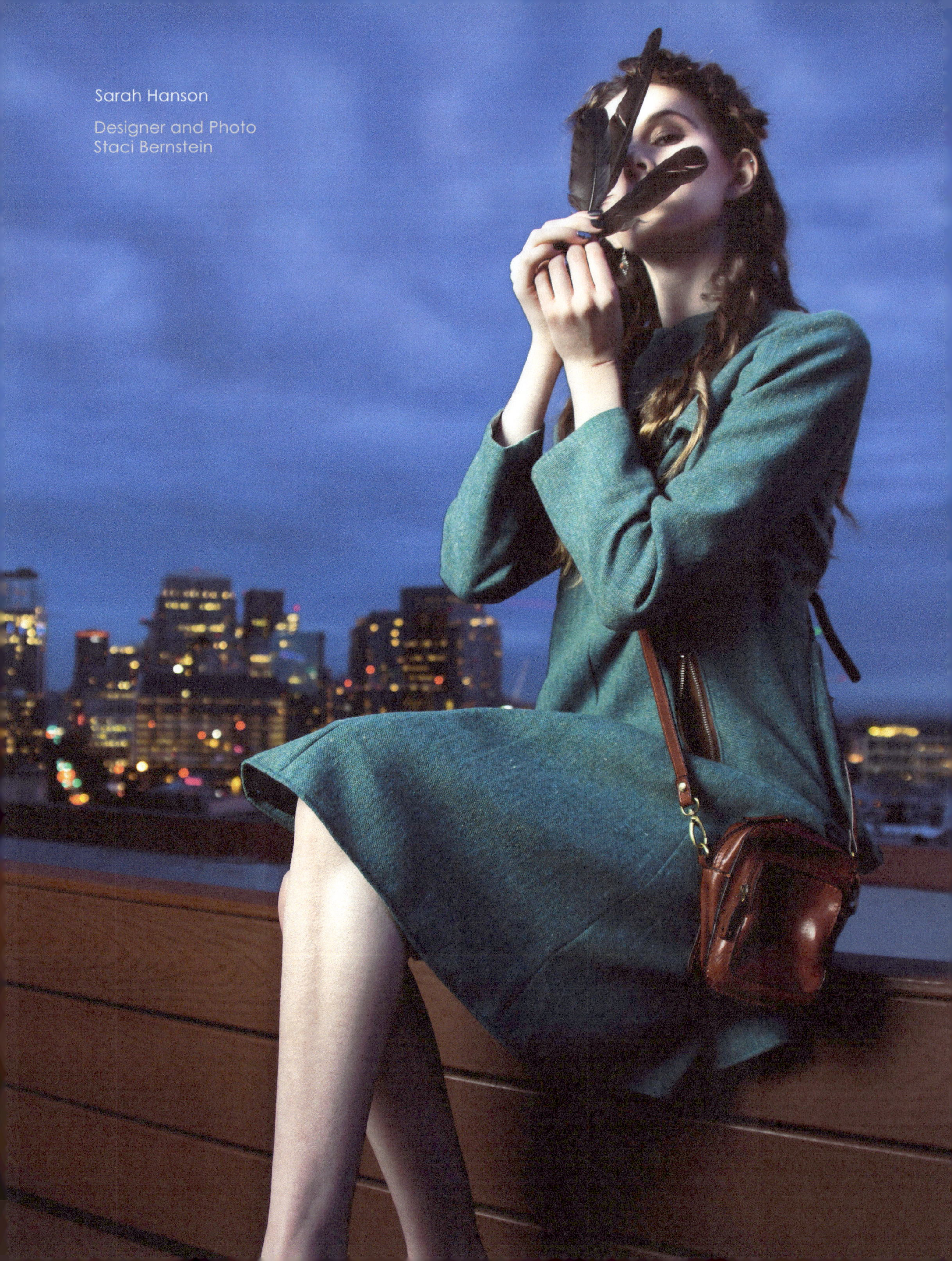
Sarah Hanson
Designer and Photo
Staci Bernstein

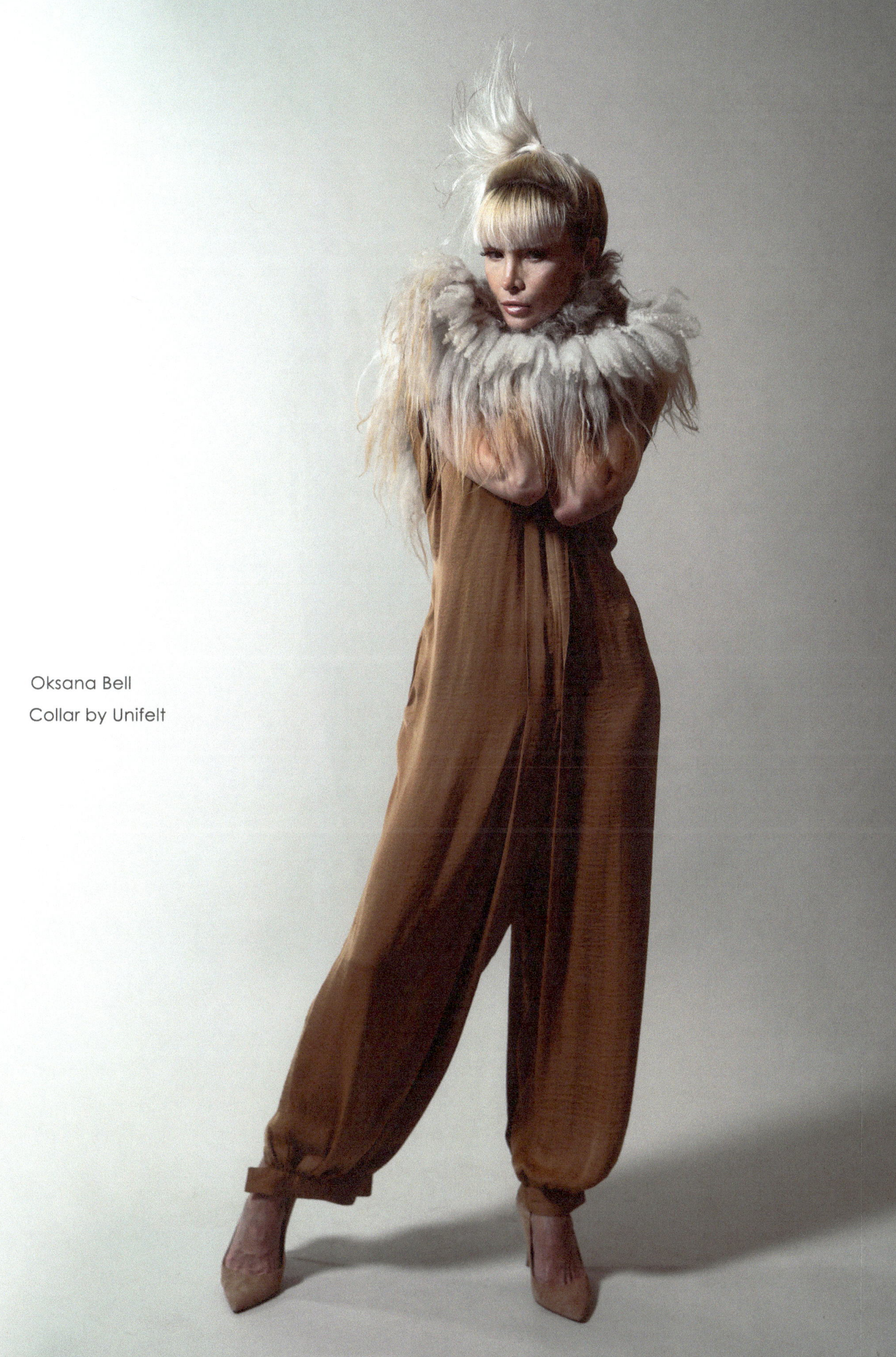

Oksana Bell
Collar by Unifelt

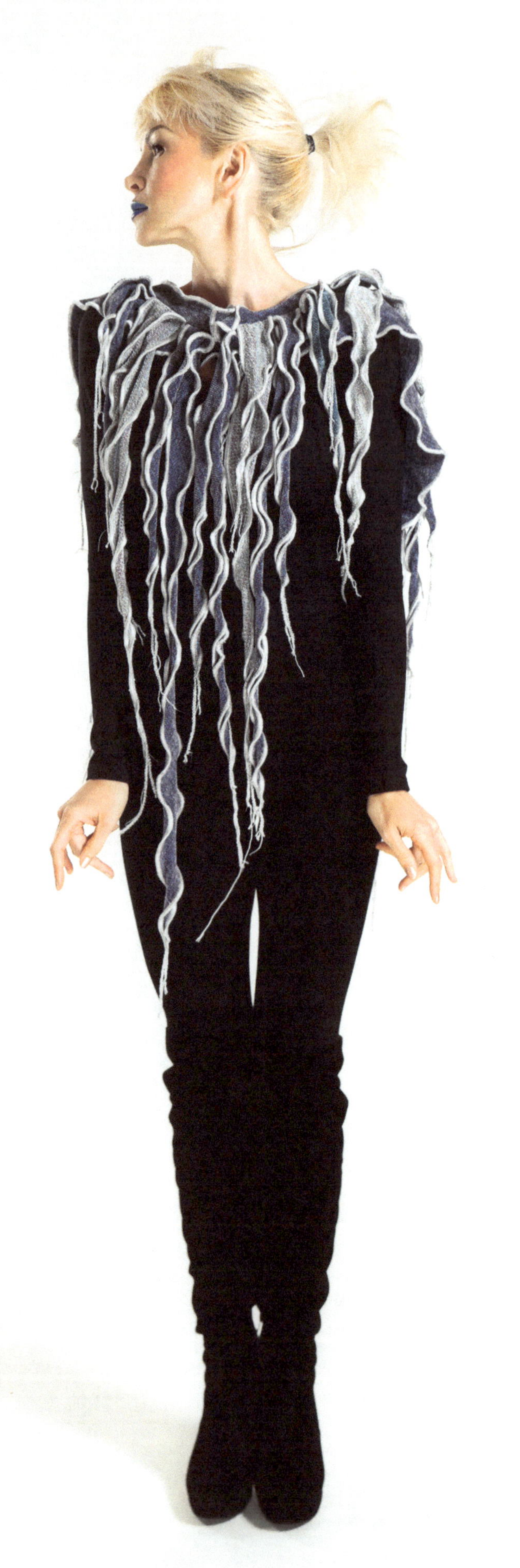

Oksana Bell
Waterfall Scarf
The Oregon Weaver

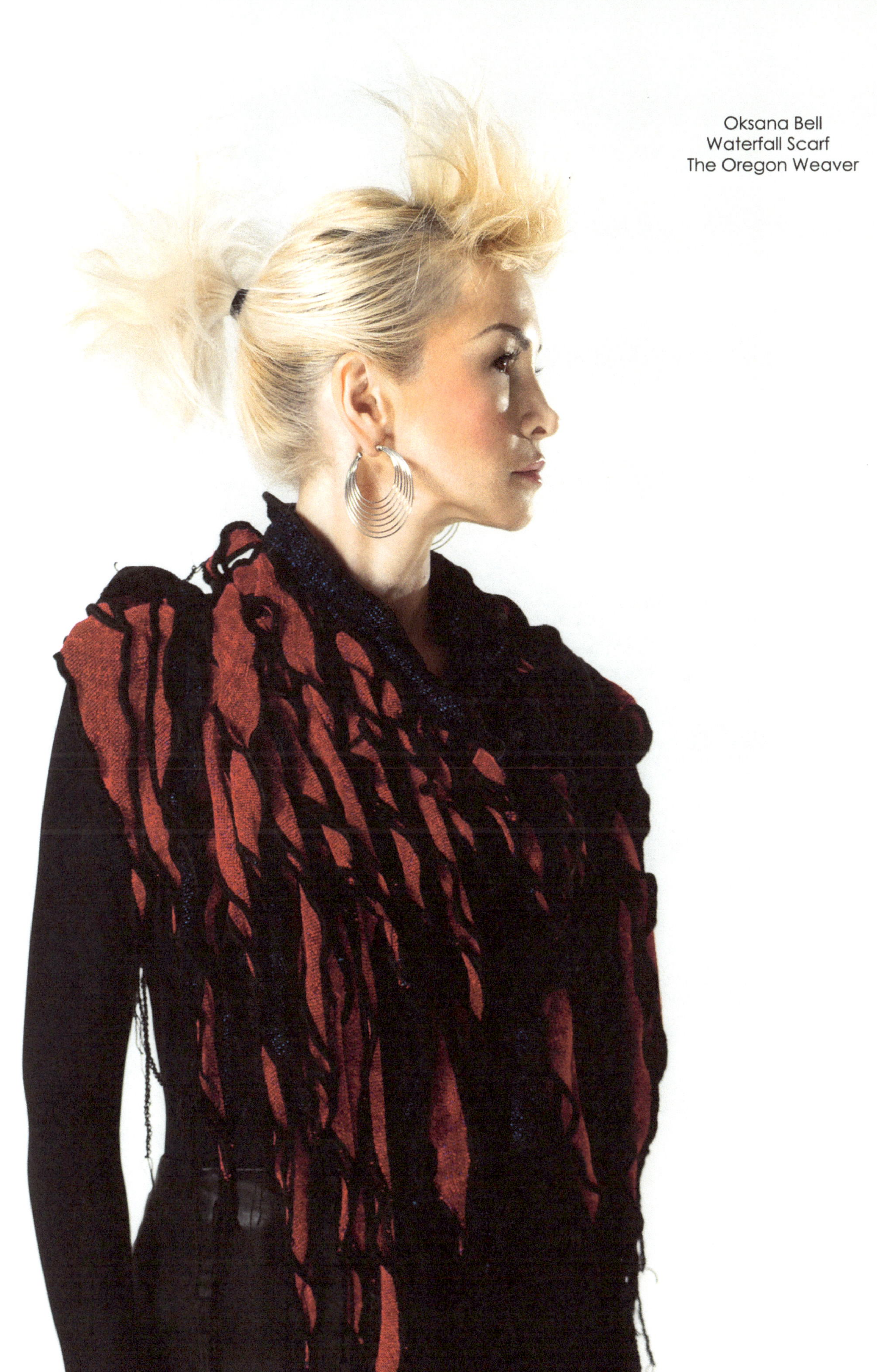

Oksana Bell
Waterfall Scarf
The Oregon Weaver

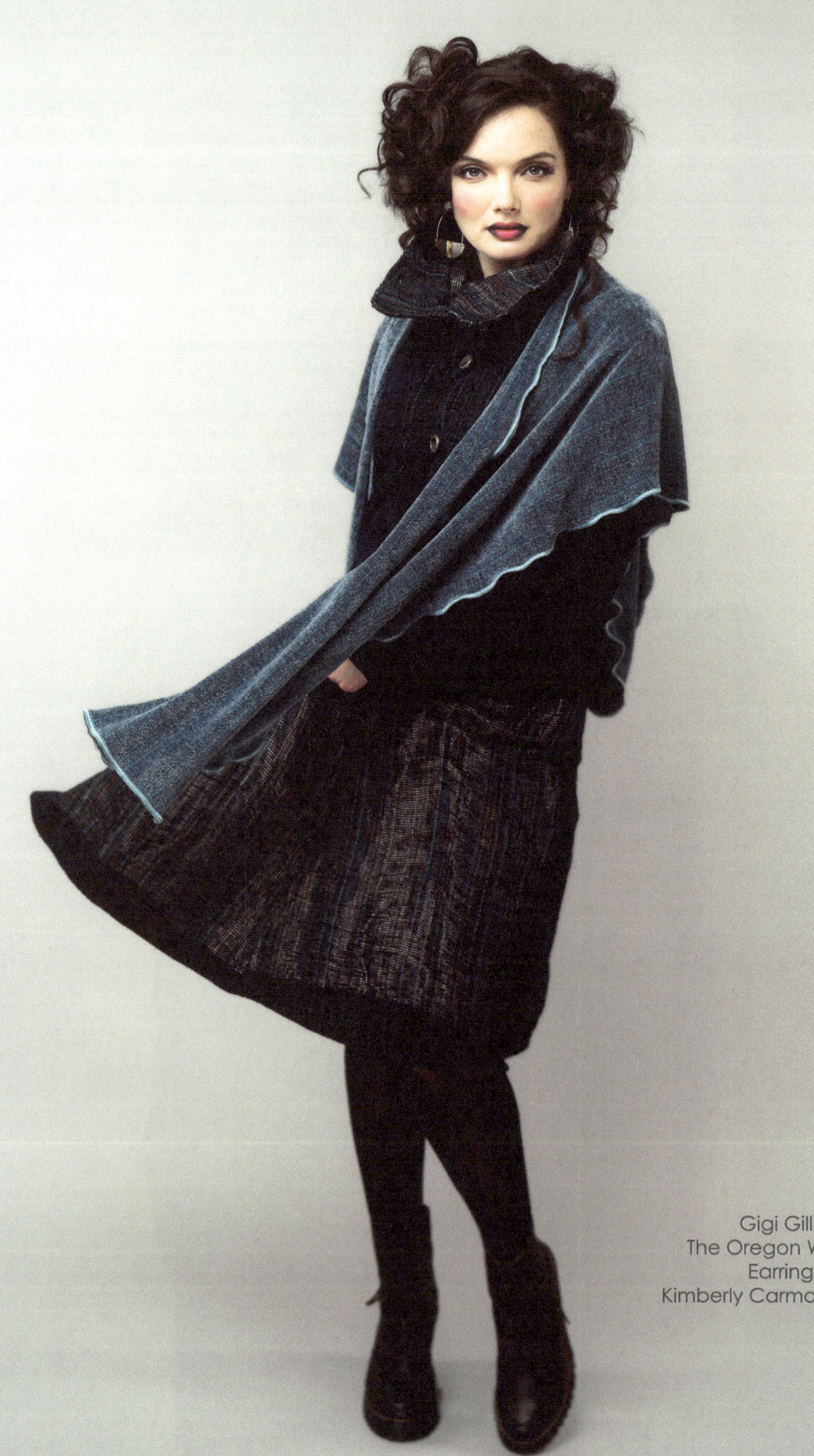

Gigi Gillie
The Oregon Weaver
Earrings
Kimberly Carman Designs

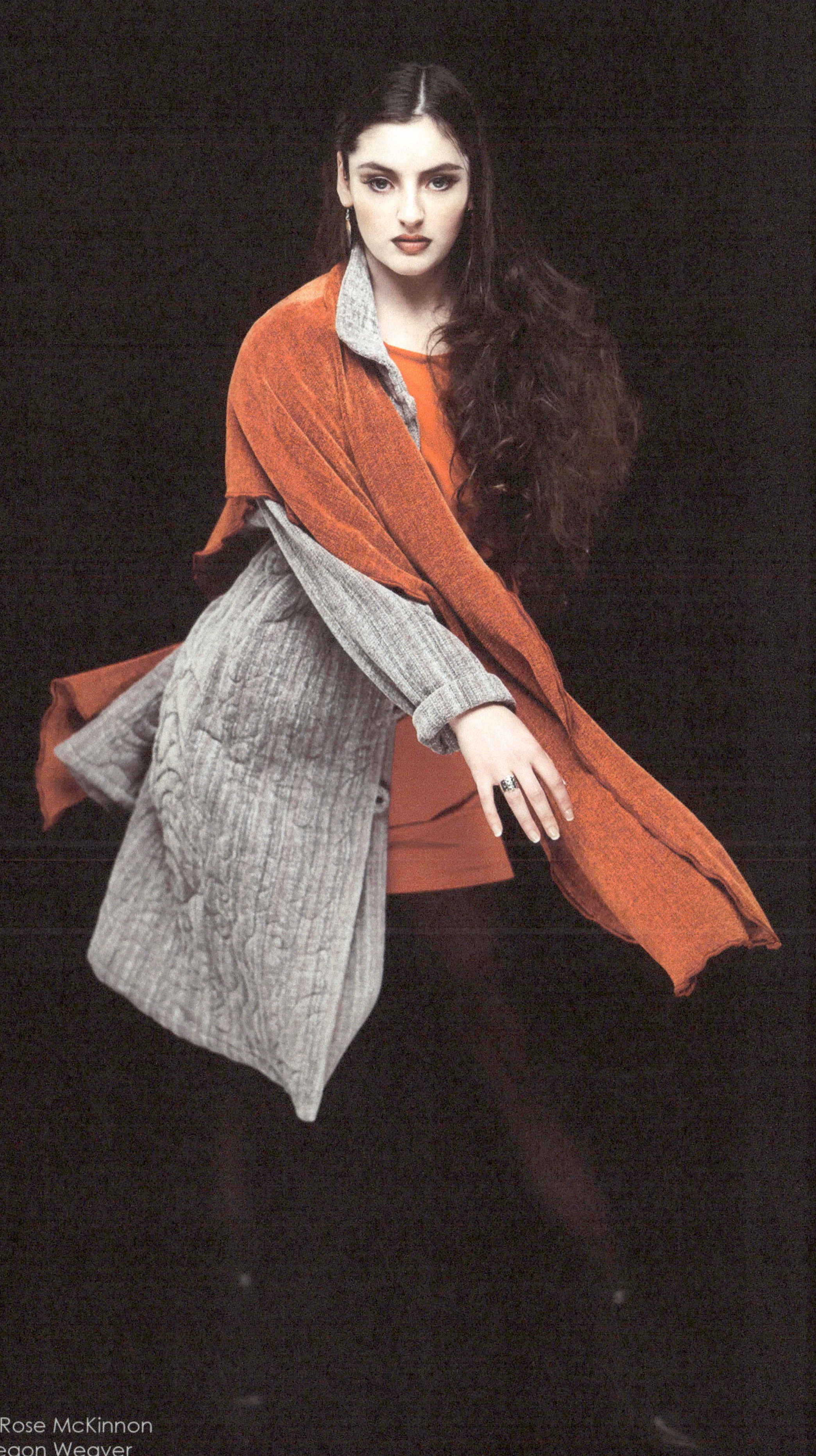

Alaina Rose McKinnon
The Oregon Weaver
Jewelry Kimberly Carman Designs

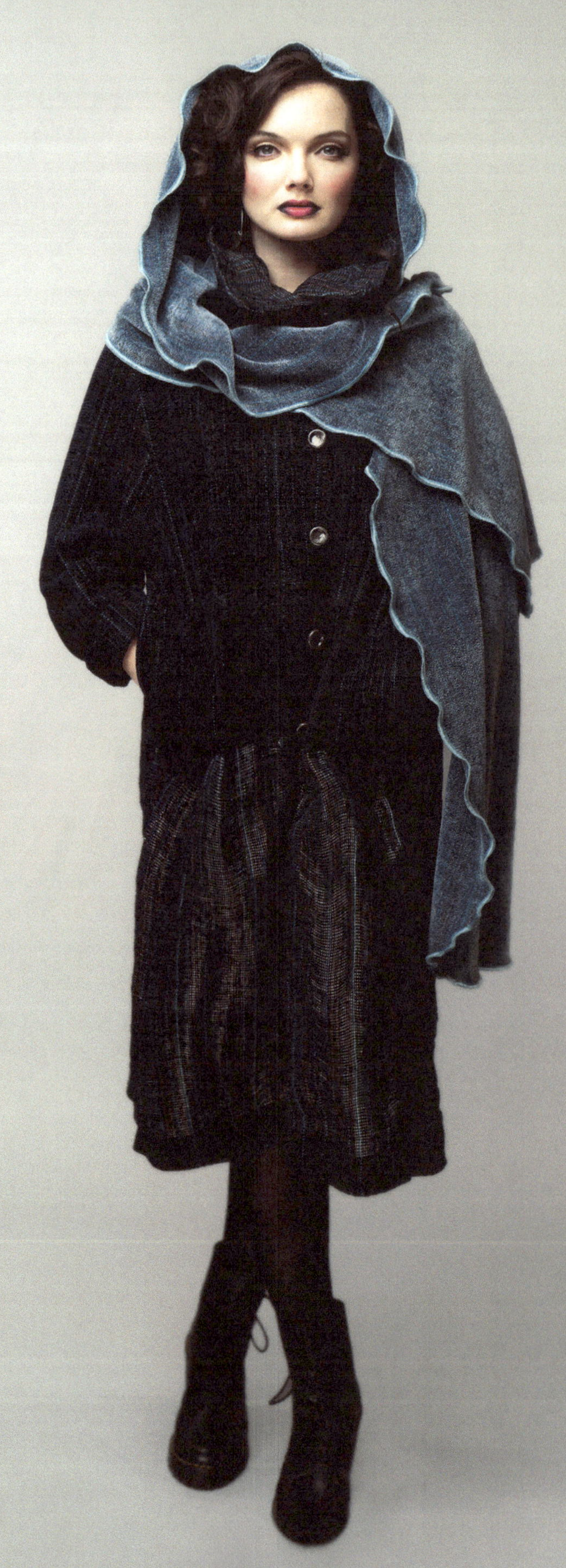

Gigi Gillie
The Oregon Weaver
Earrings Kimberly Carman Designs

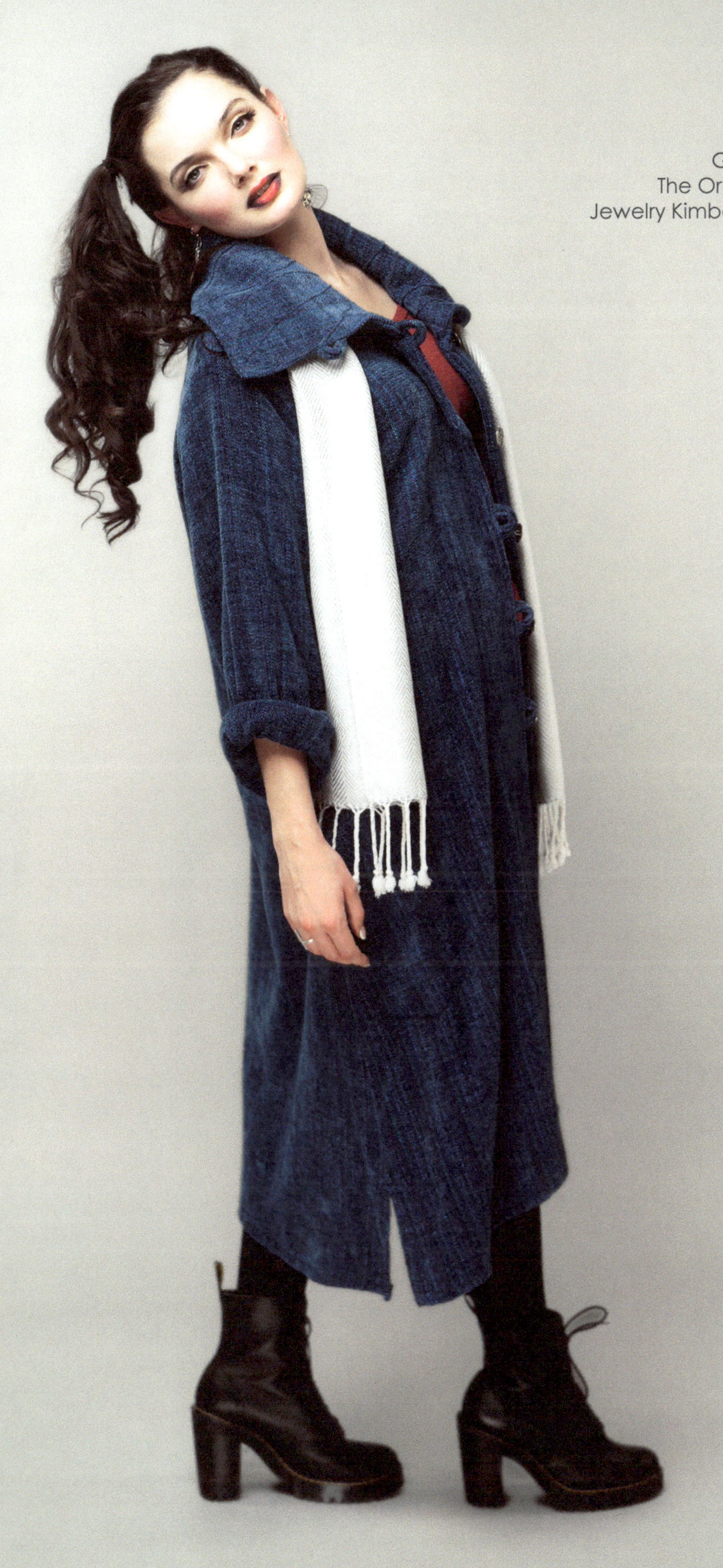

Gigi Gillie
The Oregon Weaver
Jewelry Kimberly Carman Designs

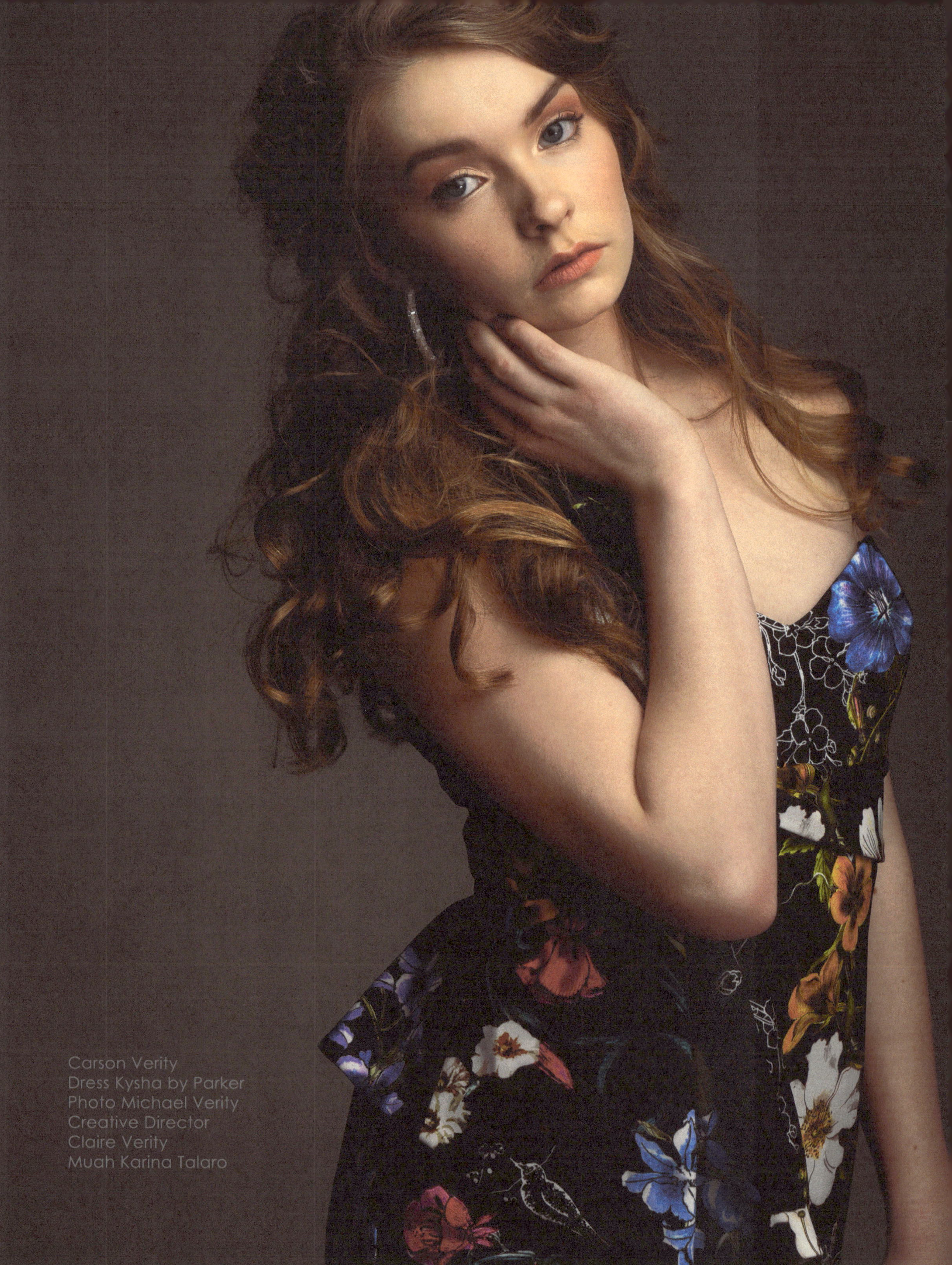
Carson Verity
Dress Kysha by Parker
Photo Michael Verity
Creative Director
Claire Verity
Muah Karina Talaro

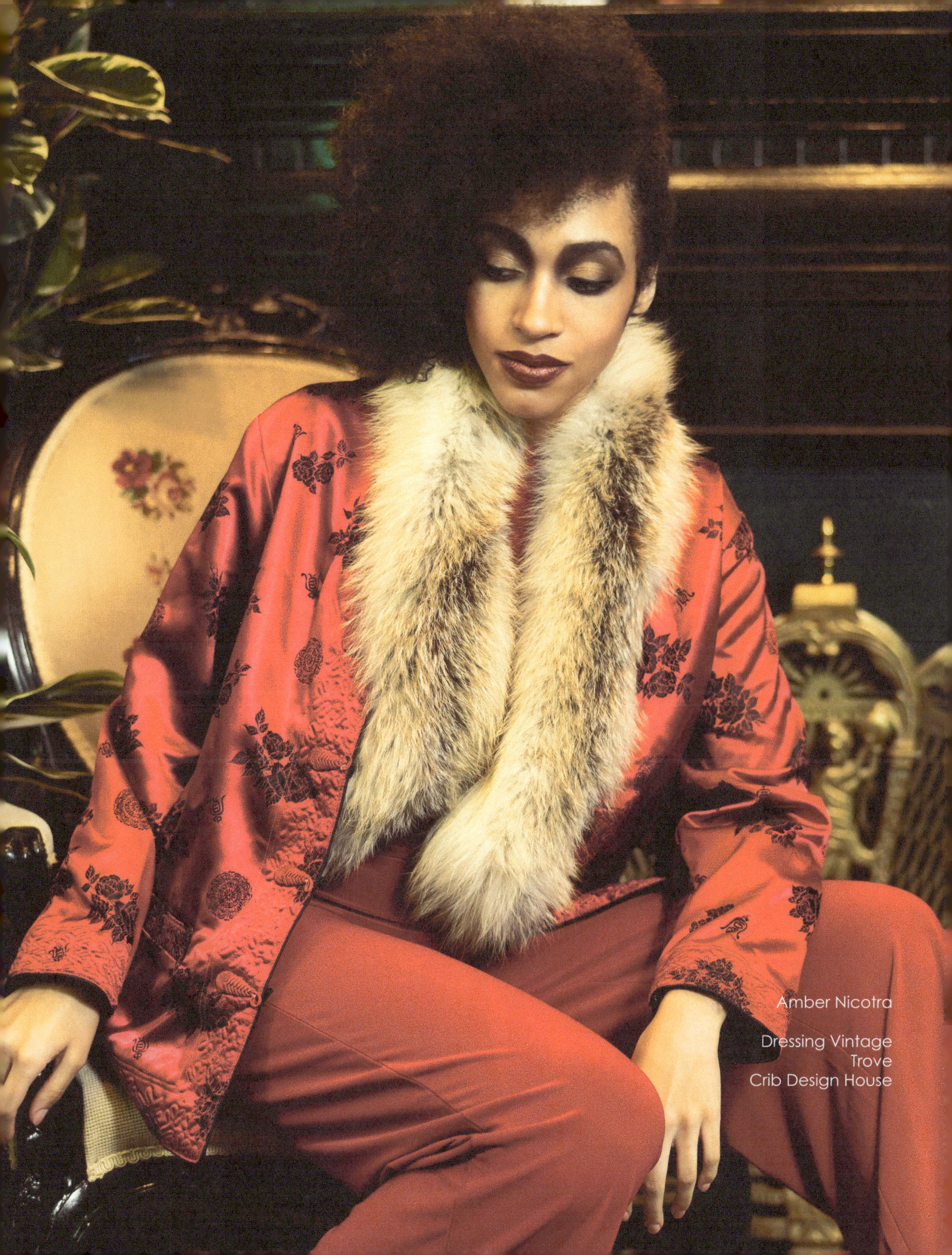

Amber Nicotra

Dressing Vintage
Trove
Crib Design House

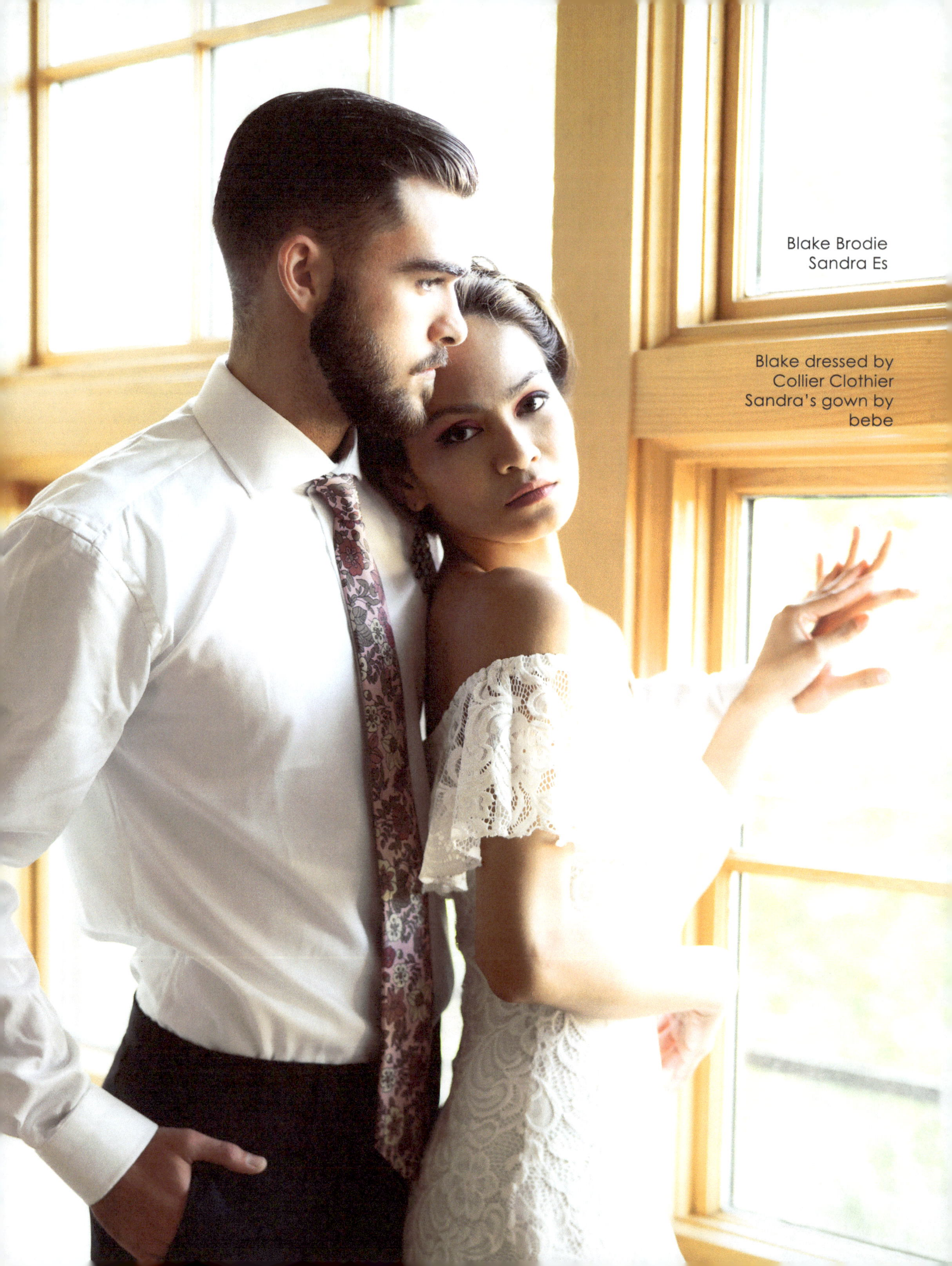

Blake Brodie
Sandra Es

Blake dressed by
Collier Clothier
Sandra's gown by
bebe

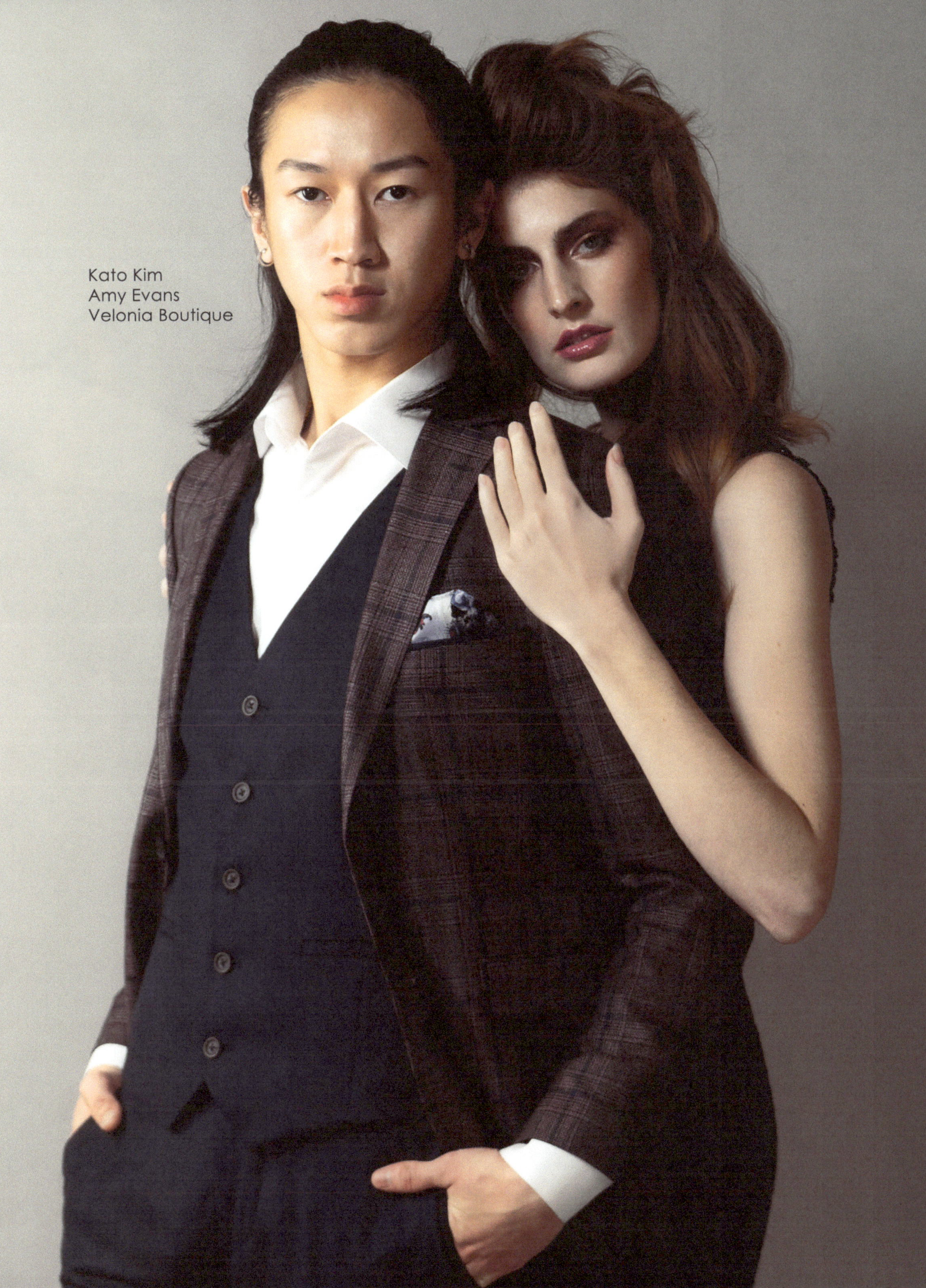

Kato Kim
Amy Evans
Velonia Boutique

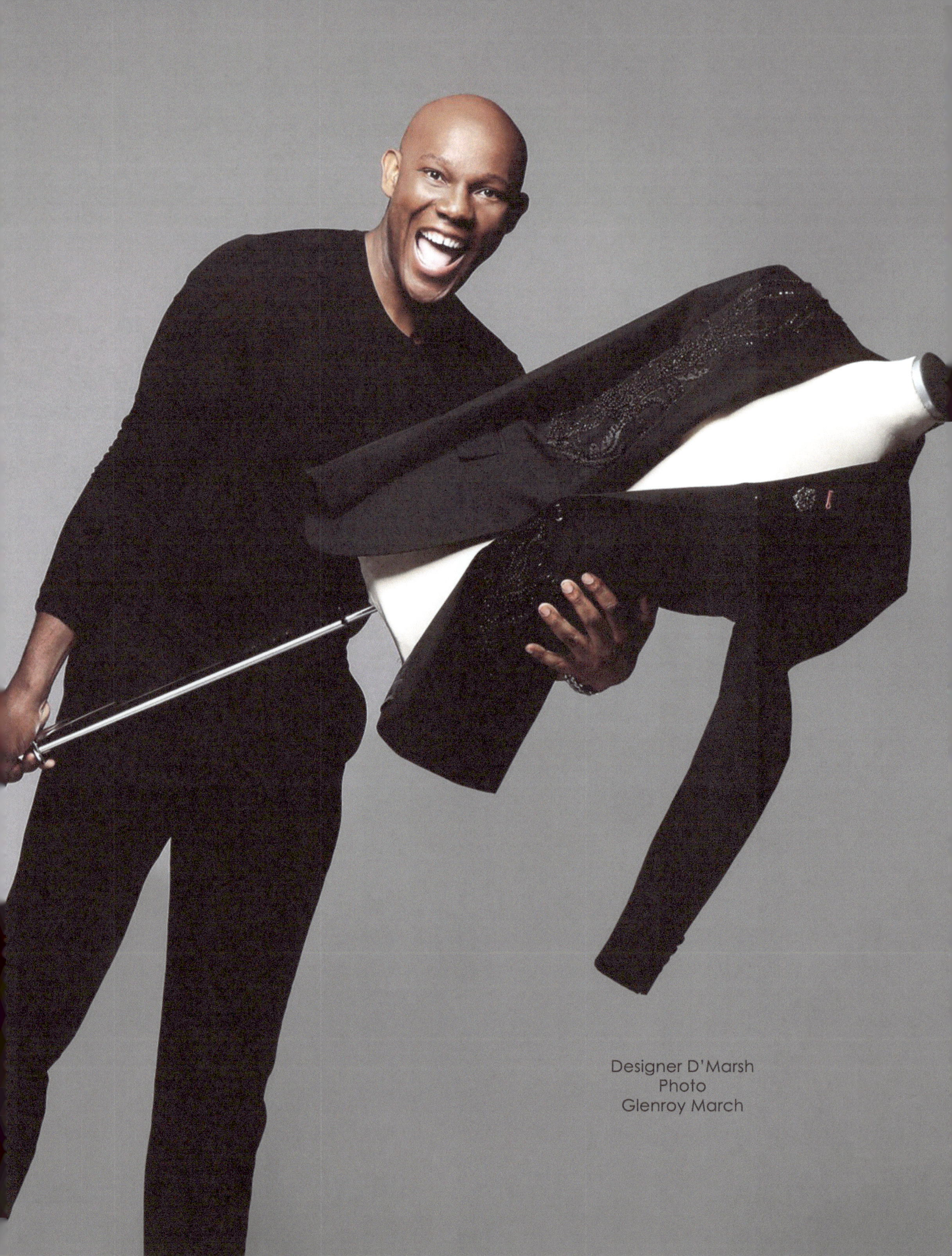

Designer D'Marsh
Photo
Glenroy March

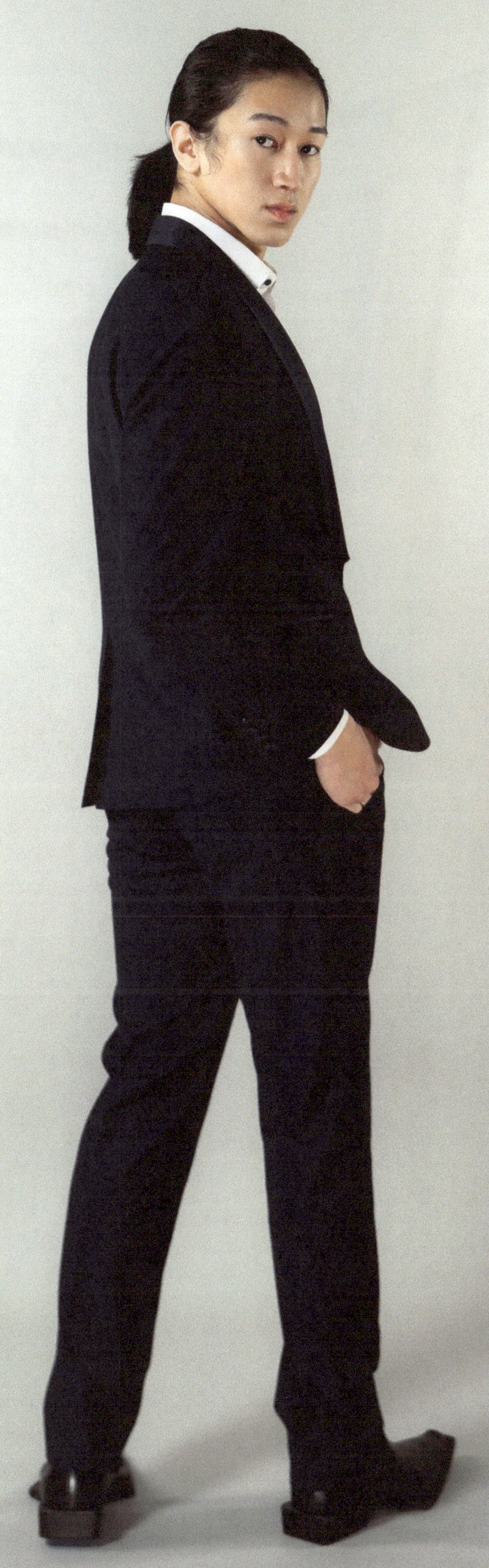

Kato Kim
Velonia Boutique
John Fluevog

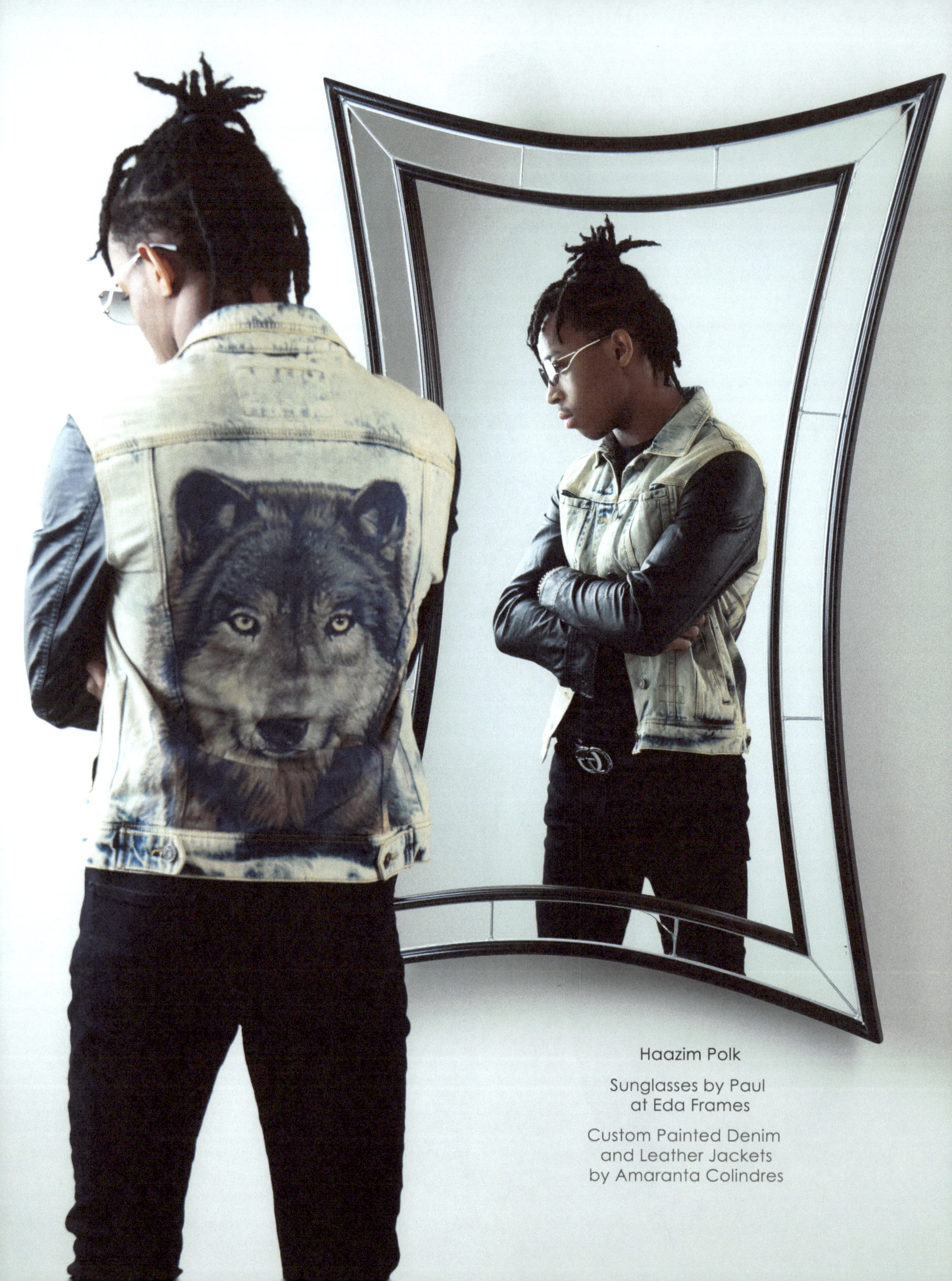

Haazim Polk

Sunglasses by Paul
at Eda Frames

Custom Painted Denim
and Leather Jackets
by Amaranta Colindres

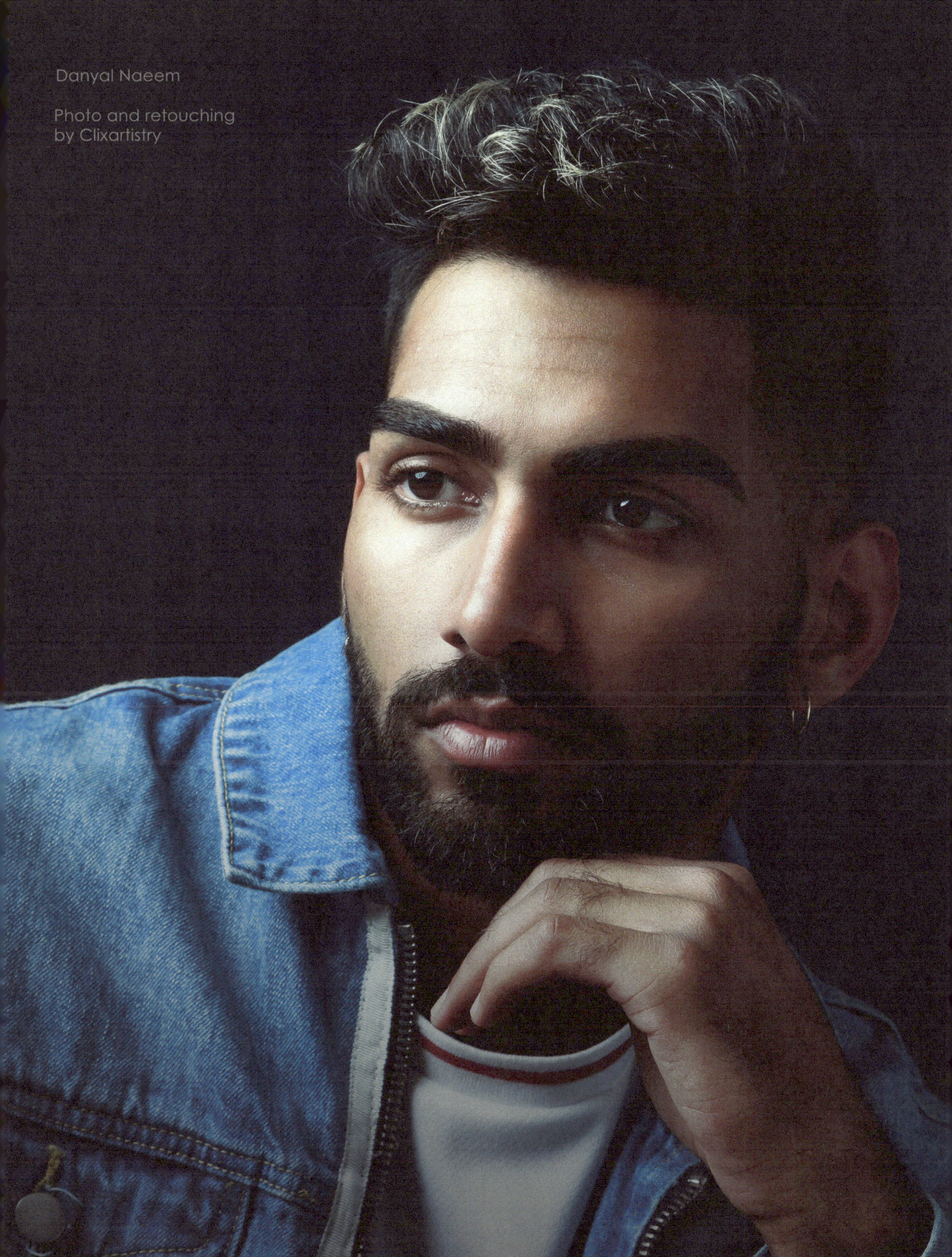

Danyal Naeem
Photo and retouching
by Clixartistry

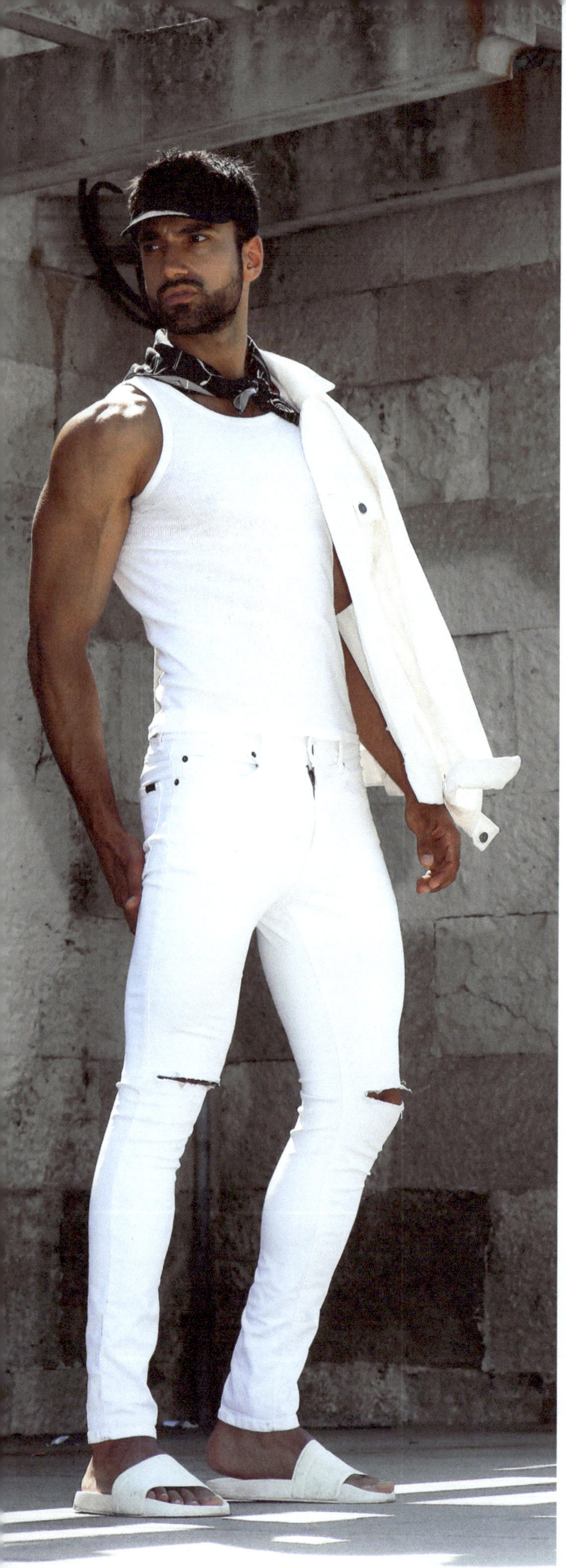

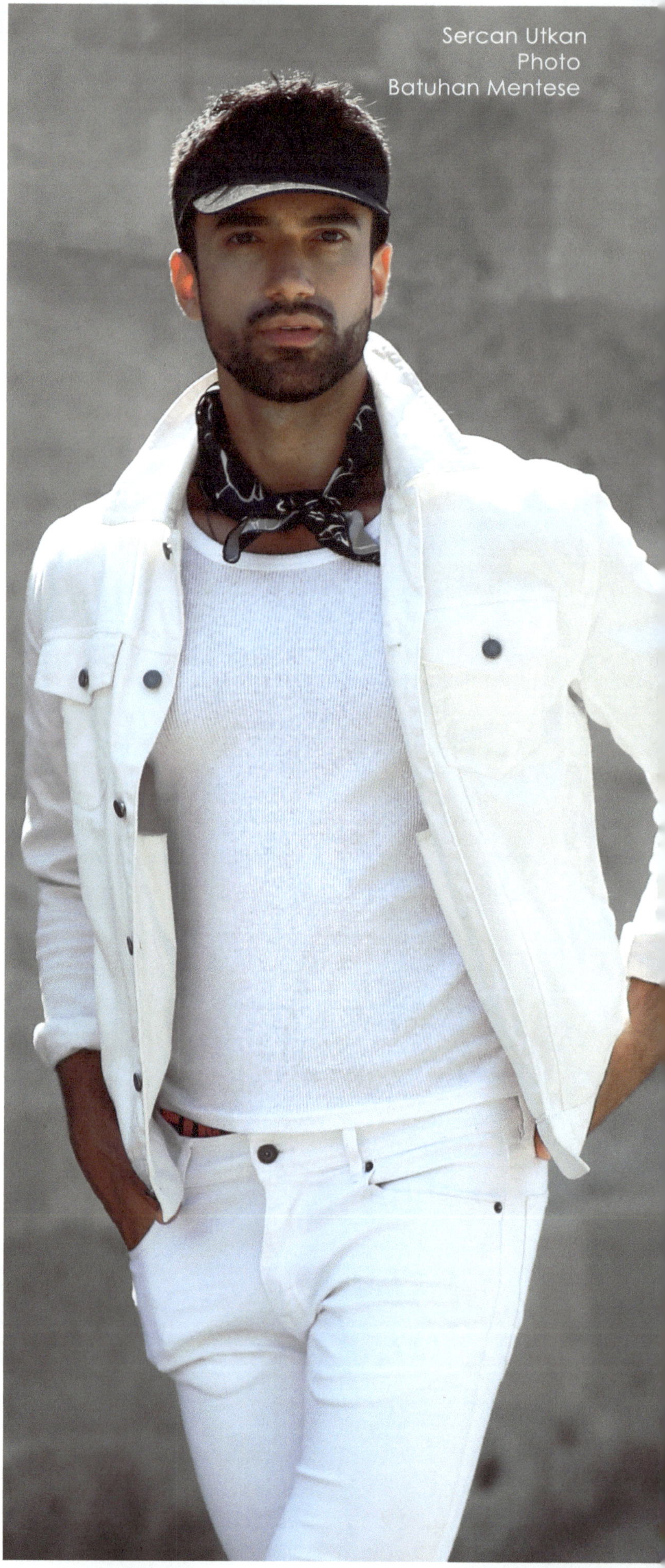

Sercan Utkan
Photo
Batuhan Mentese

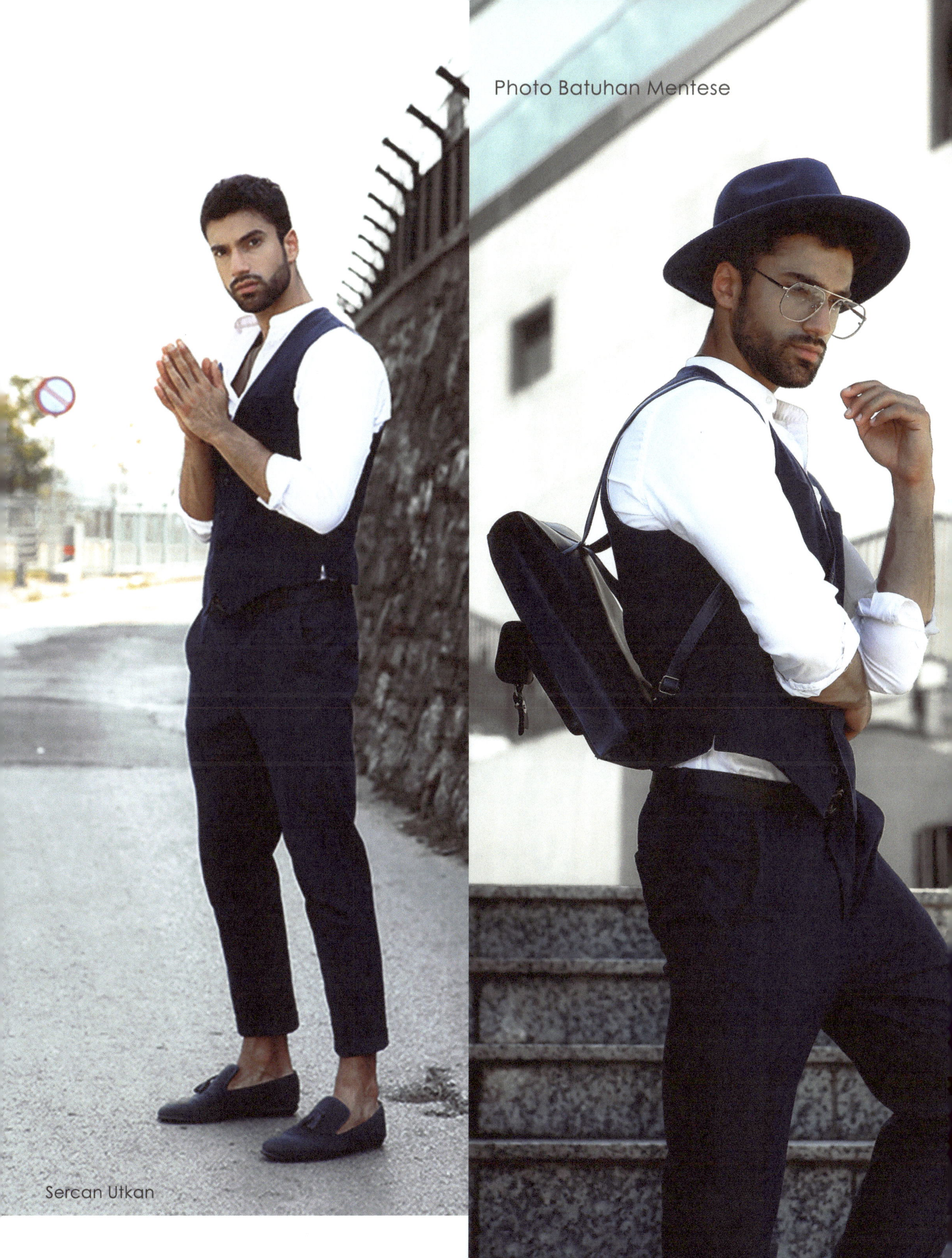

Photo Batuhan Mentese
Sercan Utkan

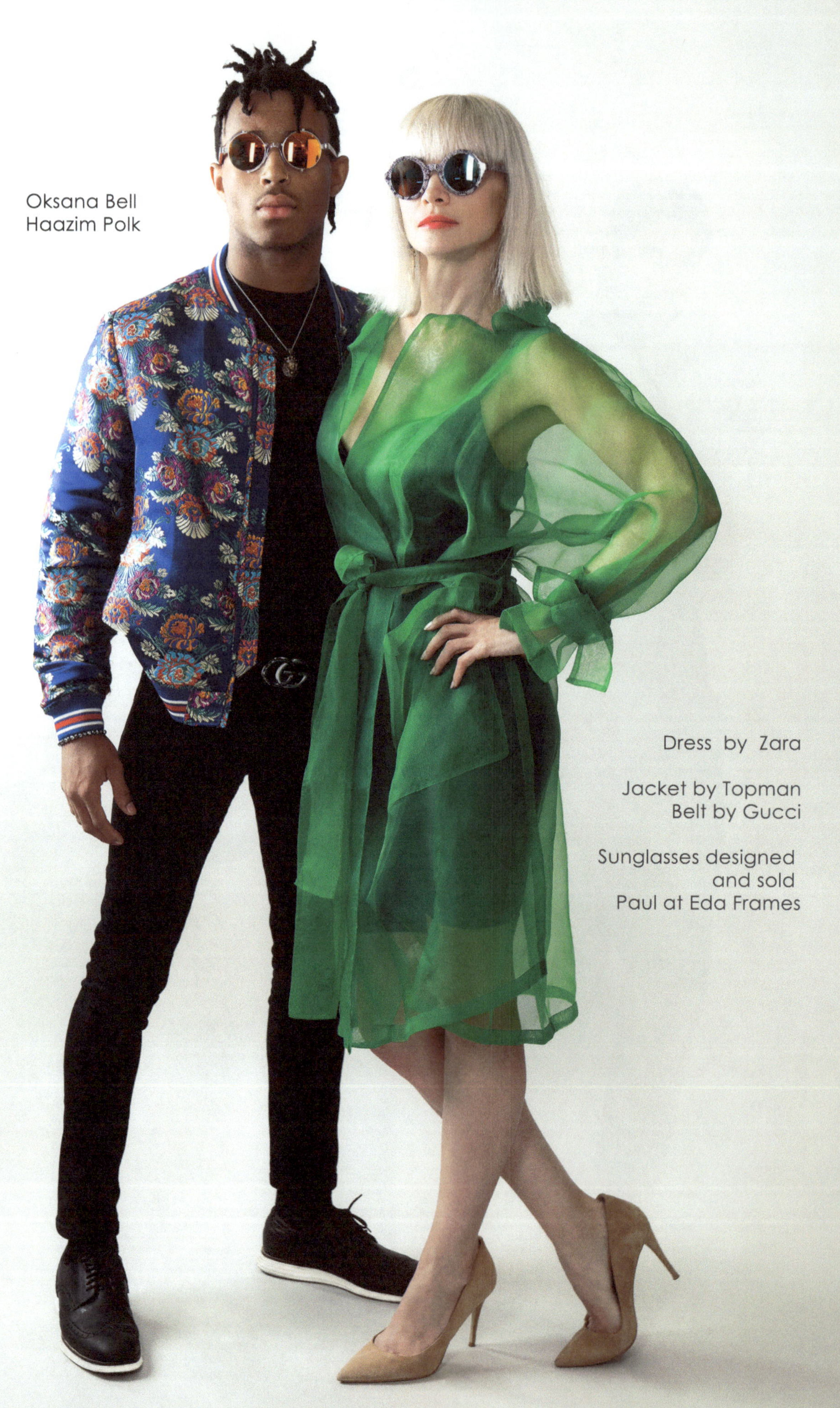
Oksana Bell
Haazim Polk

Dress by Zara

Jacket by Topman
Belt by Gucci

Sunglasses designed
and sold
Paul at Eda Frames

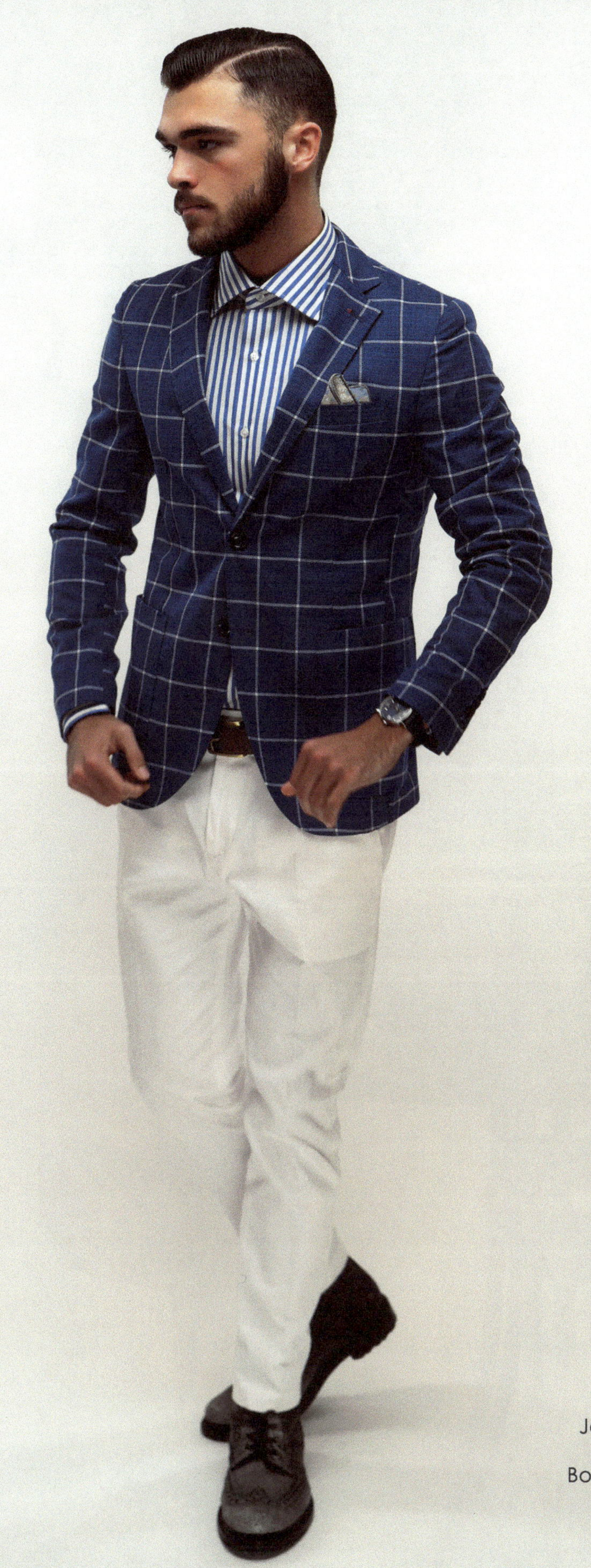

Blake Brodie

Jacket Shirt Slacks
Collier Clothier
Boots John Fluevog

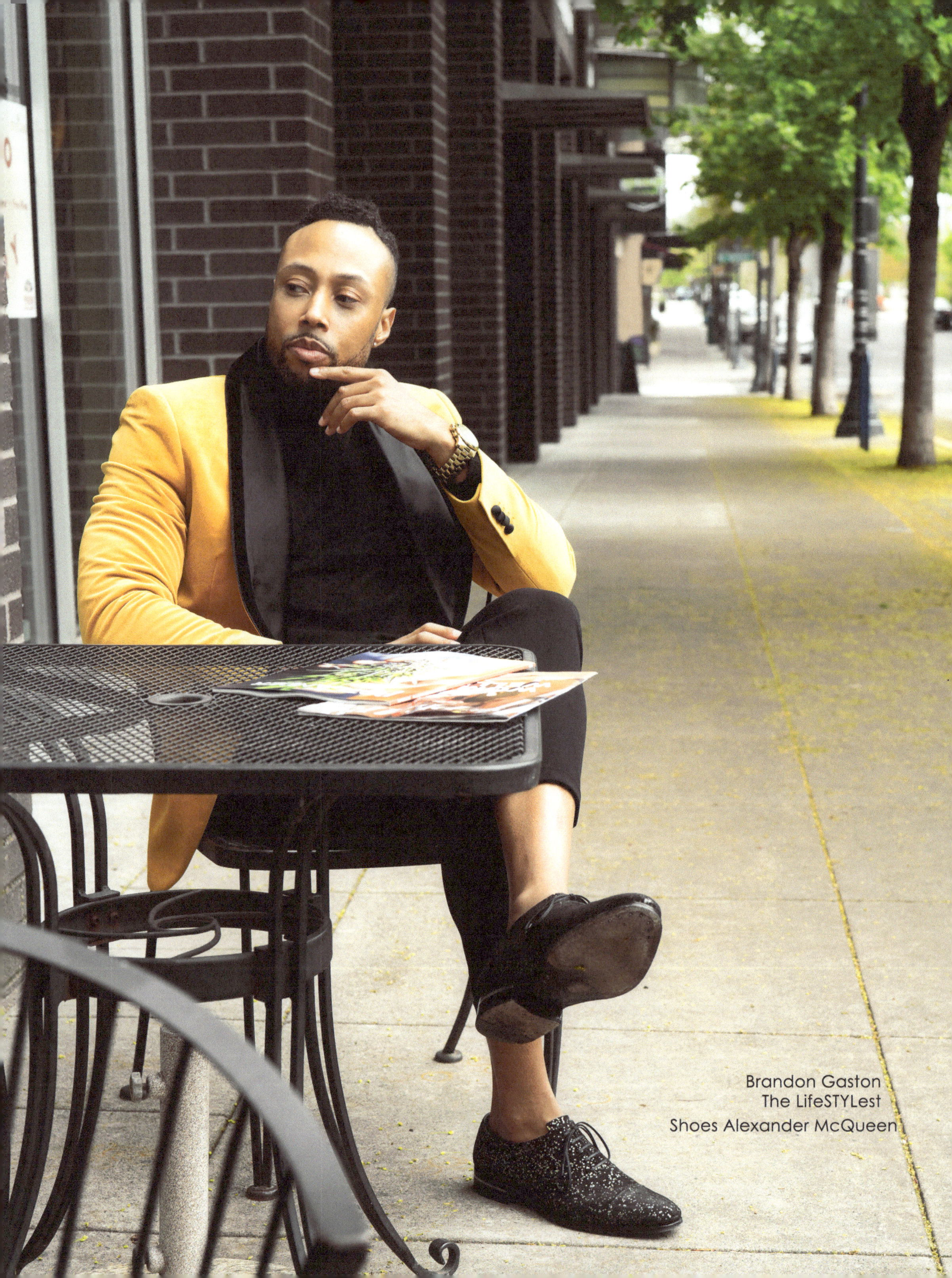

Brandon Gaston
The LifeSTYLest
Shoes Alexander McQueen

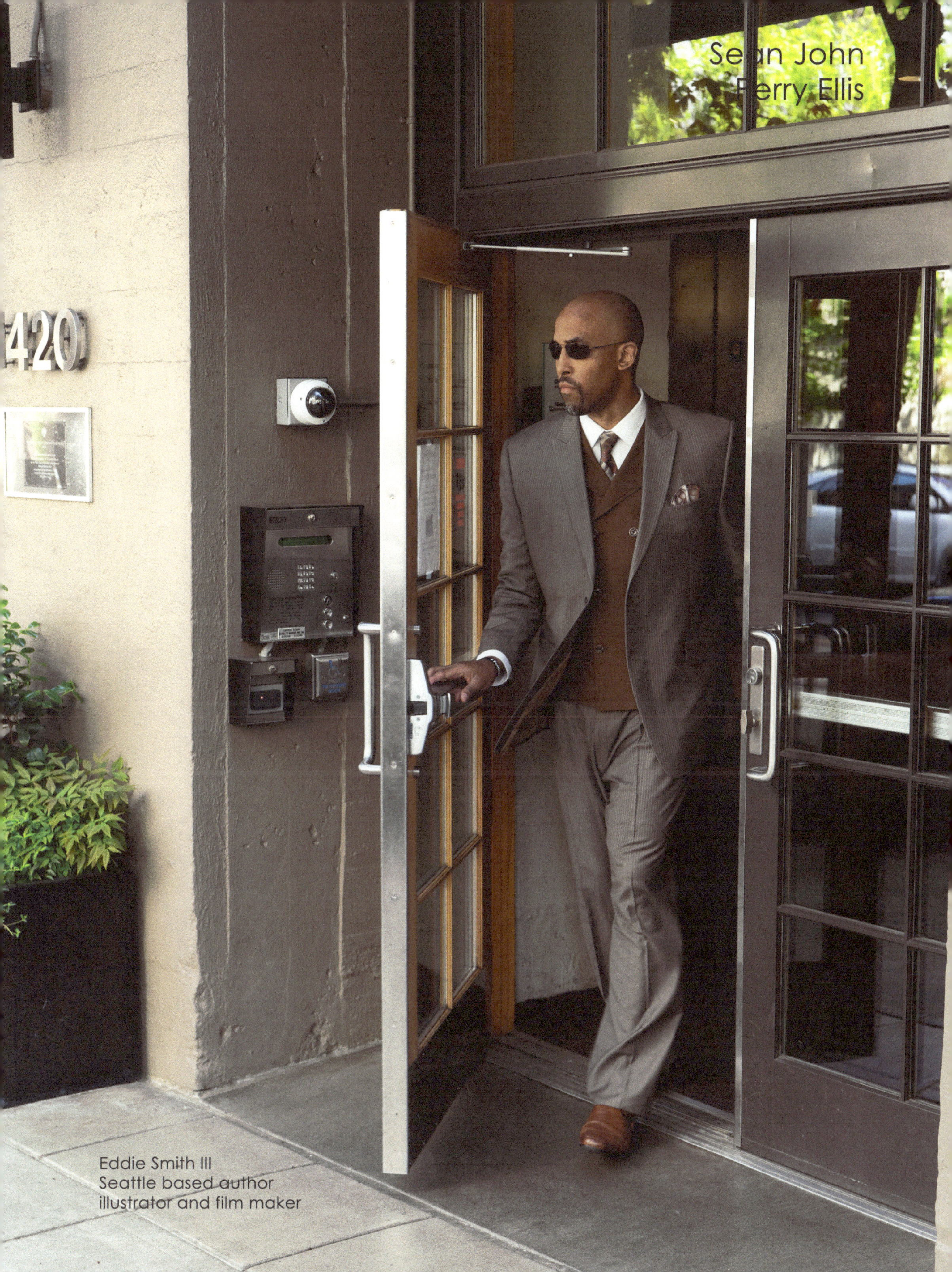
Sean John
Perry Ellis
420
Eddie Smith III
Seattle based author
illustrator and film maker

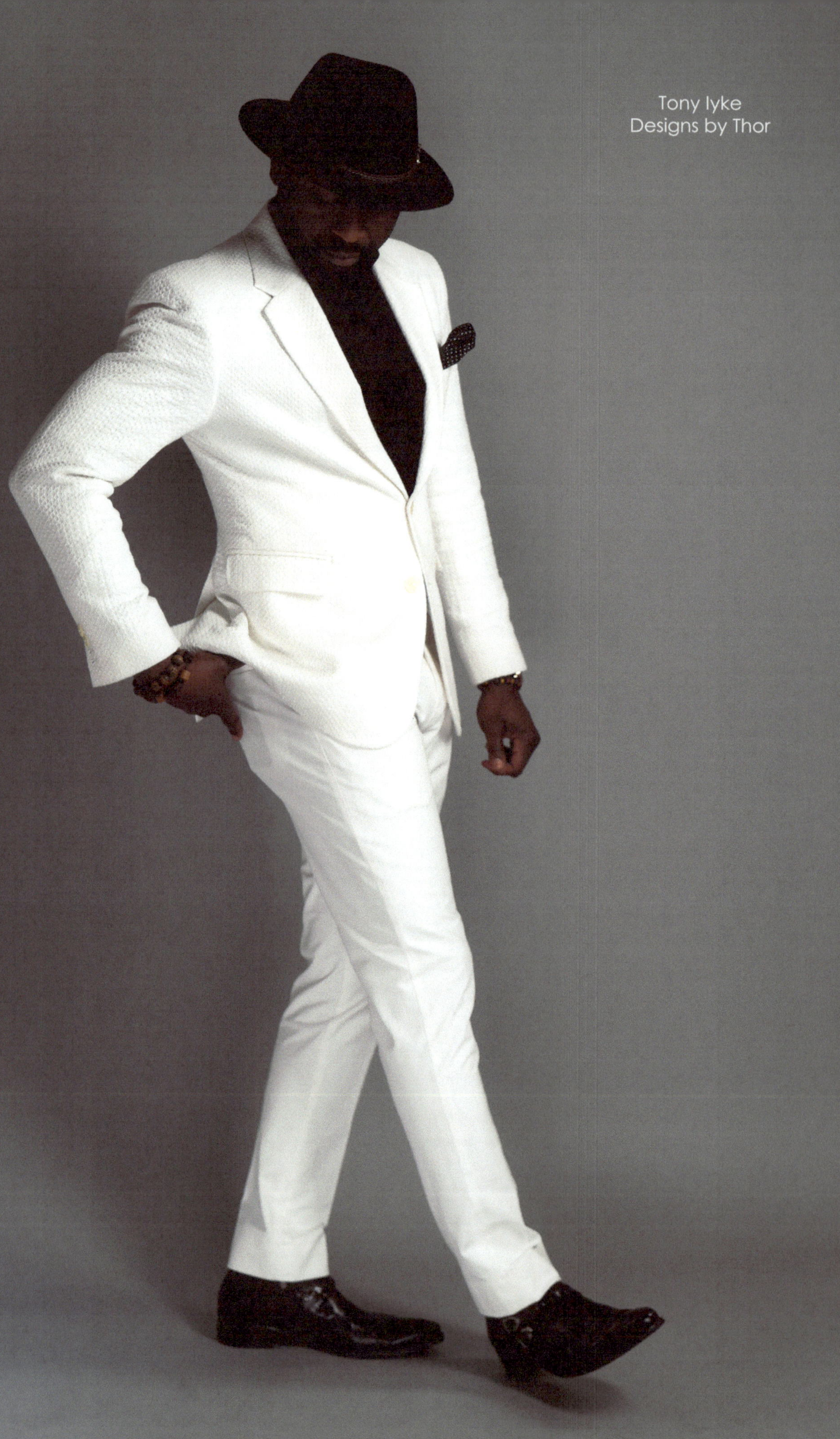

Tony Iyke
Designs by Thor

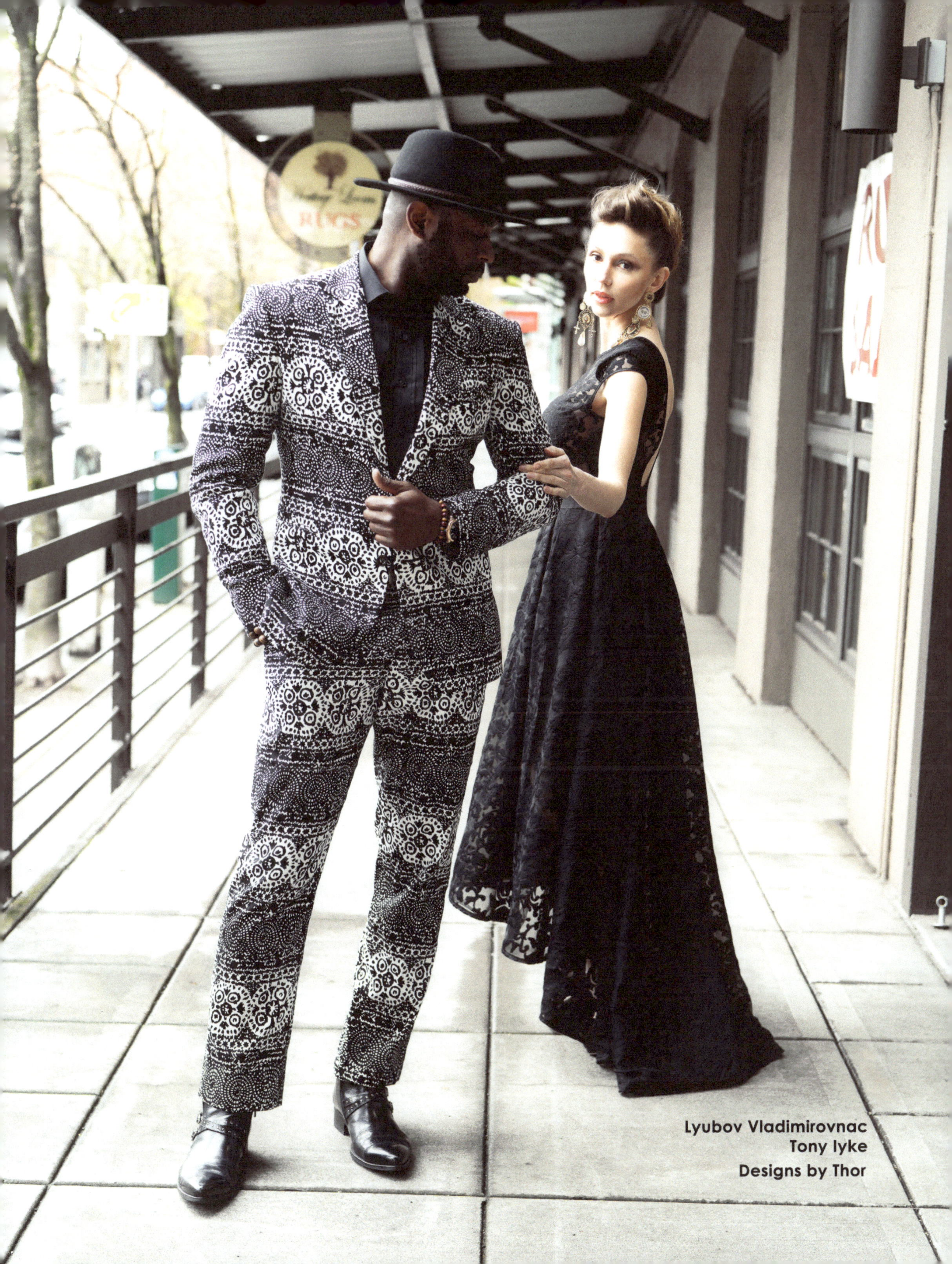

Lyubov Vladimirovnac
Tony Iyke
Designs by Thor

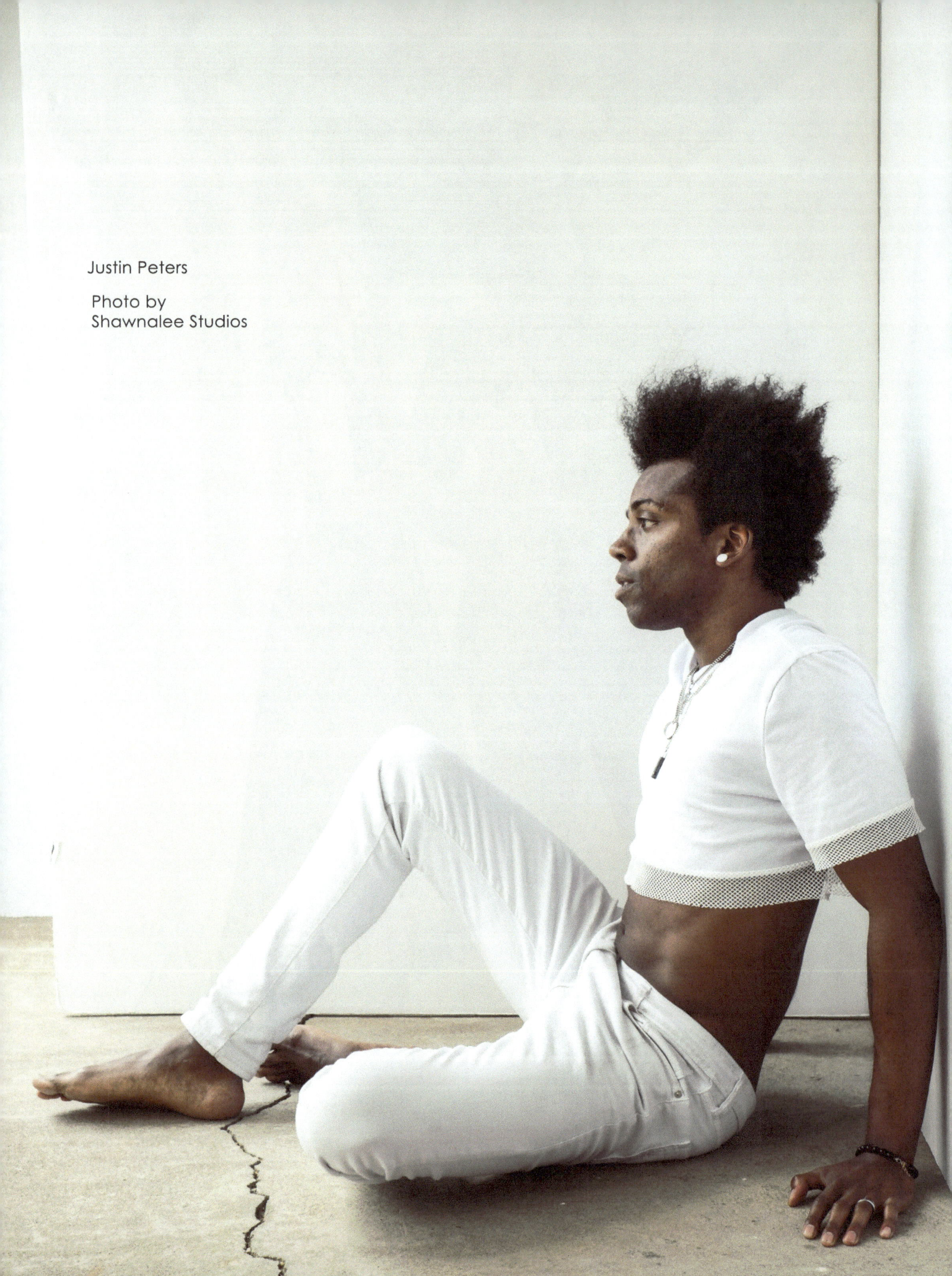

Justin Peters

Photo by
Shawnalee Studios

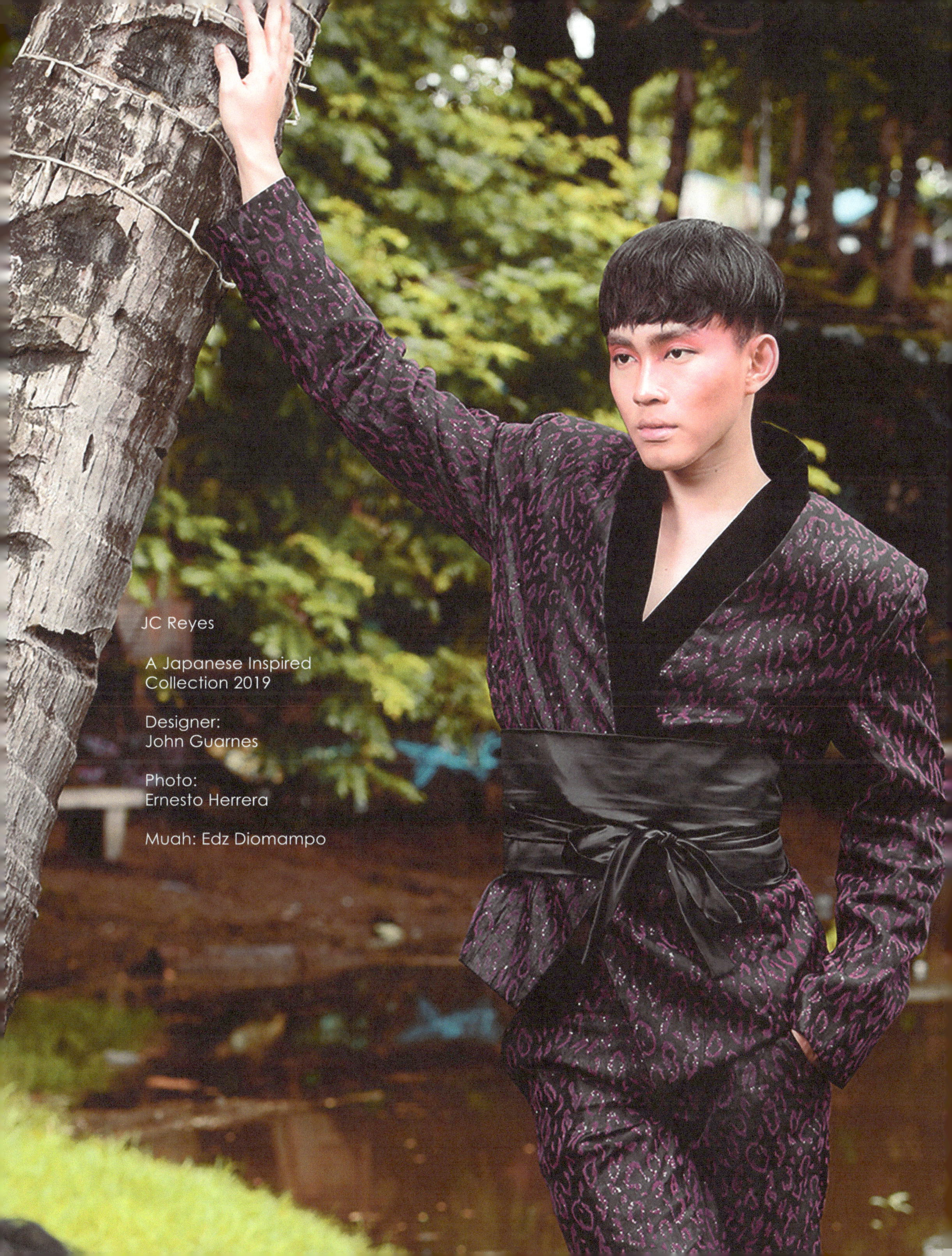

JC Reyes

A Japanese Inspired
Collection 2019

Designer:
John Guarnes

Photo:
Ernesto Herrera

Muah: Edz Diomampo

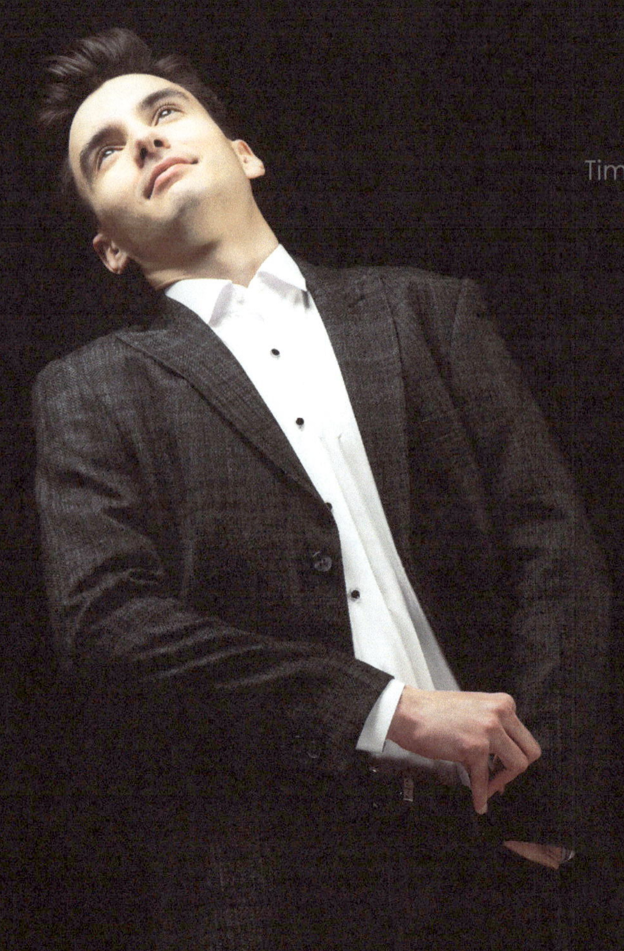

Tim Koziarovski

Jacket
Velonia Boutique

Shoes
John Fluevog

Muah Miki Willis

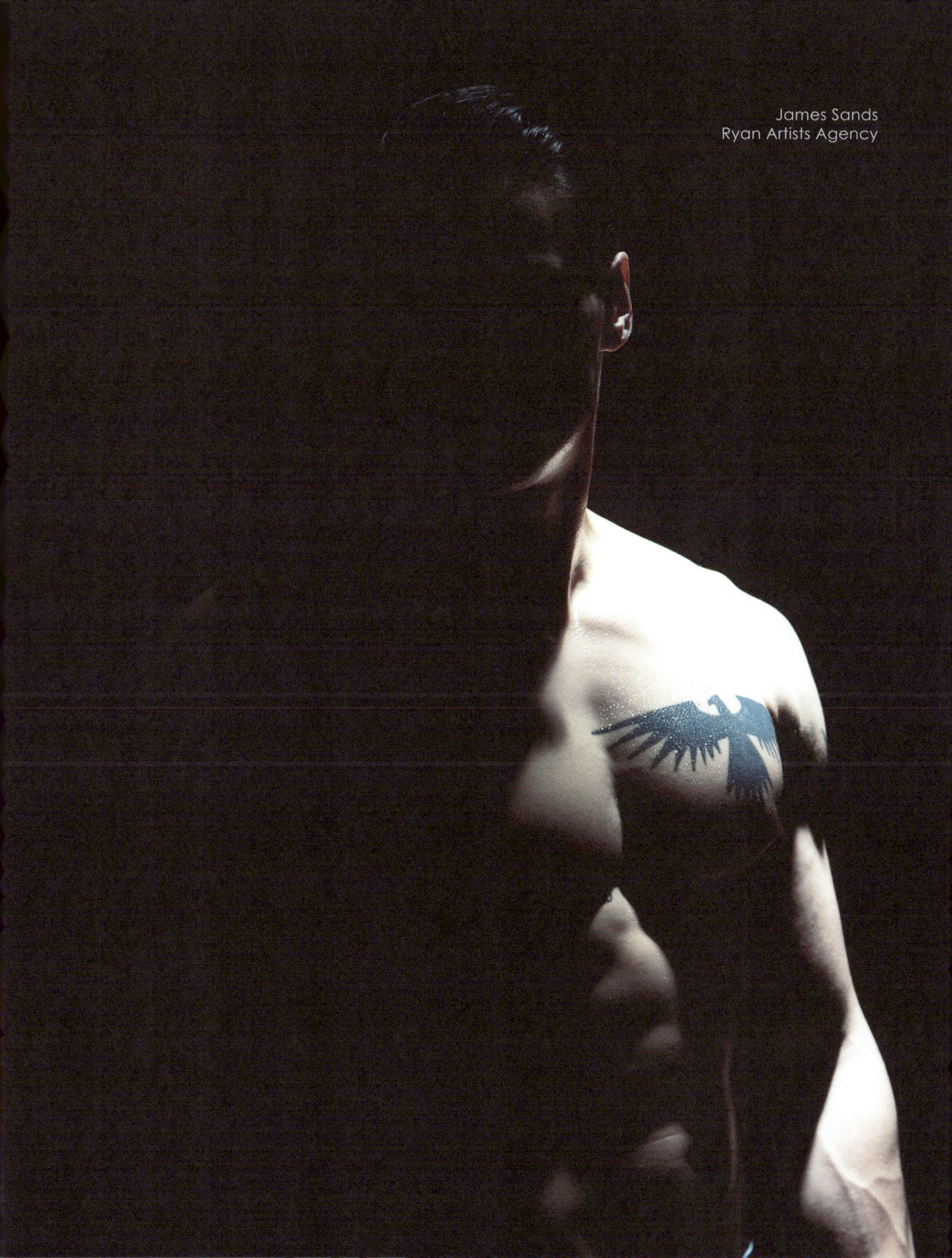

James Sands
Ryan Artists Agency

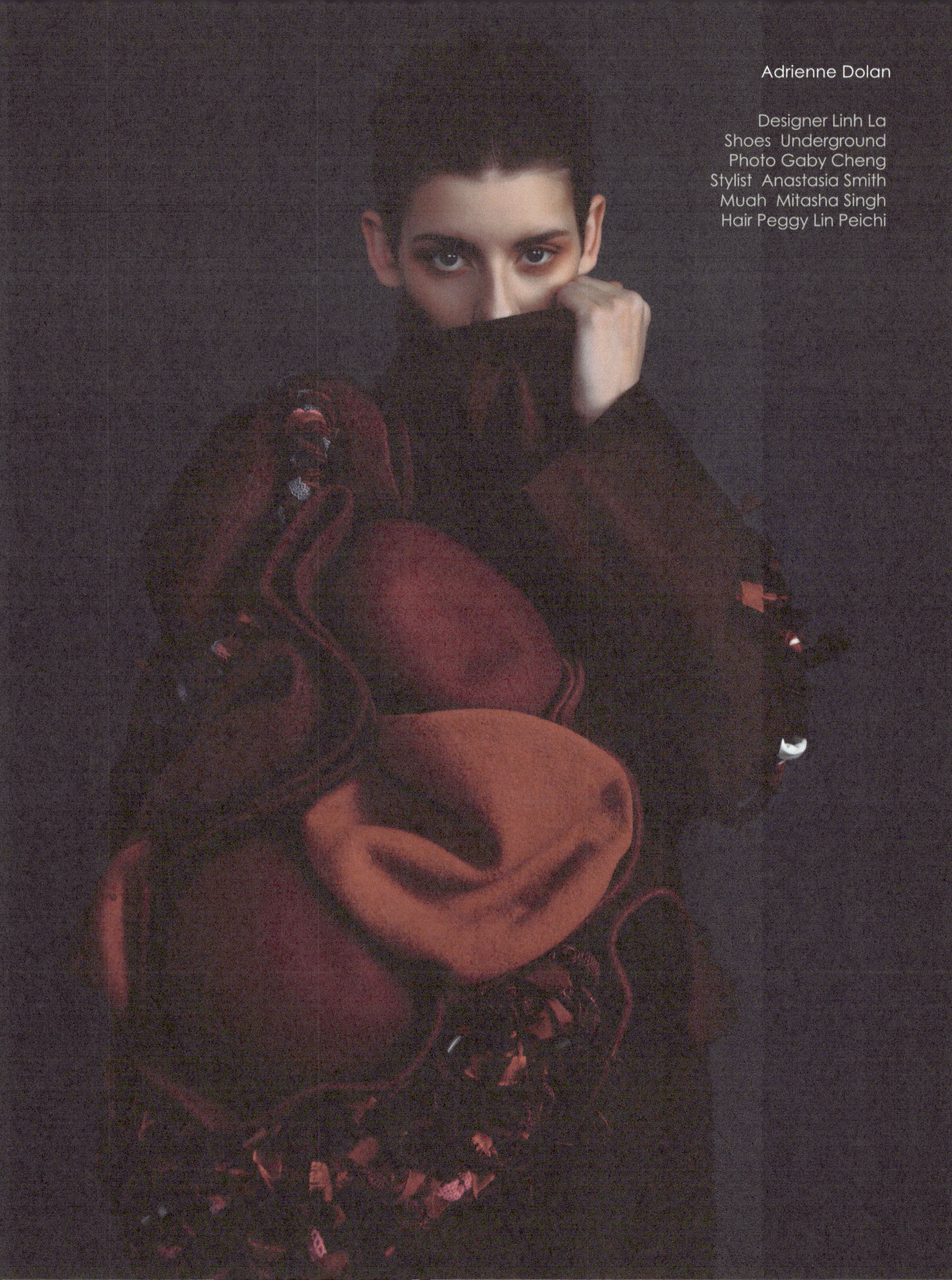

Adrienne Dolan

Designer Linh La
Shoes Underground
Photo Gaby Cheng
Stylist Anastasia Smith
Muah Mitasha Singh
Hair Peggy Lin Peichi

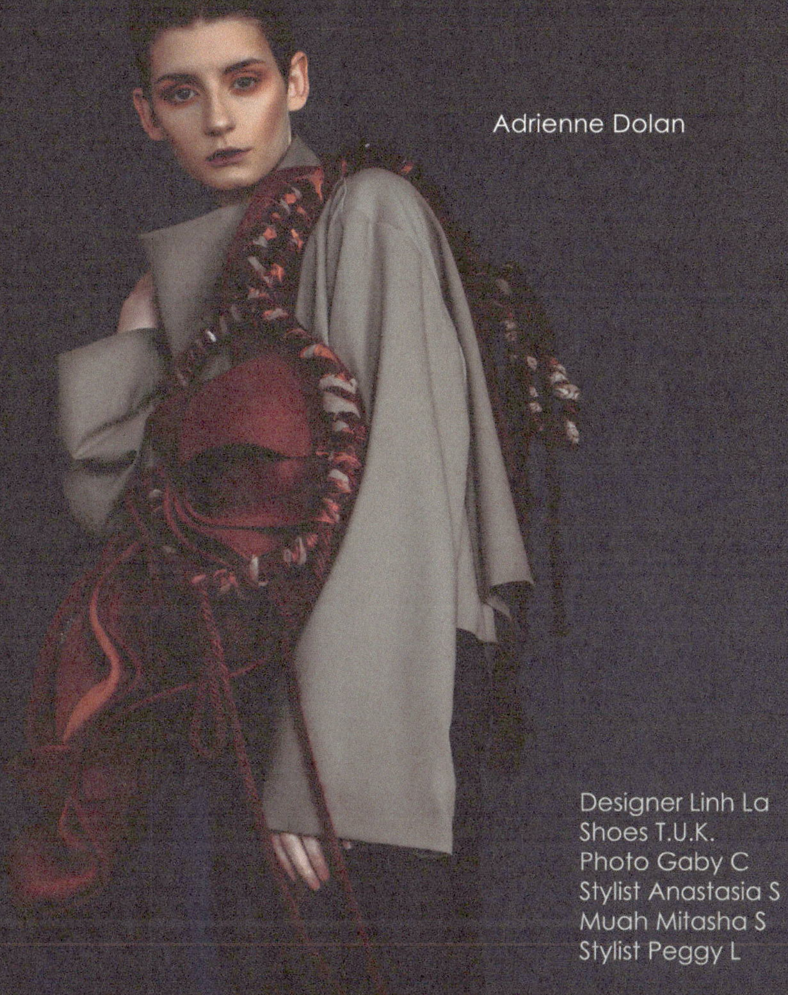

Adrienne Dolan

Designer Linh La
Shoes T.U.K.
Photo Gaby C
Stylist Anastasia S
Muah Mitasha S
Stylist Peggy L

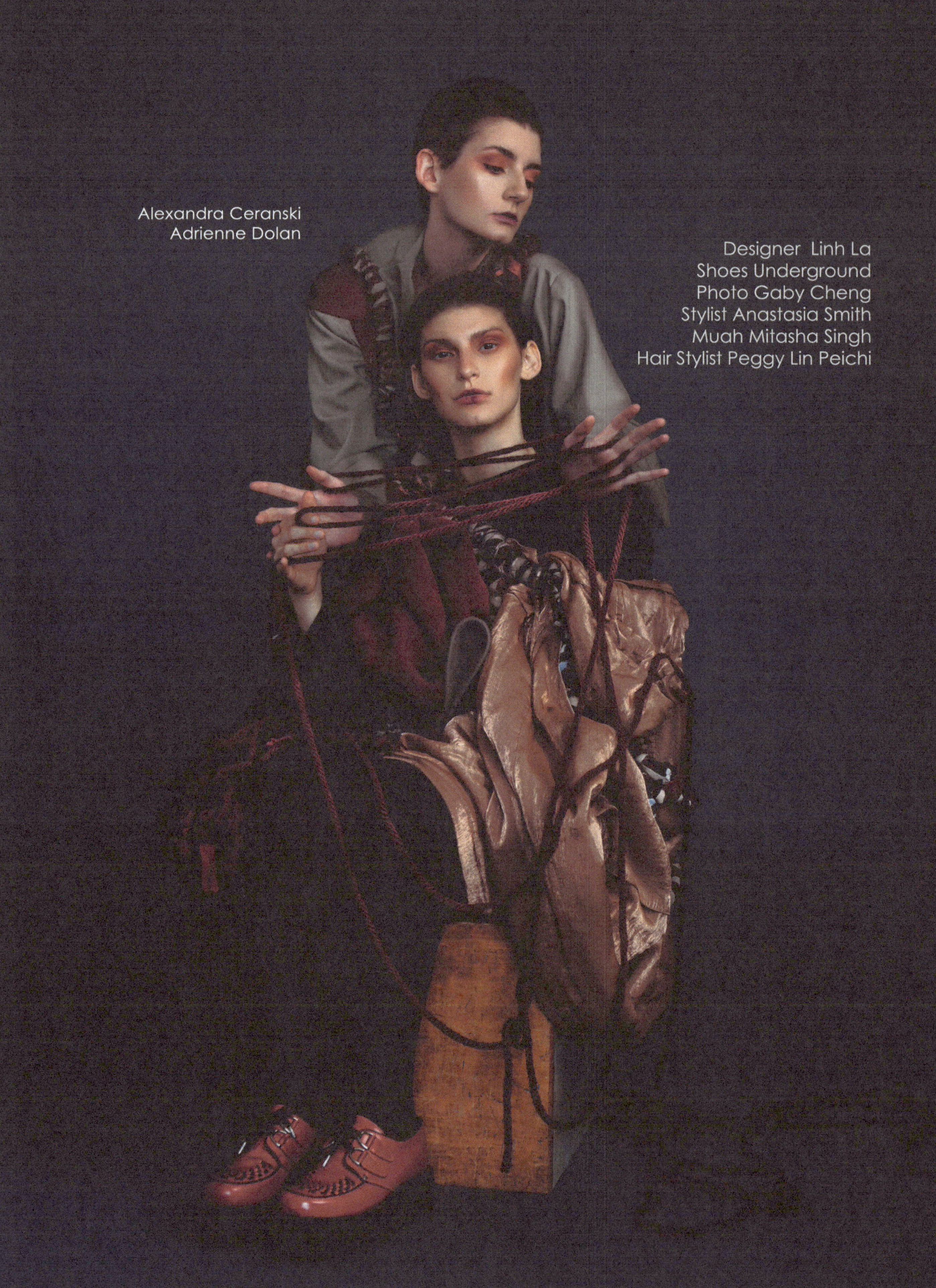
Alexandra Ceranski
Adrienne Dolan

Designer Linh La
Shoes Underground
Photo Gaby Cheng
Stylist Anastasia Smith
Muah Mitasha Singh
Hair Stylist Peggy Lin Peichi

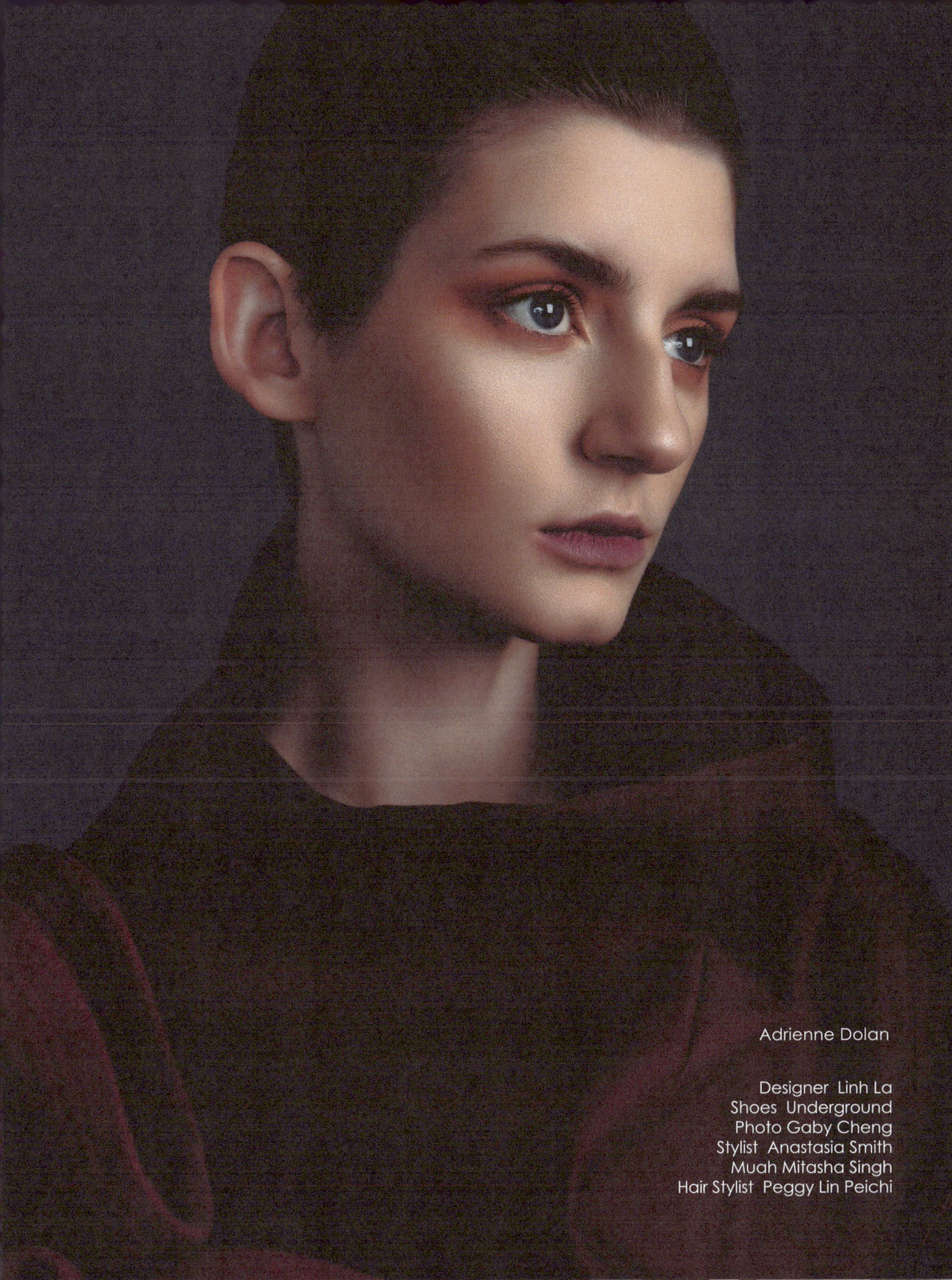
Adrienne Dolan

Designer Linh La
Shoes Underground
Photo Gaby Cheng
Stylist Anastasia Smith
Muah Mitasha Singh
Hair Stylist Peggy Lin Peichi

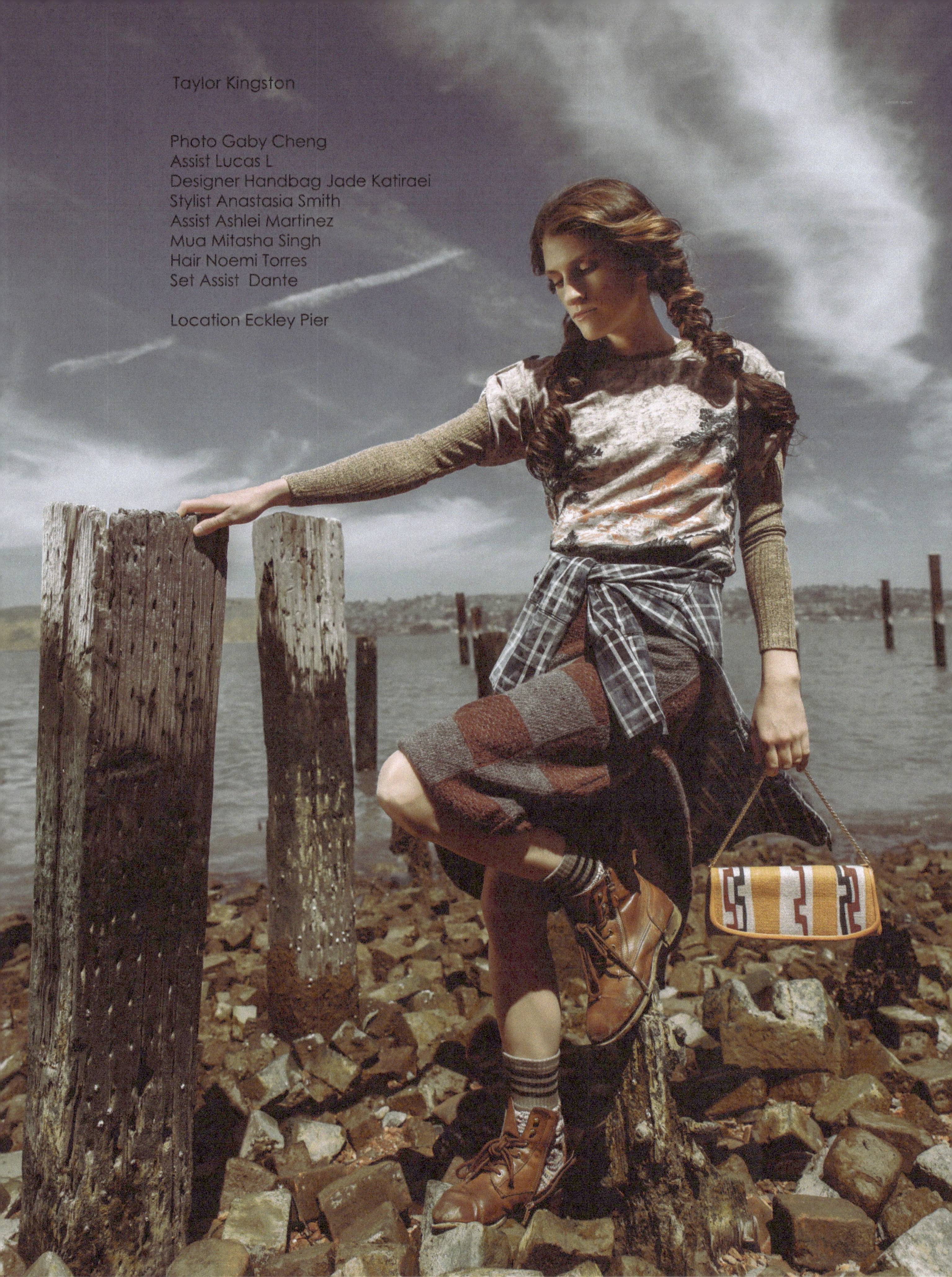
Taylor Kingston

Photo Gaby Cheng
Assist Lucas L
Designer Handbag Jade Katiraei
Stylist Anastasia Smith
Assist Ashlei Martinez
Mua Mitasha Singh
Hair Noemi Torres
Set Assist Dante

Location Eckley Pier

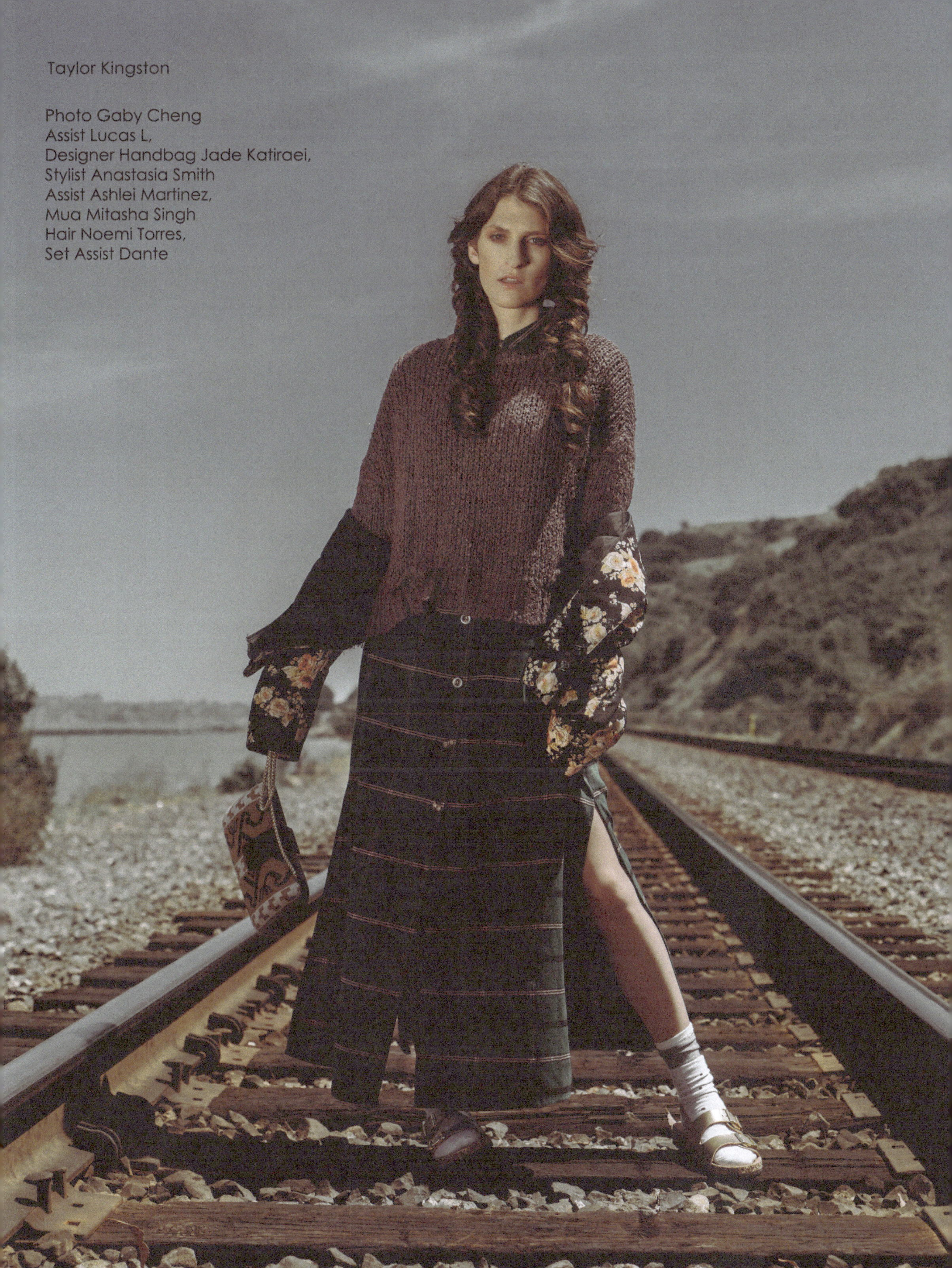
Taylor Kingston

Photo Gaby Cheng
Assist Lucas L,
Designer Handbag Jade Katiraei,
Stylist Anastasia Smith
Assist Ashlei Martinez,
Mua Mitasha Singh
Hair Noemi Torres,
Set Assist Dante

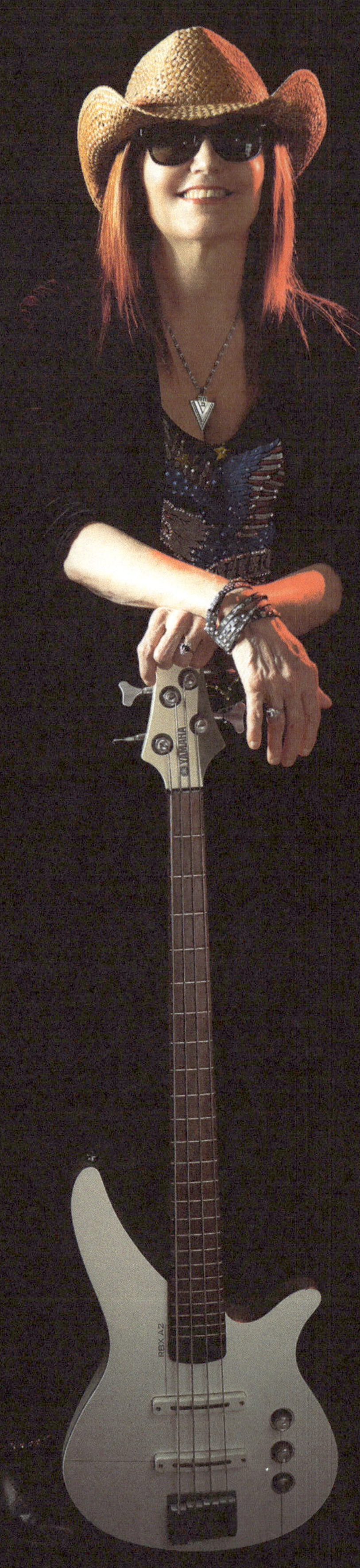

Bets Pott
Musician

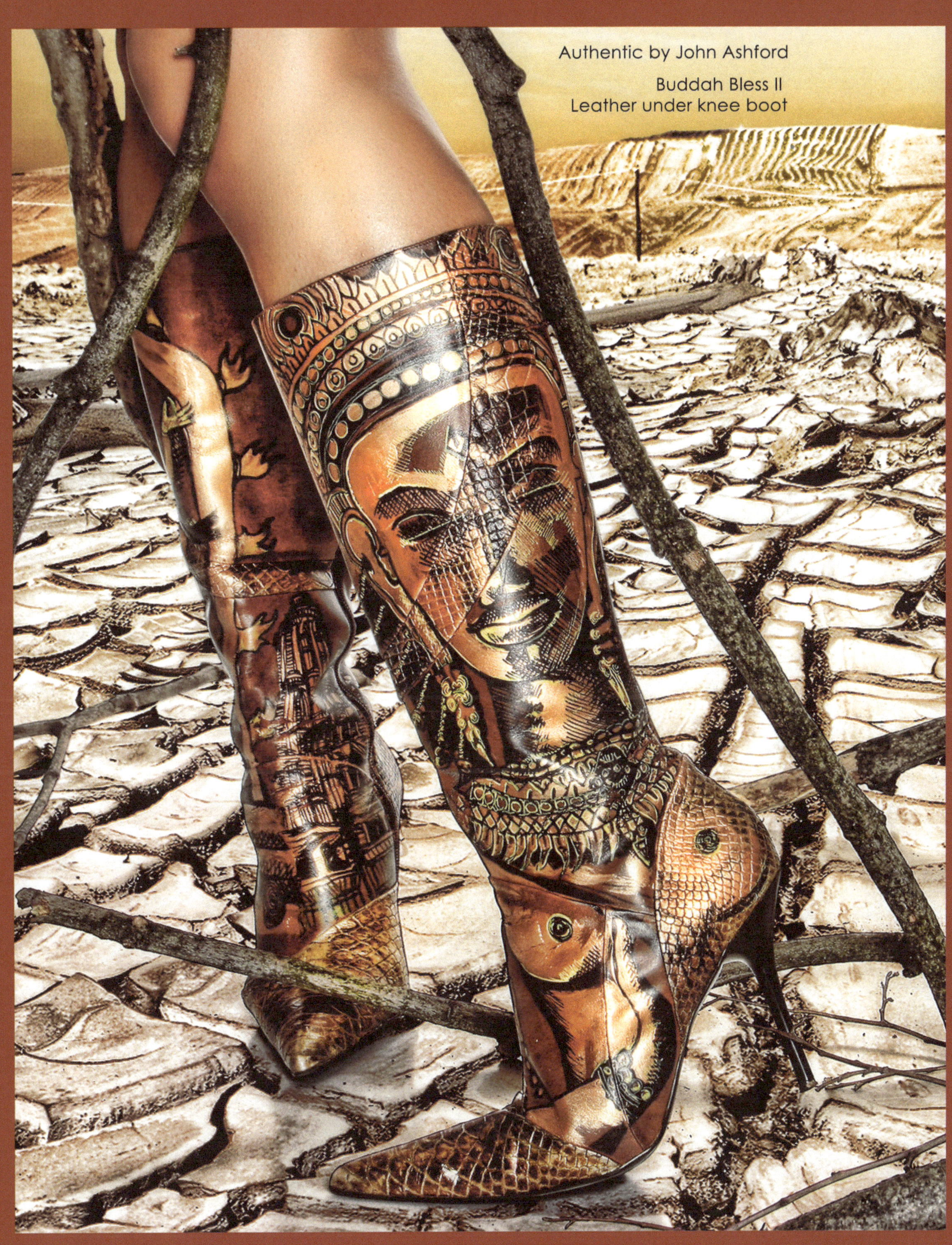
Authentic by John Ashford
Buddah Bless II
Leather under knee boot

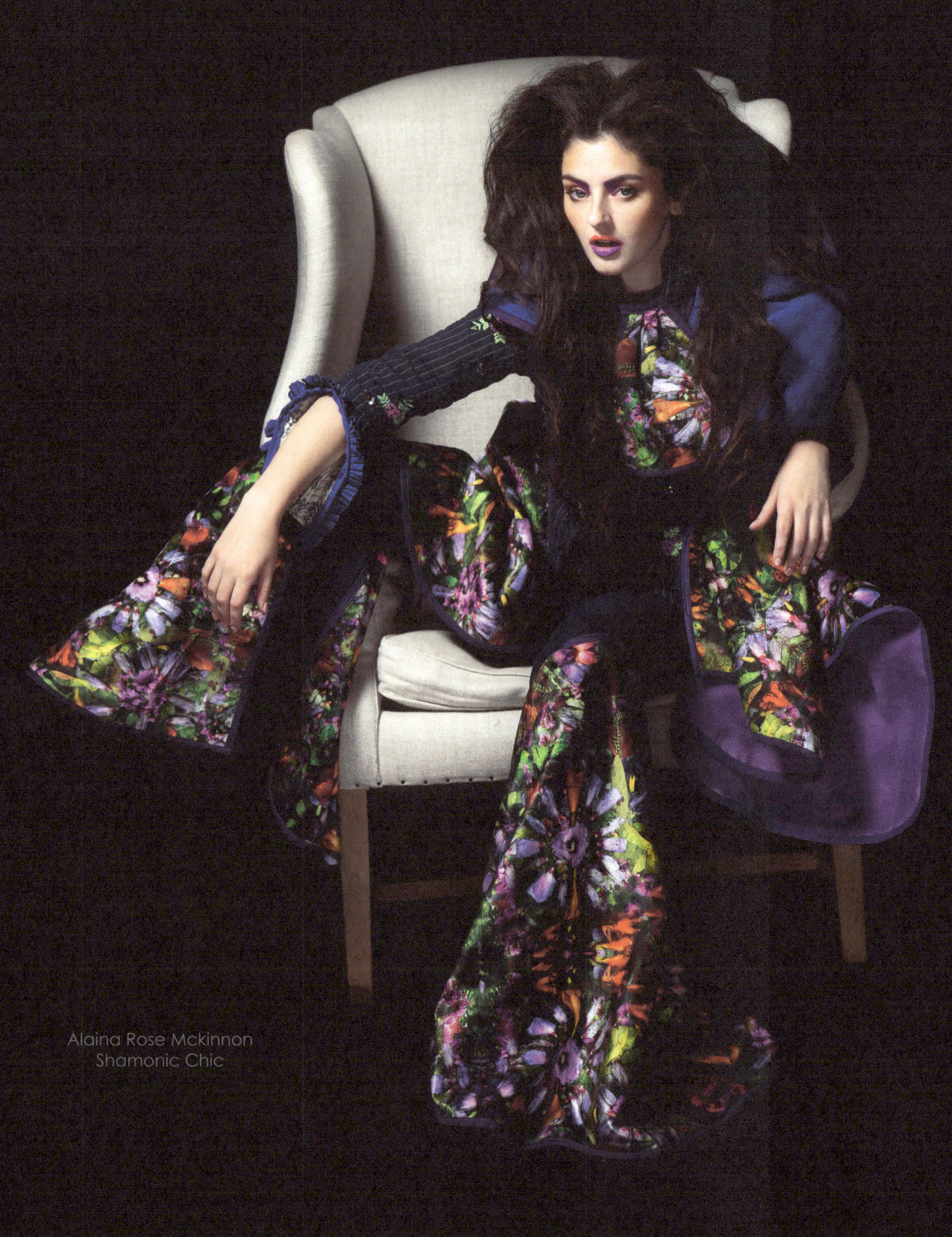

Alaina Rose Mckinnon
Shamonic Chic

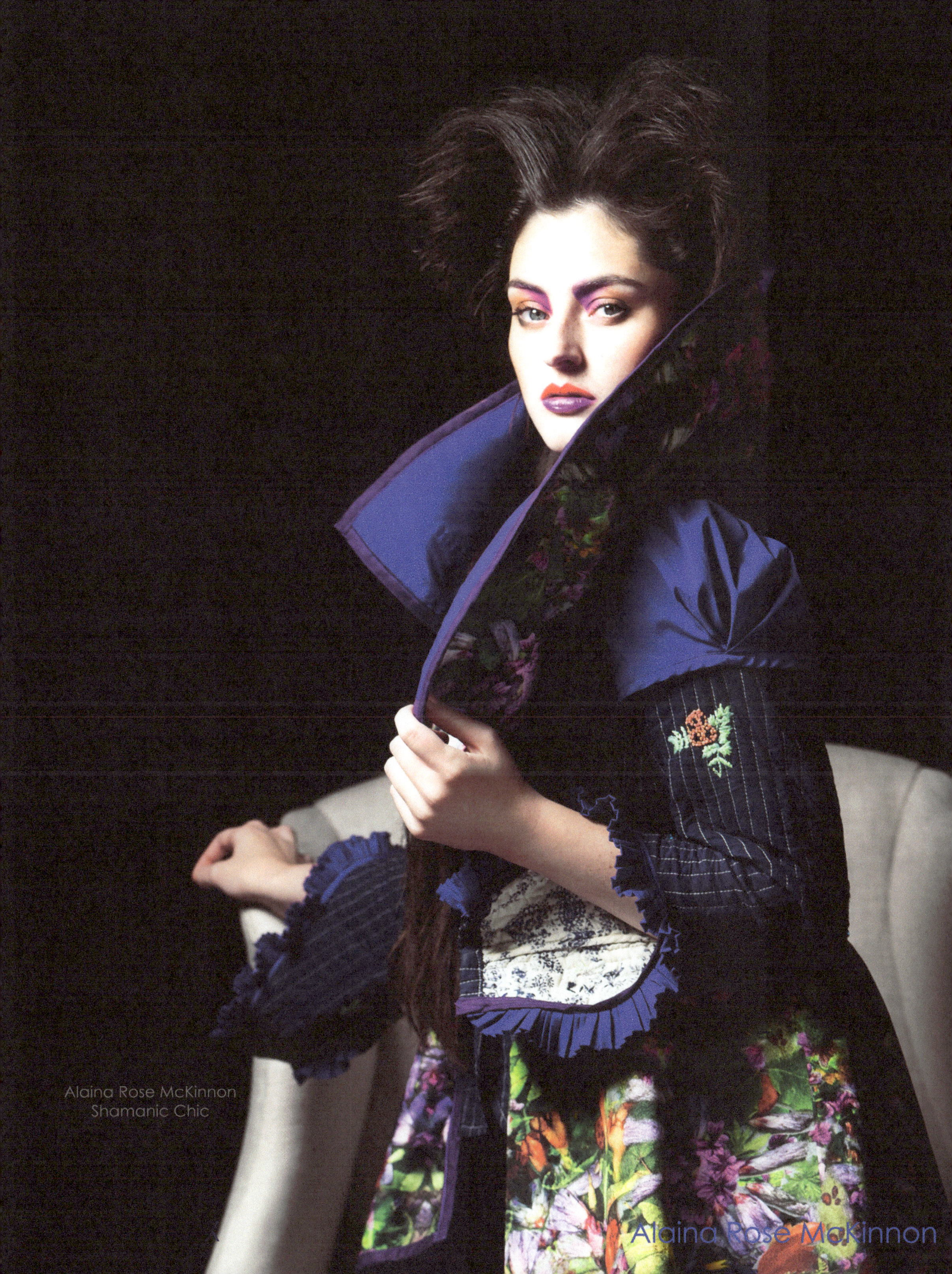
Alaina Rose McKinnon
Shamanic Chic
Alaina Rose McKinnon

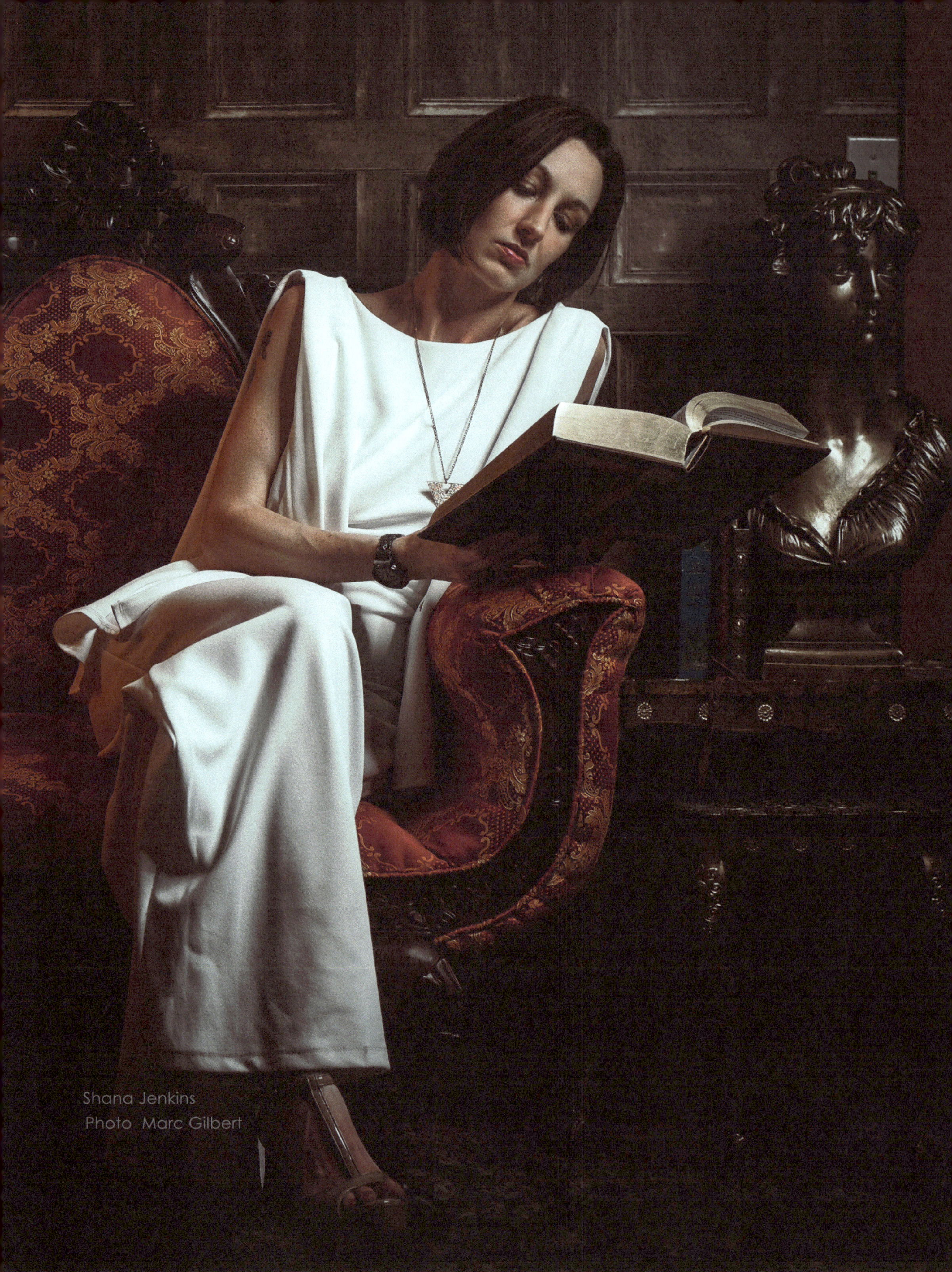
Shana Jenkins
Photo Marc Gilbert

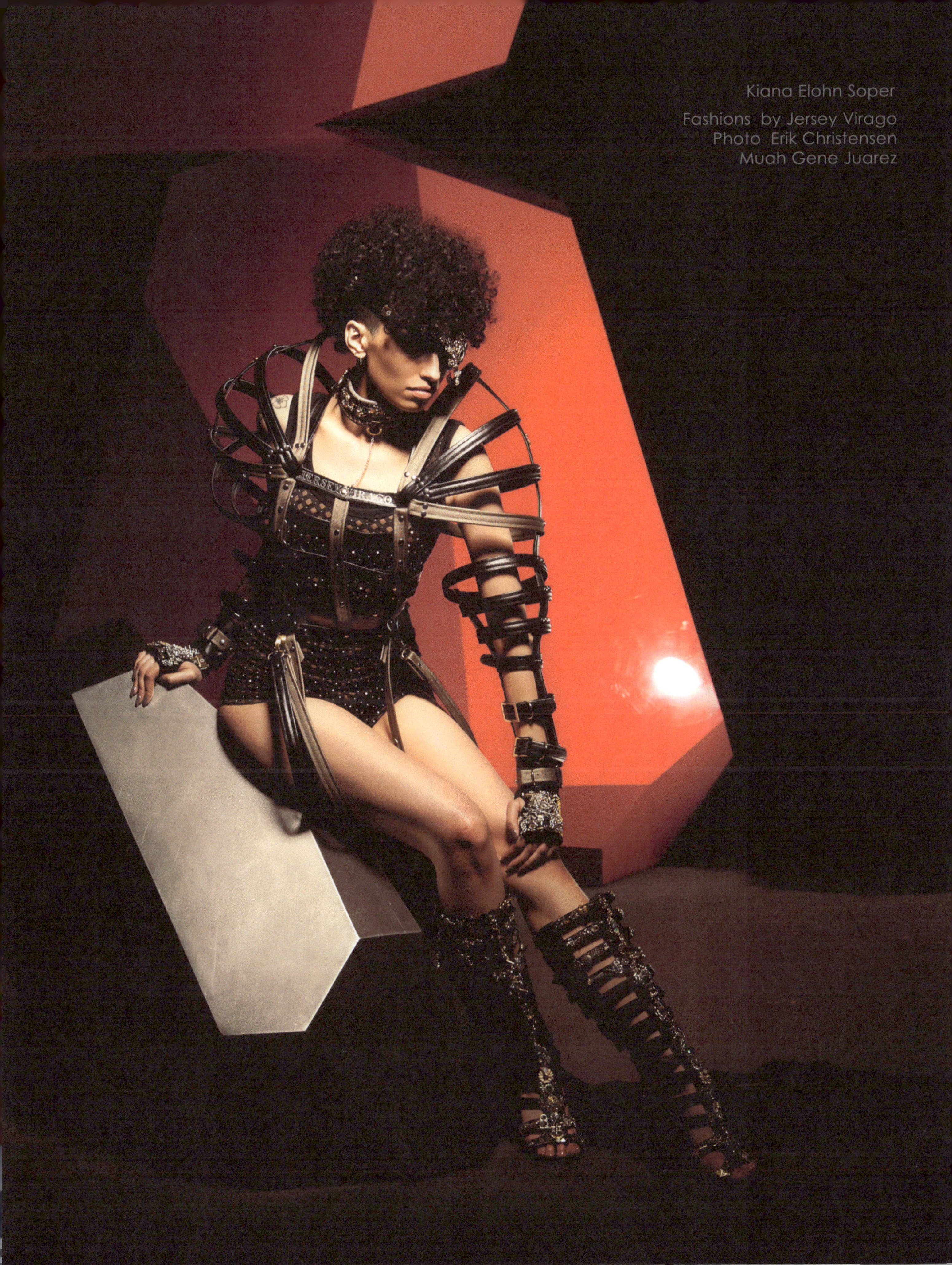
Kiana Elohn Soper
Fashions by Jersey Virago
Photo Erik Christensen
Muah Gene Juarez

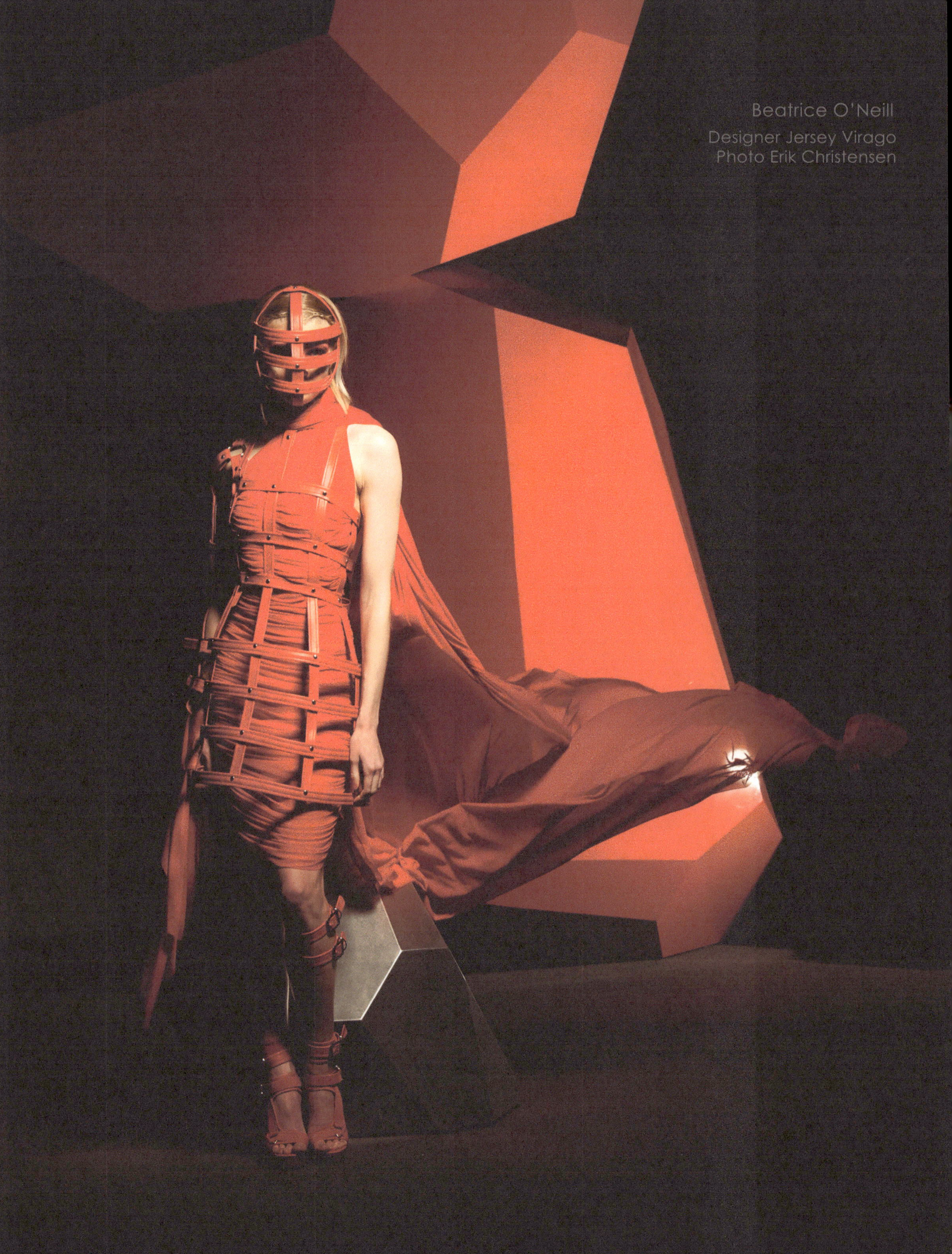
Beatrice O'Neill
Designer Jersey Virago
Photo Erik Christensen

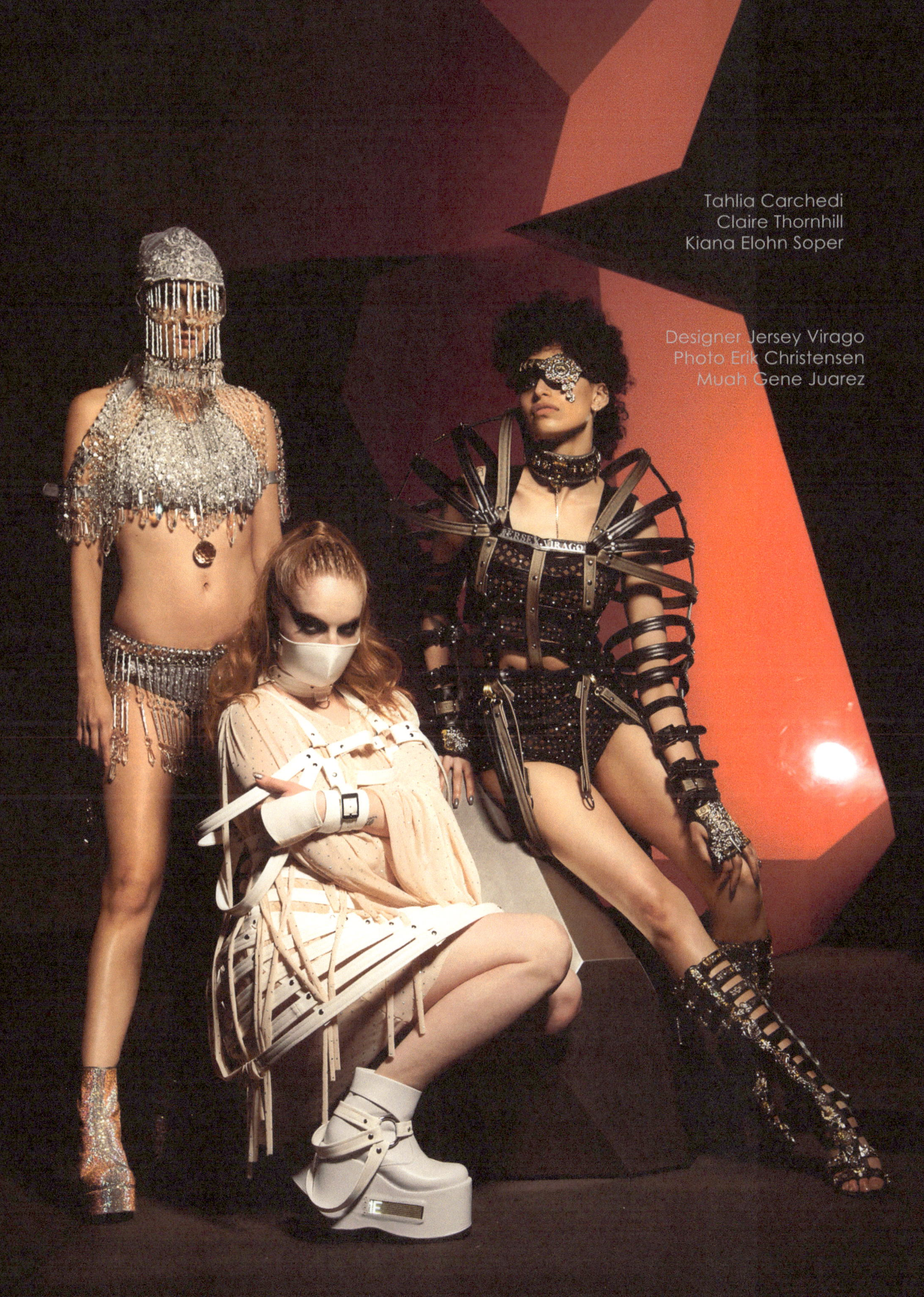
Tahlia Carchedi
Claire Thornhill
Kiana Elohn Soper

Designer Jersey Virago
Photo Erik Christensen
Muah Gene Juarez

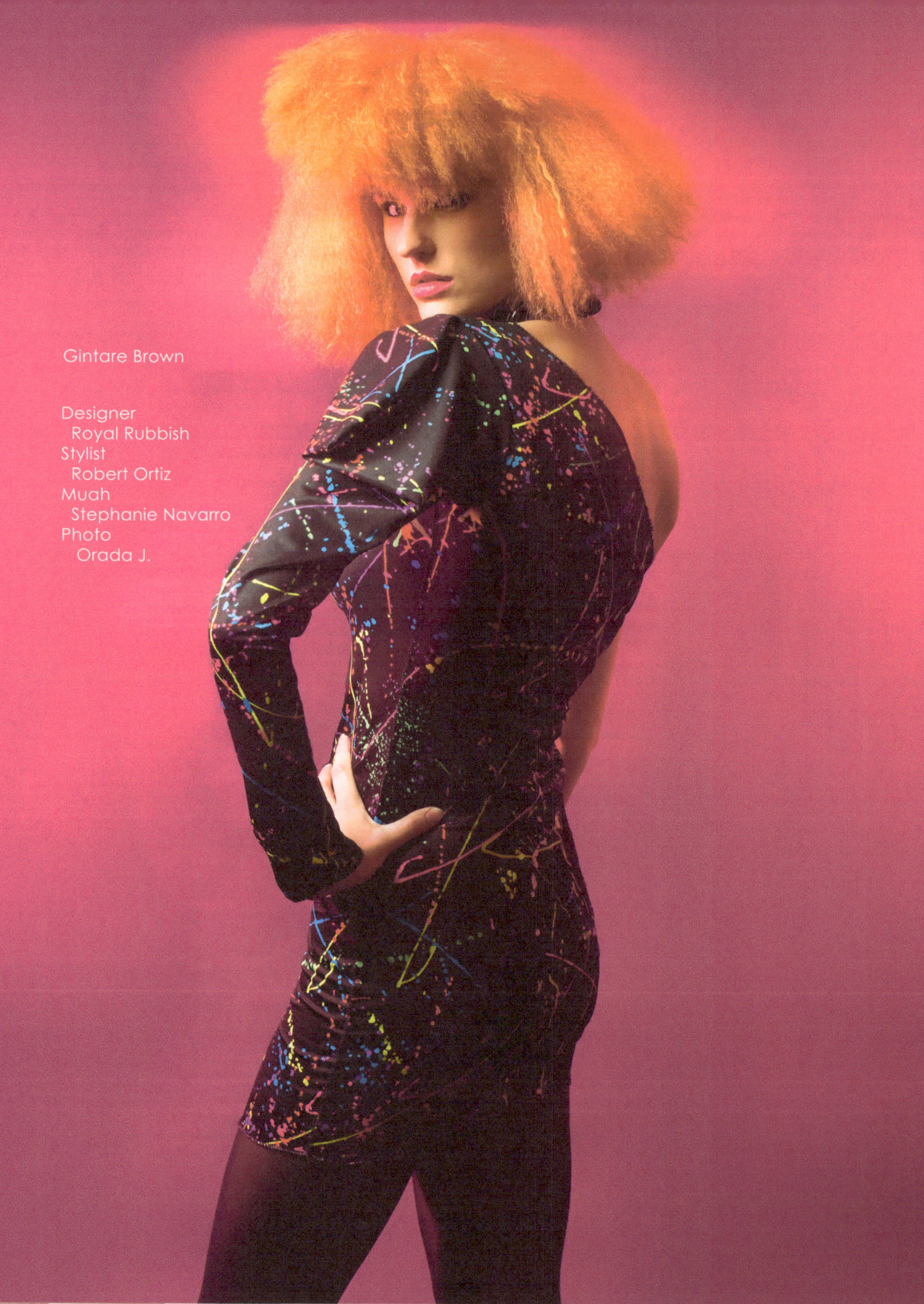
Gintare Brown

Designer
  Royal Rubbish
Stylist
  Robert Ortiz
Muah
  Stephanie Navarro
Photo
  Orada J.

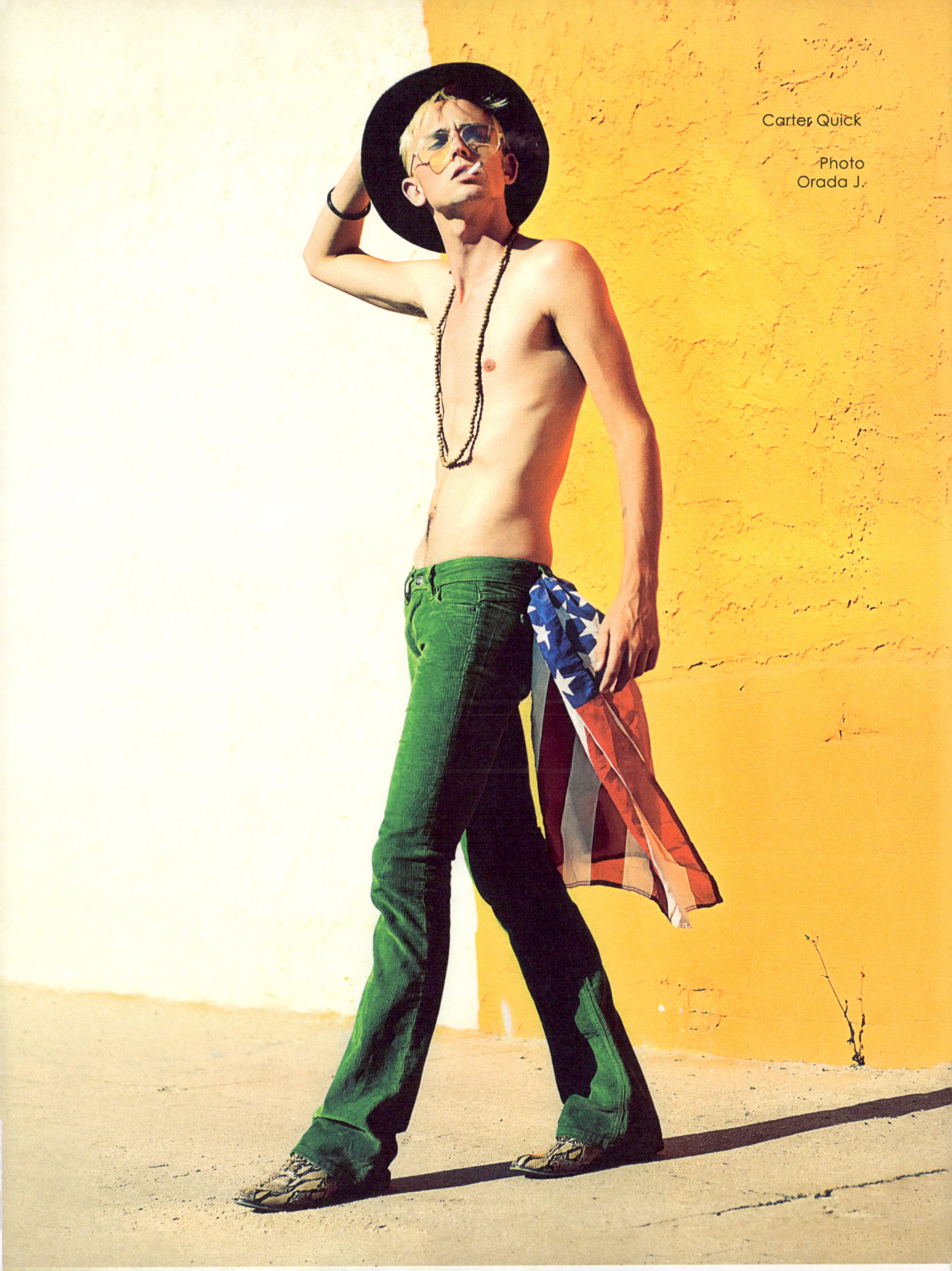

Carter Quick

Photo
Orada J.

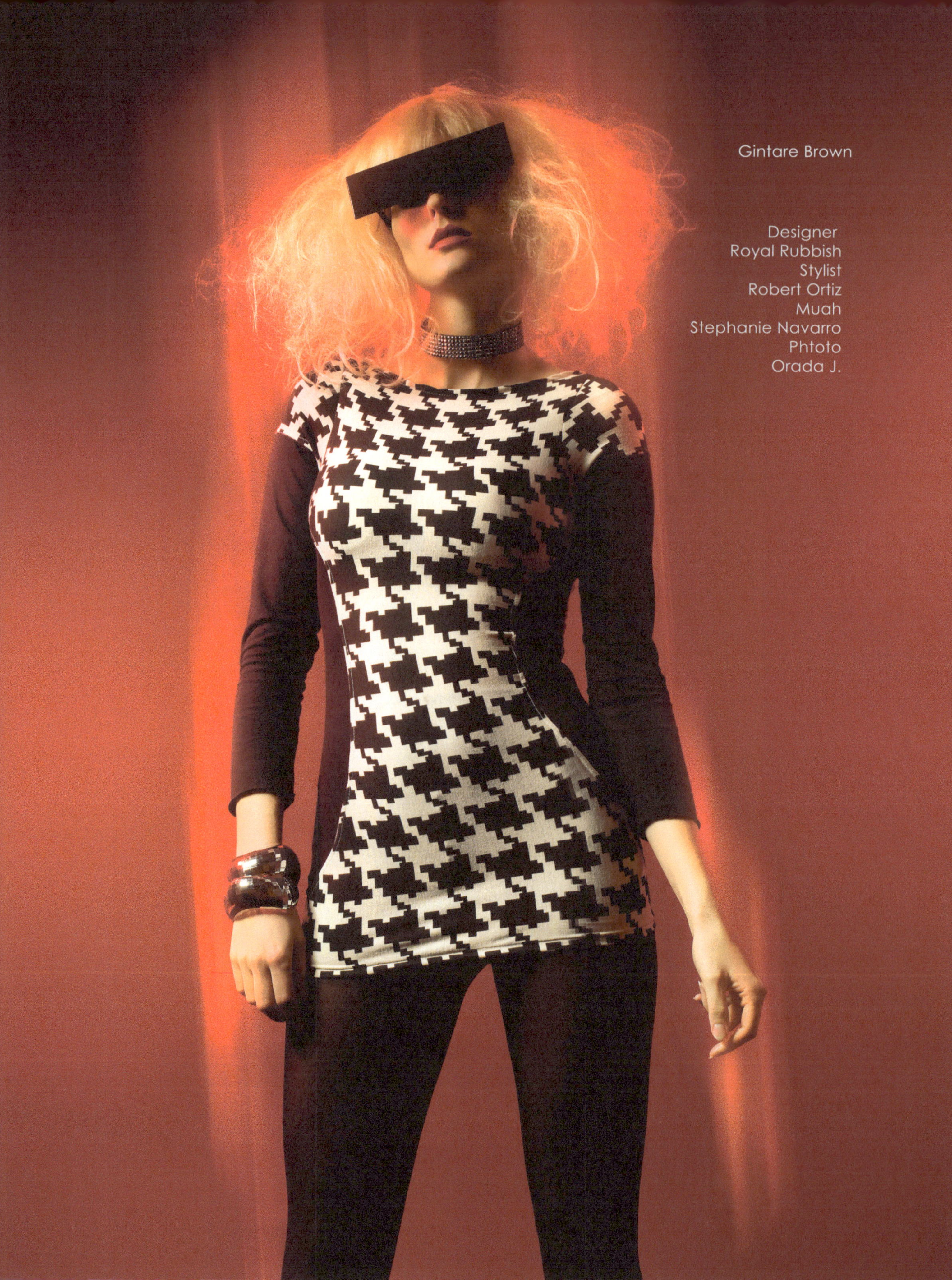

Gintare Brown

Designer
Royal Rubbish
Stylist
Robert Ortiz
Muah
Stephanie Navarro
Phtoto
Orada J.

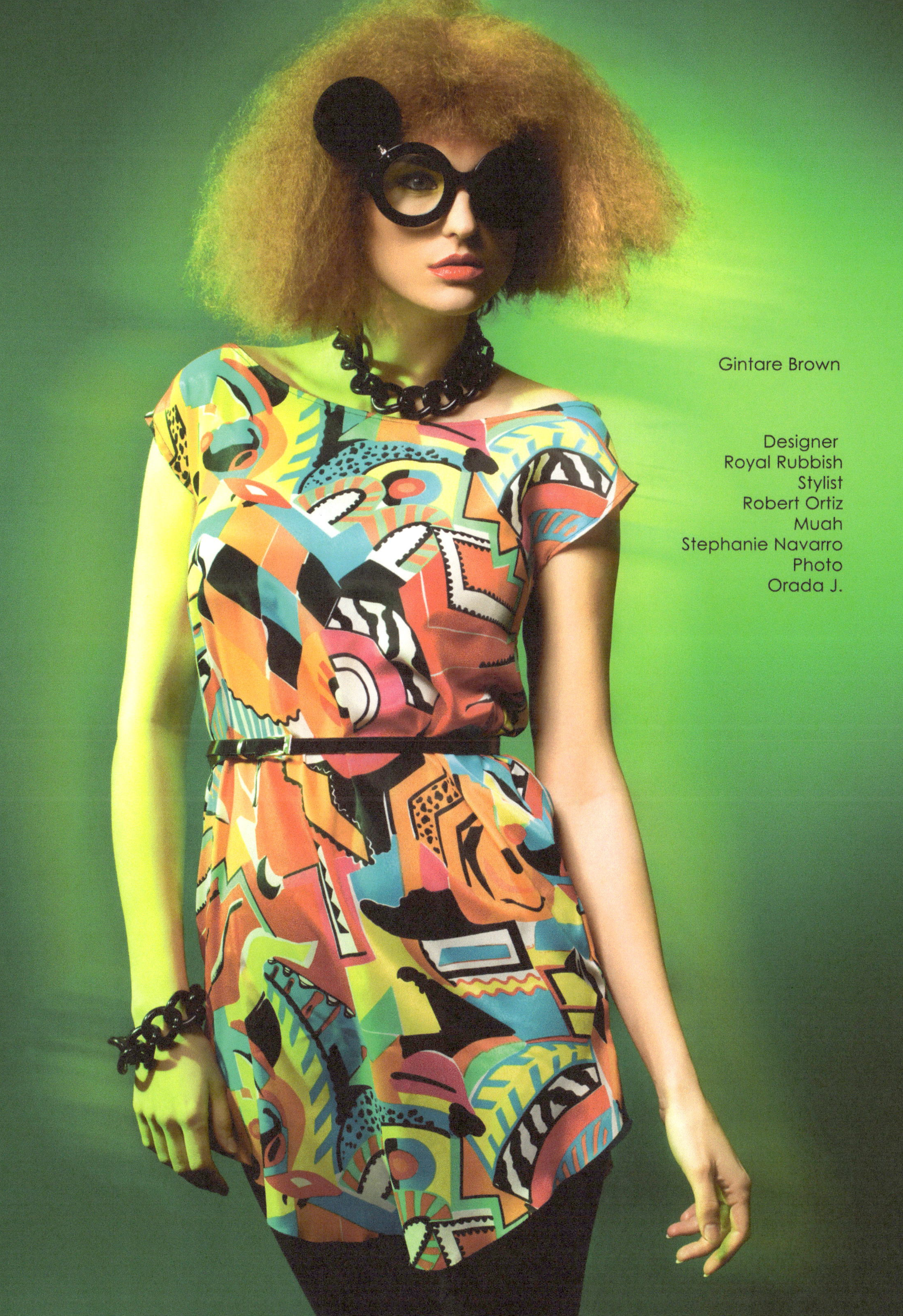

Gintare Brown

Designer
Royal Rubbish
Stylist
Robert Ortiz
Muah
Stephanie Navarro
Photo
Orada J.

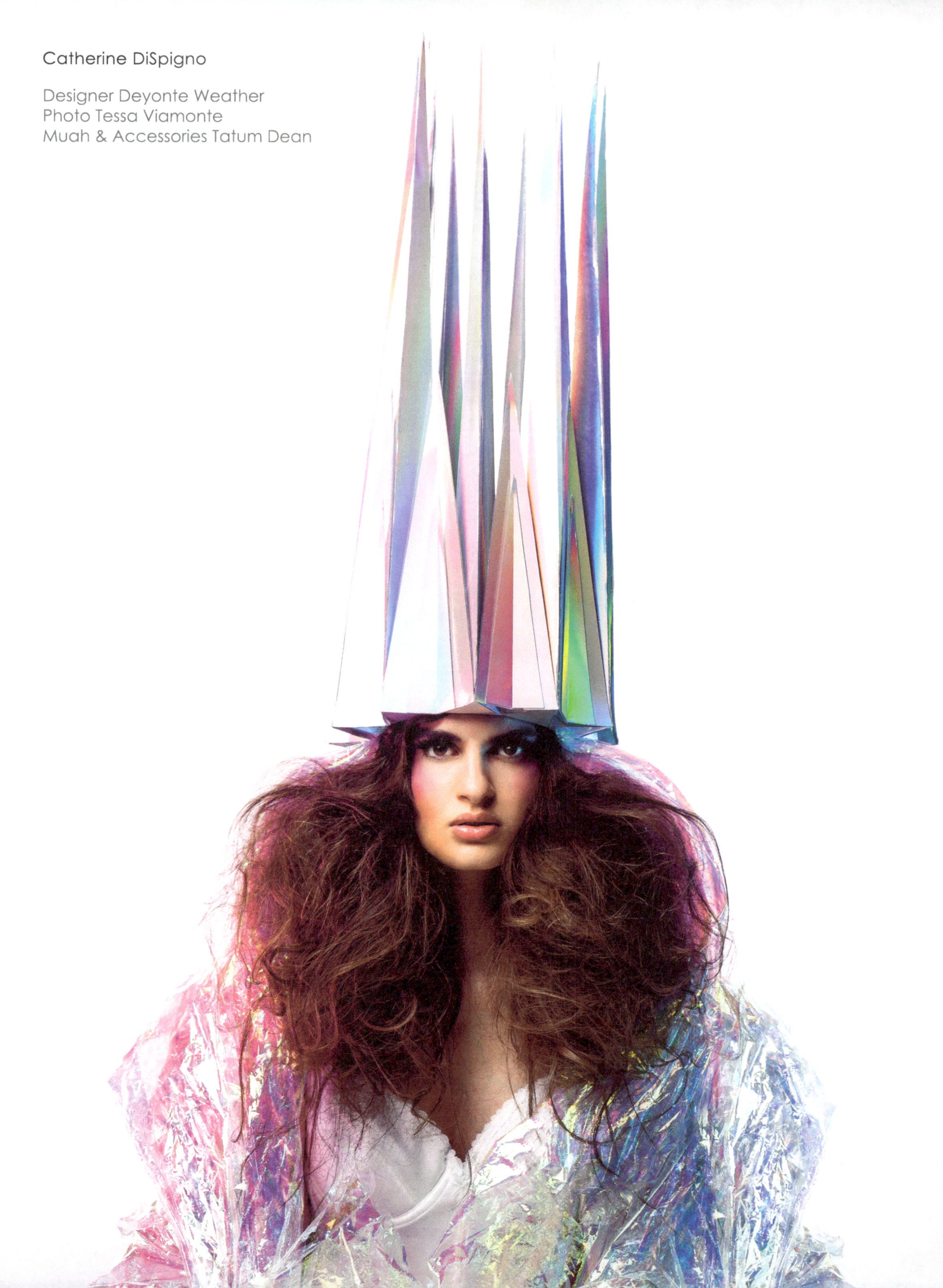

Catherine DiSpigno

Designer Deyonte Weather
Photo Tessa Viamonte
Muah & Accessories Tatum Dean

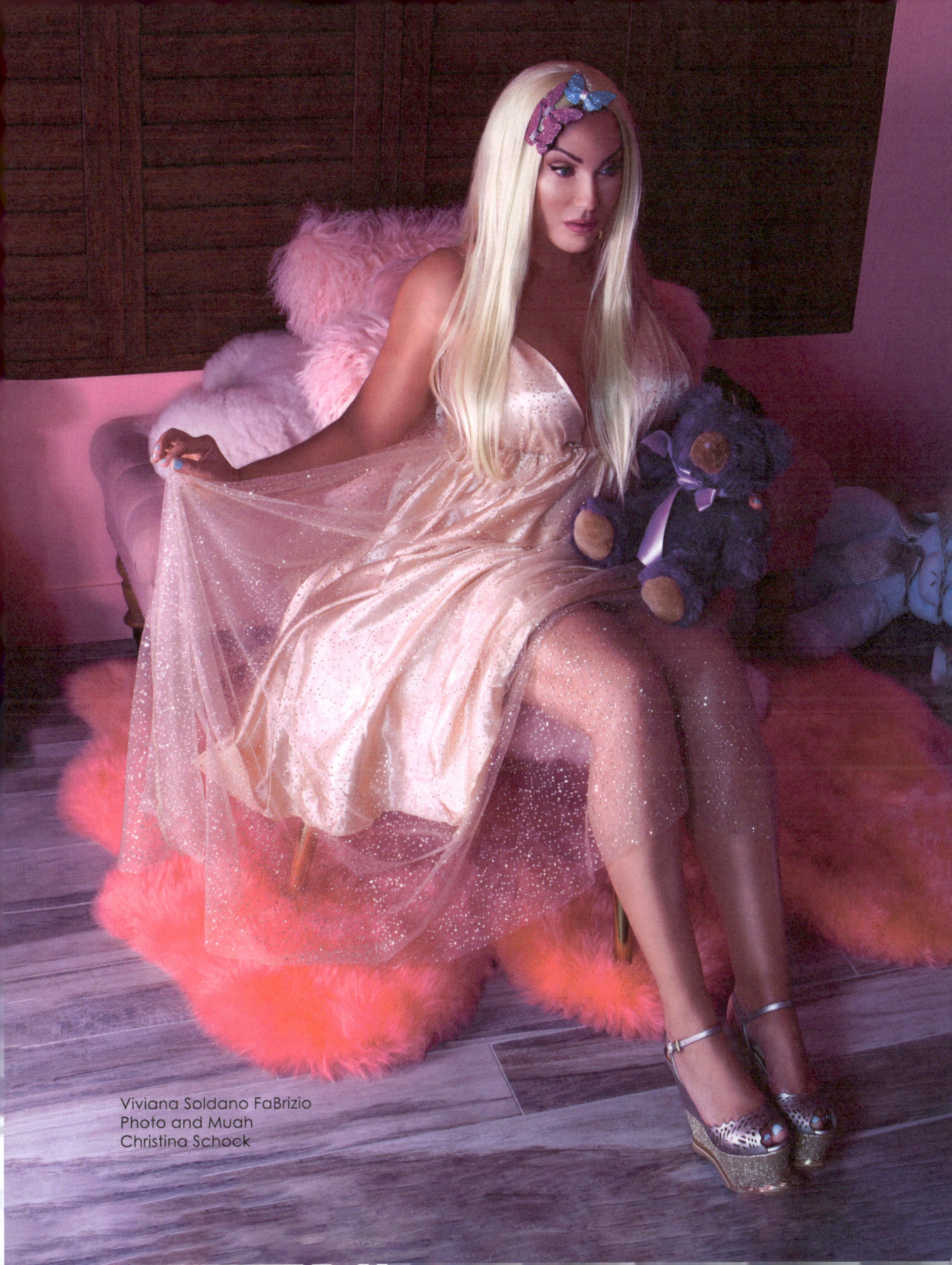
Viviana Soldano FaBrizio
Photo and Muah
Christina Schock

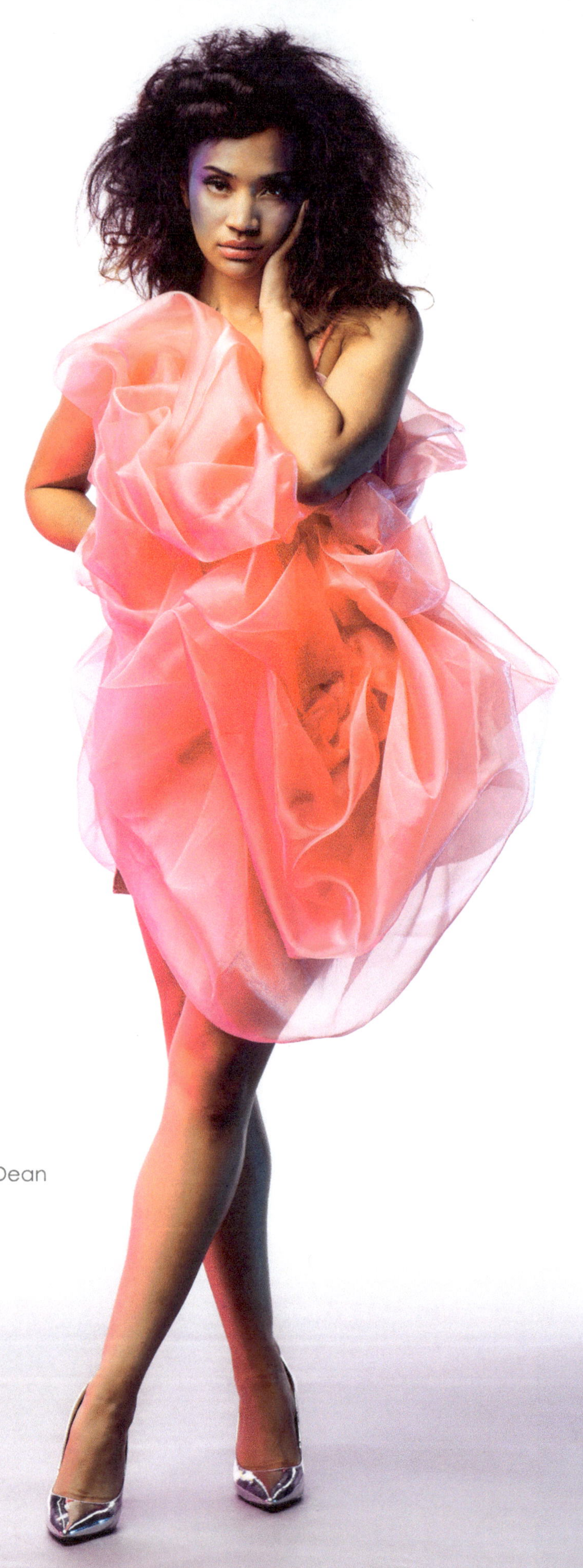

Alaina Butler

Designer Deyonte Weather
Photo Tessa Viamonte,
Muah & Accessories Tatum Dean

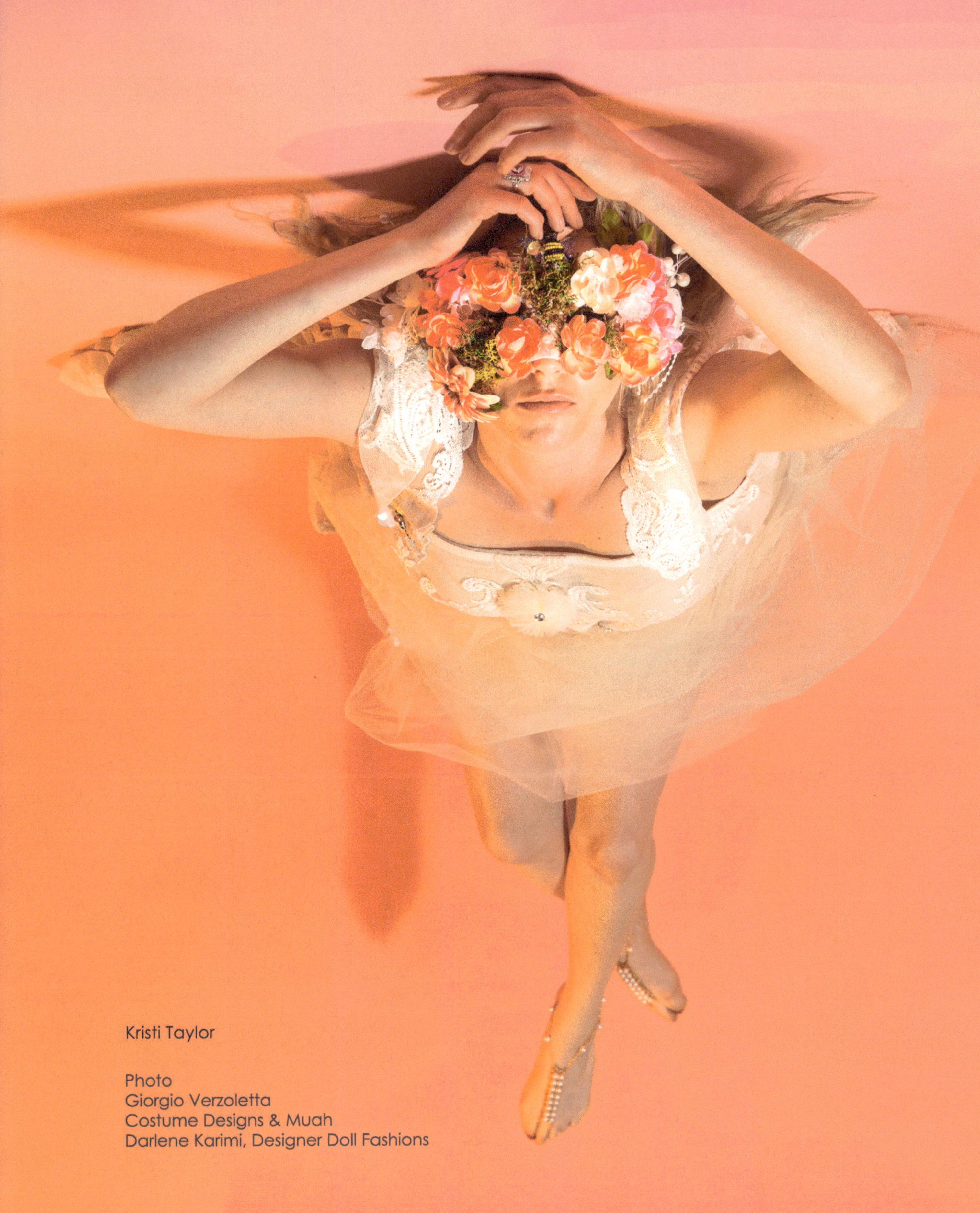

Kristi Taylor

Photo
Giorgio Verzoletta
Costume Designs & Muah
Darlene Karimi, Designer Doll Fashions

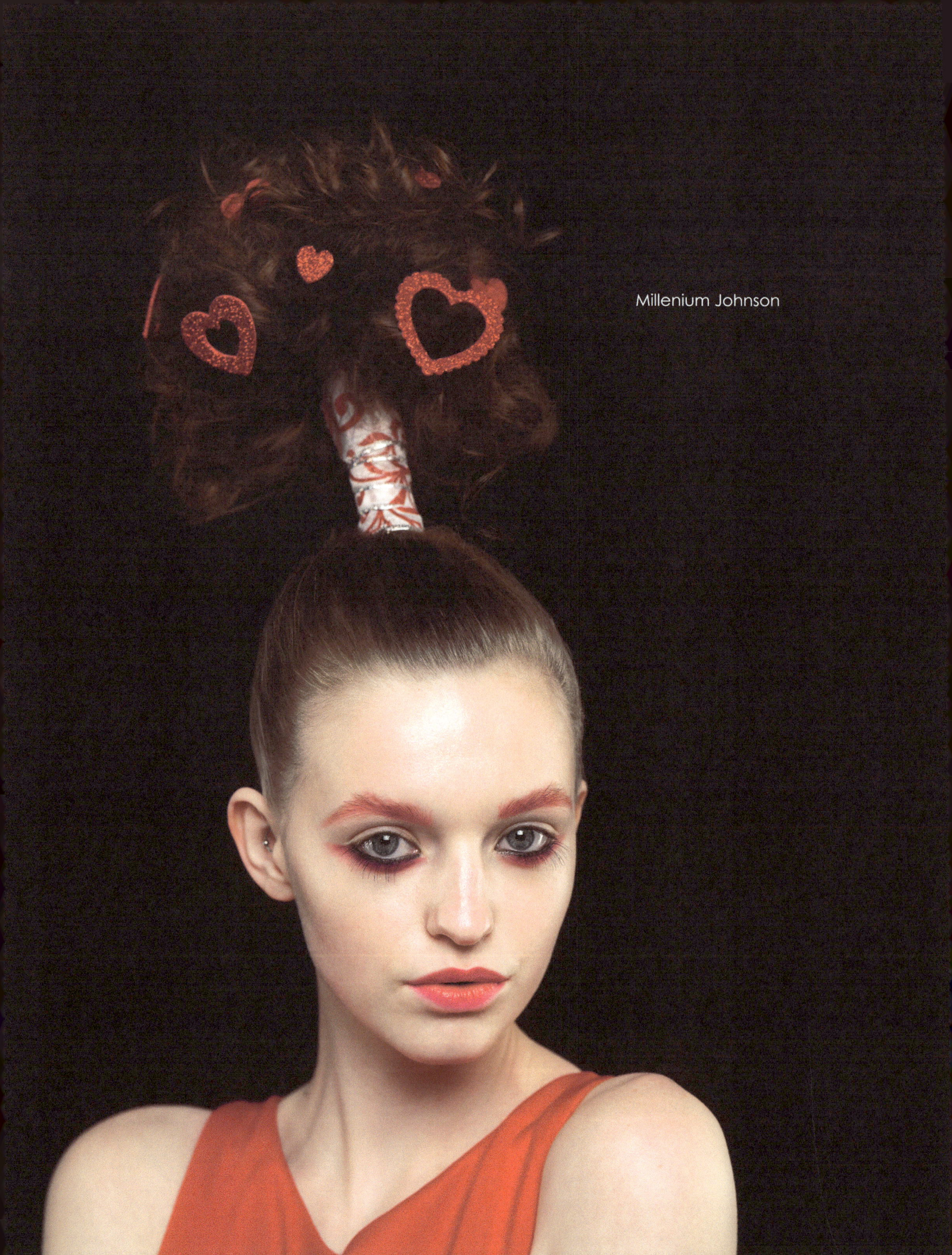
Millenium Johnson

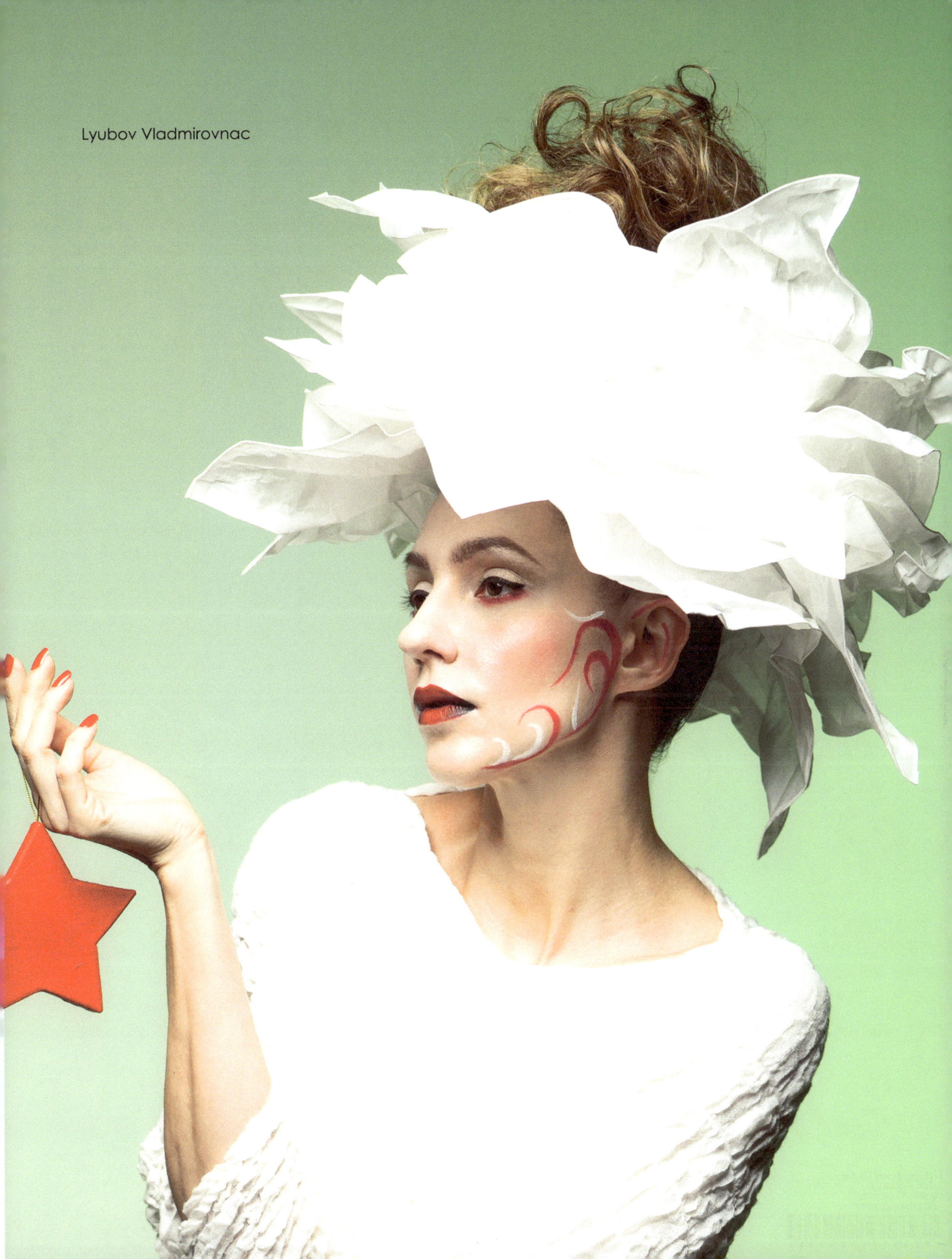

Lyubov Vladmirovnac